TWAYNE'S WORLD AUTHORS SERIES

A Survey of the World's Literature

Sylvia Bowman, Indiana University

GENERAL EDITOR

AUSTRALIA

Joseph Jones, University of Texas

EDITOR

Robert D. FitzGerald

(TWAS 286)

TWAYNE'S WORLD AUTHORS SERIES (TWAS)

*The purpose of TWAS is to survey the major writers—
novelists, dramatists, historians, poets, philosophers, and
critics—of the nations of the world. Among the national
literatures covered are those of Australia, Canada, China,
Eastern Europe, France, Germany, Greece, India, Italy,
Japan, Latin America, the Netherlands, New Zealand,
Poland, Russia, Scandinavia, Spain, and the African
nations, as well as Hebrew, Yiddish, and Latin Classical
literature. This survey is complemented by Twayne's United
States Authors Series and English Authors Series.*

*The intent of each volume in these series is to present
a critical-analytical study of the works of the writer;
to include biographical and historical material that may
be necessary for understanding, appreciation, and critical
appraisal of the writer; and to present all material in clear,
concise English—but not to vitiate the scholarly content
of the work by doing so.*

Robert D. FitzGerald

By A. Grove Day
University of Hawaii

Twayne Publishers, Inc.   : :   New York

Library of Congress Cataloging in Publication Data

Day, Arthur Grove, 1904–
Robert D. FitzGerald.

(Twayne's world authors series. TWAS 286. Australia)
Bibliography: p.
1. FitzGerald, Robert David, 1902–
PR6011.185Z63   821   73–15877
ISBN 0-8057-2311-0

MANUFACTURED IN THE UNITED STATES OF AMERICA

And under longings
man was eternal unrest that no place satisfies,
content never overtakes and no year ends;
for it is earth itself and earth's vitality
working within the bloodstream. We are earth's blood. . . .

FitzGerald, "Between Two Tides"

Dedication
To all students of poetry—especially in America
and Australia

Preface

A writer named Barron Field (inauspicious cognomen!) published in 1819 a volume called *First Fruits of Australian Poetry,* which contained the immortal apostrophe: "Kangaroo, Kangaroo!/Thou Spirit of Australia/That redeems from utter failure,/From perfect desolation,/And warrants the creation/Of this fifth part of the Earth." Since that date, more than a century and a half has passed, and later fruits of poetry, in the continent that seemed to Field "an after-birth,/Not conceiv'd in the Beginning," have ripened in profusion. In the latest one-volume anthology, *The Penguin Book of Australian Verse,* more than a hundred men and women—most of them contemporary—are deemed worthy of inclusion. Occupying the most space is a third-generation son of Irish ancestry, Robert David FitzGerald. For the past half century, he has been producing poetry that qualifies him as a classic author, worthy of wide study and deep appreciation.

My chief purpose in presenting this volume is to pay tribute to the achievement of an eminent Australian whose poetry attains power not because of its "Australianity" but because it deserves to keep company with the fine authors of the world who have used the English language to arouse the emotions and mentalities of their readers.

I first met FitzGerald and his wife Marjorie in 1955, the year I spent in Australia as a Fulbright senior research fellow studying the voluminous and fascinating literature of that nation. We encountered each other in what his fellow poet Nancy Keesing has called "Sydney Tomholt's Aladdin's Cave above Bond Street, that marvelous room full of treasures in wood, paper, friendship, and rare and valuable people." Tall and smiling, unobtrusive yet convivial, "Fitz" appeared less to be the literary celebrity than the hard-working outdoor man he was—a professional land surveyor who for most of his life had to earn a living for himself and his family, who spent five years toiling in the South Sea bush, and who weathered, along with the rest of his generation and mine, two global wars and a worldwide economic depression. Along with A. E. Housman, one of FitzGerald's favorite authors, he could say of his poetry: "Out of a stem that scored the hand/I wrung it in a weary land." Yet the main burden of FitzGerald's poetry is one of gladness and hope.

The gift of an autographed copy of *Between Two Tides,* Fitz-Gerald's epic poem about the adventures of Will Mariner in the Tongan Islands, harmonized with my strong interest in the literature of the Pacific region, and led to a correspondence that has continued to the present day. During a sabbatical year in Australia in 1965, I began in earnest to work on the present biocritical volume and then and thereafter interviewed Mr. FitzGerald and followed his career. The first two chapters herein must serve—unless the poet himself publishes an autobiography—as the most complete account of his adventurous life. All the details have kindly been verified by him in sessions at his comfortable brick and hewn-stone home in Hunters Hill, a riverside Sydney suburb, surrounded by bookshelves, chests of papers, and family portraits.

The poet's recollections, and those of his many relatives and friends, make the listener aware that his shelf of poems was not composed by an electronic computer but by a human being who labored and suffered, but unfailingly retained a sense of humor and an almost youthful spirit of hope and aspiration. If character is the sum of heredity and environment, then this poet—who had authors on both sides of his pedigree and who began his career under the best auspices—well deserves to have his biography perused by anyone at all concerned with the creation of literature. Although it is true that the master poet reveals himself in his verses more starkly than any assiduous Boswell could do in several hundred pages, this brief chronicle of a long and active life deserves to be put on the record.

The friendship begun in 1955 has endured up to the present time. When FitzGerald and his wife stopped briefly in Honolulu in 1963 on his way to teach at the University of Texas, he generously addressed a class at the University of Hawaii. Previously in that year I had revisited Australia, as I was again to go there during four later years—most recently in 1972. Each time I garnered further valuable information about the poet's career. In 1968 I supervised a lengthy and meticulous master of arts thesis by Miss Maureen

Preface

Cassidy at my university on the subject of FitzGerald's prosody, as exemplified in each of the selections in his volume *Forty Years' Poems.*

Friendship with a contemporary, however, has not, I feel, dulled my critical sense in the present study. Seldom has a commentator been free to obtain such full access to all the materials on his subject and, at the same time, been so free to express value judgments on their worth. In any event, FitzGerald's shelf of prose and poetry needs no defense by anyone. "Damn the defenders!" he wrote to C. B. Christesen, editor of *Meanjin,* on September 12, 1945. "Why can't they allow a man to be attacked in peace?" Yet I have admittedly been less concerned with picking flaws or uncovering suspected weaknesses than I have been in helping FitzGerald's many readers to discover his ideas and to appreciate the richness of the varied qualities of his work. After a life as a writer and teacher, I am mainly impressed by the glaring fact that too many people read but do not comprehend—and that many who comprehend do not appreciate.

Ironically, along with other schoolfellows who dabbled in verse, young Bob FitzGerald joked that some day he would be famous and his poems would be "set" as examinations, so that he would be execrated by later generations of students. Not too many years later, his poetry became a standard subject in Australian schools and universities—a paradoxical fate for a man who spent only two years in the science faculty of his alma mater and never took a single course in English Literature.

Yet his body of work is the most extensive in the history of Australian poetry, extending over more than half a century. It is therefore possible to examine his development during this lengthy period. One contribution of the present study is to comment upon the themes, forms, and various other qualities of every one of the more than a hundred selections in *Forty Years' Poems* (1965), as well as upon a number of verses published since that date.

Several of these more recent poems voice protests about the current scene. Discontent with various aspects of life, however, was a lifelong preoccupation with Robert D. FitzGerald. As an energetic, romantic, red-haired youth he expressed dismay that life contained injustice. All his working career was spent as an employee of one or another government agency, and he faithfully performed his duties in office and field. He was the first Australian author to be honored by his queen with the award of a merited O.B.E. for his contributions to the literature of his country, and he remarked at the time that "the monarchial system suits me very well." He was, however, like the olden fighters of the Geraldyn clan of Ireland, born to be "ag'in the government" in spirit. He was irritated by smothering bureaucracy and by the pressures that make Philistines of us all. His Celtic blood would boil at the revelation of unfairness. "Fitz with his deeper perception often saw defects in organizations, bodies, and departments which we lesser mortals had not noticed," a friend of early days told me, "and he was not afraid to speak against them." A number of his writings transmute the rebel spirit into literature; for irritability, like the sand in the oyster that forms the nucleus of a pearl, is often the genesis of a notable poem.

The two biographical chapters that open the text are followed by two that treat FitzGerald's views on the function of poetry and on its techniques. Thereafter, four chapters are devoted to critiques of all the collected items in *Forty Years' Poems,* along with some later verses published after 1965. A final chapter attempts to comment upon FitzGerald's achievements and attitudes, to remark upon his practice of composition, and to indicate the critical reception he has enjoyed in his own country over the past forty-five years. Much material—especially from unpublished sources—will be found in the Notes, a section useful beyond the mere indication of quoted passages.

A major problem in this research has been selection from the multitude of sources available to the writer. The excellent bibliography published by the Libraries Board of South Australia in 1970 contains more than 450 items by and about Mr. FitzGerald. My own Selected Bibliography, which is divided into sections and is otherwise based upon a quite different plan, has required untold days of effort to compile, and the printed materials have been drawn upon heavily for my text. However, I have drawn even more heavily upon unpublished sources, since these are all too easily lost forever. They include diaries kept during FitzGerald's five years in the Fiji Islands; private letters from and to the poet; a lengthy memoir on him by a fellow surveyor; a special, sealed collection of papers and clippings deposited in the Mitchell Library in Sydney; interviews with a number of friends of the poet; examination of unpublished recent pieces of verse; and, most of all, conversations that have taken place between FitzGerald and myself during almost two decades.

Among the many persons who have contributed to my knowledge of FitzGerald's life and work are Hugh Anderson, C. B. Christesen, R. G. Howarth, T. Inglis Moore, H. N. Murray, Douglas Stewart, H. X. Stokes, and Walter Stone. The staffs of the Mitchell and Dixson Libraries in Sydney and the National Library in Canberra assisted, as always, in providing materials for research. Dr. Joseph Jones of the University of Texas has been a valuable source of information as well as an able editor. I am indebted most of all to Mr. FitzGerald himself, who gave me the privilege of freely printing anything he ever wrote.

A. GROVE DAY

University of Hawaii

Contents

Chronology

Publication dates of only the more important books are here given; for complete list, see Selected Bibliography.

1902   Robert David FitzGerald, fourth of that name, born February 22 at Hunters Hill, N.S.W., youngest child of Robert David Fitz-Gerald and Ida Le Gay Brereton FitzGerald.

1915–   Attended Sydney Grammar School; first poem published in *Sydneian,*
1919   September, 1917, under pseudonym "Crumaboo."

1920–   Studied Faculty of Science, Sydney University; abandoned course
1921   in 1922 and became articled as surveyor to firm of Dobbie and Foxall.

1922   Poems appeared in *Australian University Verse, 1920–1922,* and in following year in *Poetry in Australia, 1923.*

1920–   Contributed to *Hermes,* Sydney *Bulletin, New Outlook, Forum,*
1924   *Triad,* and *Vision.* Peripheral member of important group that founded *Vision* in 1923, including Norman Lindsay, Jack Lindsay, Hugh McCrae, and Kenneth Slessor.

1925   Qualified as licensed surveyor and Member of Institution of Surveyors, New South Wales.

1926   Entered private practice as surveyor; the following year became partner of Athol Blair, with office in Pitt Street, Sydney.

1927   *The Greater Apollo: Seven Metaphysical Songs,* privately distributed edition issued as memorial to mother.

1929   Published *To Meet the Sun* (verse), awarded bronze medal of the Festival of Arts and Letters sponsored by the Panton Arts Club in England.

1931   Married Marjorie-Claire Harris, librarian, at Hunters Hill. Started work as surveyor with Native Lands Commission, Crown Colony of Fiji, in Seaqaqa District, Macuata Province, Vanua Levu. Wife joined him in July and stayed with him in camps and native villages until close of field season in December.

1932   Wife returned to Sydney. Continued surveys of Seaqaqa District. Wife came back to Suva with infant daughter Jennifer Kerry at close of field season.

1933   Completed Seaqaqa surveys and took over and finished two others that had been left unfinished in Macuata Province. Wife and child rejoined at Vunimoli village in Sasa District. Took over unfinished district of Wairiki in Cakaudrove Province; wife in Labasa.

1934   Wife returned to Sydney before field season started. Daughter Rosaleen Moyra born. Brief season before going on leave. In May ascended Mount Nasorolevu, highest mountain on Vanua Levu (3,386 feet), spent eight days awaiting clear weather in company with Henry Stokes, first European to ascend this peak. Completed Wairiki survey after considerable labor trouble at the isolated valley of Lovo. Left field in August and left Suva in October.

1935   Wrote long poem "The Hidden Bole" at Lane Cove, suburb of Sydney, while on leave and convalescing from severe operation for appendicitis. Returned from sick leave in June, assigned to Veivatuloa District, Namosi Province, Viti Levu, near Suva.

1936   Completed Fiji service. Worked for private surveyor for several months until joining Manly Council Staff, N.S.W., and then worked until 1939 as employee of Municipal Council of Ryde, N.S.W. Studied for examinations for local government engineer certificate. Resumed acquaintance with literary friends.

1938   Awarded Australian Sesquicentenary Prize for "Essay on Memory," long poem. Published *Moonlight Acre* (verse), awarded gold medal of Australian Literature Society, Melbourne, for best book of year.

1939   Only son, Robert Desmond, born.

1940   Joined Commonwealth Department of the Interior, Property and Survey Branch, as surveyor. Work during World War II mainly concerned with defense tasks such as laying out airfields.

1942   Third daughter, Phyllida Mary, born. Compiled *Australian Poetry, 1942.* Purchased present residence, 4 Prince Edward Parade, Hunters Hill.

1947   Hon. Secretary, Institution of Surveyors, N.S.W.

1949   *Heemskerck Shoals,* long poem, privately printed.

1951   Awarded O.B.E. (Officer of the British Empire Order) for services to literature.

1952   *Between Two Tides* (long poem) published.

1953   *This Night's Orbit* (verse) published.

1959   *The Wind at Your Door,* long poem, privately printed. Advanced to Fellowship of the Institution of Surveyors (Australia). Delivered three lectures in July at University of Melbourne under auspices of Commonwealth Literary Fund. These, rewritten, were delivered in June, 1961, at the University of Queensland, which published them in 1963 as *The Elements of Poetry.*

1962   Published *Southmost Twelve* (verse).

1963   Visiting lecturer in English, Humanities Section, University of Texas. Published *Of Some Country* (verse collection). Traveled around world with Mrs. FitzGerald, via United States, Ireland, Europe, and Hong Kong.

1964– Supervising Surveyor, New South Wales Branch, Department of
1966   Interior, Sydney.

1965   Published *Forty Years' Poems* (verse). Awarded £2,500 Encyclopaedia Britannica Australia prize for literature.

1968   Participated in Arts Vietnam festival, October.

1970   Published the edited *Letters of Hugh McCrae.*

1972   Second trip to Europe and Asia.

CHAPTER 1

Surveyor and Poet

R OBERT David FitzGerald, acknowledged during the past quarter of a century to be Australia's most prominent poet, did not spend his life in a classroom or library. As a land surveyor whose labors took him as far afield as the Fiji Islands, he enjoyed running a traverse through unmapped countryside on a clear day. The only task he enjoyed more was sitting up nights wrestling with words and hammering out unforgettable lines of verse.

Both surveying and poetry were in his blood as well as in his heart and mind. Of an Irish family, he was the fourth son to bear the same name. His most distinguished ancestor, Robert David FitzGerald (1831–1892), his grandfather, was born at Tralee, County Kerry, and educated at Queen's College, Cork, as a civil engineer. He came to Sydney in 1856 and soon thereafter entered the Lands Department as a draftsman. He sent for his father and family to join him, and married Emily Hunt, a granddaughter of Martin Mason, the doctor who is the main figure in the poet's "The Wind at Your Door" (*Forty Years' Poems,* pp. 236–40).[1] This grandfather was a man of letters and a scientist. He visited every Australian colony to study varieties of orchids, on which he published the first authoritative book in 1882, dedicated to Charles Darwin. A second volume, also a collector's treasure, with hand-colored illustrations, was assembled by two friends in 1895, three years after the author's death. He had retired in 1887 as Deputy Surveyor-General of New South Wales.[2]

I   *Two Uncles at the University*

The poet's father, born in 1864 in Balmain, N.S.W., was also an engineer, a member of the Institution of Civil Engineers, and a licensed surveyor. Like most Australians, he had a passion for sports and was a member of the first New South Wales Lawn Tennis Team. In 1891 he married Ida Le Gay Brereton, who also came of a distinguished Australian family.

Young Robert's mother was a daughter of John Le Gay Brereton the elder (1827–1886), a well-known Sydney physician who published five volumes of verse between 1857 and 1887. Ida's brother (1871–1933), bearing his father's name, became an even more noted poet, as well as the foremost Australian authority on Elizabethan drama. He graduated from Sydney Grammar School and Sydney University (1894) and became librarian and Professor of English (1921) at his alma mater. Of his poetry it was said: "A master of rhythm, there is nothing academic about him; his verse is compact of sincerity and the spirit of natural comradeship."[3] Brereton the younger was a friend of the fine Australian author Henry Lawson, as well as of dozens of lesser writers who needed a friend. Another daughter of the Brereton family, Ruby Millicent, became the mother of Sir Victor Windeyer, whom FitzGerald called "the most distinguished relative I can claim, High Court judge, privy counsellor, and much-decorated soldier."

The FitzGeralds have lived in the old Sydney suburb of Hunters Hill for more than a century, ever since the poet's botanist grandfather moved there from Balmain in 1871. Still a literary center, Hunters Hill lies on a peninsula on the northwestern shore of the harbor. Some families there have known each other for generations and are proud to live in modernized homes built of yard-thick, weathered blocks of stone still bearing the chisel marks of convict laborers from the upriver quarries. To be a member of a Hunters Hill family, surrounded by uncles and cousins, was an education in itself.

The nephew remembered the Breretons especially on Sundays, when his grandmother's buggy would be sent for his eldest brother and sister and himself, and they would be driven to the Gladesville estate to visit with those uncles and cousins. "I recall those Sundays as spacious and gracious days when I would be forcibly removed from putting the finishing touches on mud pies, and compressed into a sailor suit with a white front that tied on with silly tapes, and with a lanyard that wisely, but provokingly, had no whistle on the end. . . . We would ride gleefully over to Osgathorpe with its fifty acres of paradise for children: garden, orchards, paddocks, wilderness. There were cows, waterholes, and a hay shed."[4] The whole family would sometimes rush to view the road as an early-model motor car roared by in a fog of dust.

Young Bobbie grew up at his birthplace in a family where, on both sides, science and poetry were taken for granted as honorable and inspiring occupations. His father wrote verse, mainly humorous rhymes or bits for his children, whom he brought up on "Horatius at the Bridge," "Hiawatha," and the galloping ballads of Adam Lindsay Gordon. His youngest son attended local schools and nondenominational Sydney Grammar School, one of the city's oldest and best. FitzGerald was delighted years later to discover that his only son strongly desired also to attend this school with a proud tradition.

Tall, gangling, with a mop of chestnut hair almost obscuring his dark Irish eyes, Bob showed the normal enthusiasm for team sports. But he was also unable to repress his urge toward verse, and his first efforts were published in the school monthly, the *Sydneian,* of which he became a staff member. During his five years at Sydney Grammar (1915–1919) he published a baker's dozen of poems, all under the *nom de guerre* of "Crumaboo"—a war cry of the Geraldyns of Desmond.[5] In this activity he was abetted by a shining fellow student, Tom Inglis Moore, destined to become an outstanding journalist, novelist, poet, critic, and the first professor to offer in Australia a course in Australian literature. Another schoolmate was Ross Gollan, who for years gave careful critiques of most of FitzGerald's poems. The lads severely commented upon each others' writings—a practice that became a lifelong habit for which the researcher into FitzGerald's theory of composition should be grateful.

To disinter his juvenilia would be, in FitzGerald's simile, "like poking sticks at something dragged out of the river." Again in his own terms one finds a description of the schoolboy writer's tone. "There was a bloke called Crumaboo, who was a dreadfully diffuse emotionalist and romanticist," he wrote to Moore on December 30, 1938. "Severity has been my constant deliberate aim, as a corrective. . . . Frigidity is the result rather than the desired classical severity. Wasn't cut out for a classicist." Haunting the Sydney Public Library, young FitzGerald came upon the early Provençal and other translations of Ezra Pound made in Europe, at a time when even few Americans had ever heard of that American poet. Bob enjoyed the swinging, braggadocio cadences of the pre-Mauberley Pound, a taste surprising to those who picture FitzGerald as nourished on nothing later than Browning. The Romantic strain in FitzGerald lingered through his *Vision* period in the early 1920s and cropped up frequently in his later best work, despite the attempted severity that led some reviewers to label him as a cold, neoclassical intellectual.

Bob determined not to go to the university at the expense of his family. Fortunately, his "leaving certificate" marks qualified him for an exhibition, or scholarship, and he spent two years at Sydney University in the Faculty of Science. His roving mind was repelled by the physics textbooks, and in all areas he was more likely—as happened all his life—to try to invent new solutions to problems rather than to memorize formulas or parrot the professor. He did not sit for "posts" and left the university, feeling that a life in a laboratory would kill the fascination for writing poetry.

Always preternaturally shy, the youth once shared a railway carriage with Henry Lawson but did not introduce himself to his uncles' friend. One of Bob's uncles, Ernest Le Gay Brereton, was a lecturer in chemistry at the University, and the other, as has been said, was Professor of English and librarian. The influence of J. Le Gay Brereton, the English professor, was bound to exert itself on his nephew.[6] Bob contributed to *Hermes,* the university literary magazine, and came on the staff in 1921. He was happy to have three poems selected for *Australian University Verse, 1920–22,* and five more for *Poetry in Australia, 1923.*

II *Money from the* Bulletin

Fitz, as he was usually called by his friends, dropped out of the university in 1922 and, in the paternal pattern, became articled as a surveyor to the Sydney firm of Dobbie and Foxall. In 1925 he qualified as a licensed surveyor and member of the Institution of Surveyors of New South Wales. He then entered private practice and in 1926 became partner of Athol Blair, with a small office in Pitt Street, Sydney. He often admitted, however, that he did not have the personality that attracts and impresses clients, and few came to the door. Yet he did not hold against the capitalist economy his failure to prosper, and all his life—unlike some of his early friends—FitzGerald had the plain sense never to swallow a morsel of Marxism.

Even during his apprentice days, Fitz revealed his dislike of officialdom and his championship of the underdog. He often tells a story about himself at this stage. On his way home one night he saw two policemen trying to arrest a drunk. The twenty-year-old and his two friends thought the drunk was putting up a rather good show and gave him a bit of encouragement by cheering. Finally the drunk was collected, and then one of the policemen grabbed Fitz, who was the nearest, and said, "And I'll just take you along too!"

FitzGerald was introduced at this time to H. M. Green, librarian and historian of Australian literature, who later helped him to get *Moonlight Acre* published. The lack of great demand for the firm's services left plenty of time to continue writing poetry and to become acquainted with the most active poets in Sydney. Before he was twenty-one Fitz became a casual member of the only *avant-garde* circle of the early 1920s in Australia, the group which founded the little magazine *Vision* in 1923. The publication ceased after one year, but its influence spread and the founders all have high places in the history of Australian poetry. The two older men were Norman Lindsay, novelist, philosopher, and artist,[7] and Hugh McCrae, a lovable, long-lived poet then producing his finest verse. The younger men were Lindsay's eldest son, Jack; Kenneth Slessor, journalist, destined to become Australia's finest modernist poet; and FitzGerald, then still in training as a surveyor.

FitzGerald himself has given a picture of the shabby atmosphere in which *Vision* was founded:

A gentleman named Mockbell established a line of coffee-shops in Sydney. They were mostly cellars dignified by the title of basements; and though they were lit by murky electric globes, not gas, I feel sure it must have been these haunts that Kenneth Slessor had in mind when he wrote of 'the gas-lit cellules of virtuous young men.' Certainly we were all virtuous enough then (our pockets demanded it); and Mr. Mockbell encouraged virtue by charging only fourpence for a tin jug from which you could squeeze two, or with luck two and a half cups, of passable coffee. And you could stay as long as you liked at the marble-topped tables, at ease in good chairs or in leather-upholstered seats with backs safely to the wall, quite unlike those stiff, tightly packed little cubicles that restrict you everywhere today. Did everything good like that go out in the 'twenties, or was it only youth? At any rate it was to one such cellule (in Castlereagh Street, near King Street) that Jack Lindsay invited me early in 1923 to meet Slessor (for the first time) and himself (for the second or third) to discuss the newly projected

and now memorable journal *Vision*. They had considered (with some mis-
givings) that I might perhaps be admitted as a contributor. Thereafter it
became habitual for me to frequent the place between five and six o'clock
in the afternoon. There was always company.[8]

Jack Lindsay described the young recruit as "a tall, somewhat
clumsy fellow with an engaging humility and a ready mind. I liked
him, and perhaps it was only my liking that made me feel sure his
verses would get better. At that time they were rather tame. He did
quickly develop, and so he was one of the few cases in which a wish
of this kind came true."[9]

FitzGerald was even more intimate with Jack's brother Phil,
then only seventeen, but a bohemian, friendly soul with whom
the young surveyor enjoyed conversing for hours at a time, in the
surveying office or out. From Phil comes a good picture of Fitz-
Gerald in the early 1920s:

Impatience is his keynote, an impatience with flesh and bone that with-
holds the luxury of dissolution, the return to earth. In life, too, he was impatient, boisterously thumping his fist on the marble-topped tables of
Mockbells, or the linoleum covering of a bar, while he insisted that *Vision*
found a new school, the pre-Kiplingites, escape from the modern mathe-
matics of verse, from the intellectual cottonwooling of emotion. Huge,
lean, gaunt Fitz, with his bright dark eyes and tousled hair, striding down
Pitt Street—I can see him now—a theodolite tossed carelessly over one
shoulder, roaring suddenly at sight of a friend, and swinging round, theodolite and all, so that had he been of ordinary height, he'd have brained at
least a dozen passers-by: Fitz bellowing in the Angel or some other pub,
or trying to fold his long legs under a restaurant table.[10]

A decade later, dejected when his surveying labors in Fiji were
going very badly, FitzGerald wrote to his friend Henry Stokes:
"Phil Lindsay, who wrote the novel [*Here Comes the King*, 1933],
used to be a great cobber of mine; many and many a drink has he
cadged off me, many and many a two-bob has he 'borrowed.' Ah
well, he's gone up in the world and I've gone down. It's my own
fault. If I had had any guts I'd have gone to London with him—he
wanted me to—instead of which I took the easier course and came
to Fiji."[11] Philip Lindsay's career was short and self-destructive.
Fitz, the literary tortoise, was to continue to build a reputation
through the next forty years.

Since his *Vision* days, which will be discussed later, FitzGerald has published a variety of poems, reviews, and articles in various magazines, as well as more than a dozen books. His style has naturally changed and his powers improved, but his association in his formative years with a highly talented group put the poet's mark upon him for life. With an uncle who was a center of literary ferment at Sydney University, and with such friends as the Lindsay family, McCrae, and Slessor, the young man could not help being convinced that the bringing of happiness and contemplation to readers through the medium of verse was an aspiration worthy of any man's most exacting effort.

FitzGerald therefore continued to write and publish. His first collection, *The Greater Apollo: Seven Metaphysical Songs,* a fourteen-page sheaf, was privately distributed in 1927 as a memorial to his mother. These were incorporated into his first solid volume of verse, *To Meet the Sun* (Sydney, 1929), along with a selection of poems that had appeared in such journals as *New Outlook, Forum, Triad, Spinner,* and the famed pink-covered Sydney *Bulletin.* This weekly's first editor, the eccentric and dominant J. F. Archibald, had created a whole school of authors proud of their Australianism, and throughout his life Fitz usually offered his verses first to the "Bully." Unlike some other periodicals, they paid money for poems—no small consideration, especially in depression days. An early unpublished version of *To Meet the Sun* won recognition in Britain when it was awarded the bronze medal of the Festival of Arts and Letters, sponsored by the Panton Arts Club. John Drinkwater was the final adjudicator of the prize.

III *"What Am I Doing in Fiji?"*

The world depression struck Australia as it did the United States and many other countries, and in 1931 FitzGerald took three momentous steps. He gave up his Sydney practice, got married, and left Australia to work as a surveyor with the Native Lands Commission, Crown Colony of Fiji.

With the exception of his family background and his association with the *Vision* poets, the strongest influence in FitzGerald's life and work has undoubtedly been his years in the islands of Fiji. His experiences in various parts of those tropical bushlands were to supply him with plenty of subjects for verses; as much as thirty years later the recollection of an old chief's grave on a ridge would be given form as a fresh poem—"Relic at Strength-Fled" (229–33). It gave him, as well, plenty of time to recollect his emotions in tranquility. His later verses, vehicles for contemplation rather than lyrical outbursts, often were the result of his solitary pondering while sitting with his surveying crew in a "fly-camp" on a jungle river, without having seen another European for half a year. It will later be shown that the knowledge of the Fijian language acquired by FitzGerald affected the English style of some of his poems by giving them a rhythm somewhat strange, loose, and percussive to citified ears.

This Fiji interlude, which was to have such a major effect upon his life and writing, came about by chance. On the busy little ferry plying to Hunters Hill, Fitz met a fellow surveyor, Harry Eve, who had been offered two jobs—one in New Guinea and one in Fiji. "I'm taking the New Guinea one—it pays better and is a bit closer to home," the friend said. "You can apply for the Fiji one if you like." Harry Eve went to New Guinea and after a distinguished but brief career died of scrub-typhus. Fitz went to Fiji and spent five years at hard work, but lived to write many a notable poem and at least one short story with a Melanesian setting.

Early in 1931, FitzGerald was married—in Hunters Hill, of course—to Marjorie-Claire Harris, whom he usually called Manon. She also came from a Hunters Hill family, although the poet liked to tell how he "swept her out of the Sydney Public Library," where she was a librarian. Her father had been an engineer too, and had been killed during the construction of the old shipping wharf at Suva, so that Fiji was not a completely unknown land to her. The marriage was a love match, and Manon became the poet's only muse; his 1965 volume of collected poems is dedicated to her. The marriage was to produce three daughters and one son.[12]

The staff of the Native Lands Commission in the early 1930s consisted of about a dozen surveyors. These men were sent out, around the end of March, from the capital at Suva to spend most of the year in the field, returning in the wet season to map their results in the office. After a terse interview with the cool, thin-lipped assistant commissioner, FitzGerald was assigned to survey at Seaqaqa, Macuata Province, and embarked, with his luggage and instruments, on the little steamer *Sir John Forrest* to Naduri, on the coast of Vanua Levu, second largest island of the Fiji group.

When the little ship reached Naduri in the Macuata District, Fitz was met by a young Englishman named Herbert Norman Murray, who volunteered to truck his gear inland eight miles to the village of Natua, which would be the surveyor's headquarters for many months. Fitz settled into the thatched open house of the *buli,* or district official. Murray, then on assignment by Morris, Hedstrom, Ltd., largest merchants in Suva, to manage an experimental plantation for the Hawaiian Pineapple Company, had his camp just across the ford, and most evenings were spent together. Sometimes Murray would explore the country in the daytime by following the traverse line being laid out by the surveyor and his Fijian aides, assigned to the task by the *buli.*

The two men became lifelong friends. "I liked him at sight," Murray recalled:

Tall, slim, with his balding chestnut hair unkempt and a grin on his face, he was always good-humored—gleeful, in fact, although there was nothing much at the time for him to be gleeful about. He liked the Fijians and they liked him. At times he was forced to be stern with them to get his job done, but at the end of a dust-up, when he got his way, he would always soften the defeat by cracking a joke. We chatted about everything in the world, except his family background. He introduced me to Roget's *Thesaurus,* a handy dictionary of synonyms that I have kept by me ever since. He read the Sydney *Bulletin* and seemed to know most of its contributors. I had the impression that at the time he was interested in forming phrase patterns, in words for their own sake, in finding the telling turn of sentence. He was not reticent in talking about the poems he had finished and published. An early one, "A Date," was inspired by his waiting for his wife to cross the sea and join him in Fiji.[13]

A not uncommon trait in a poet, the enjoyment of a good song or tune, was a pastime of FitzGerald's, and he listened for many evening hours to Murray's gramophone beside the Fijian river. The two men studied the language together from a battered copy of David Hazlewood's *A Fijian and English Dictionary,* and Murray started his friend on several years of concentrated practical work that ended with his attaining a high skill in grammar and a wide vocabulary that frequently crept into his letters thereafter.

Later he seldom even had the energy to read the books sent him by a monthly club. He wrote to Tom Inglis Moore from Seaqaqa on November 16, 1932:

I have not seen or spoken to a white man since June and my reading has been limited to Shakespeare, Montaigne, and *Na Mata,* the latter being a monthly publication in Fijian, the only language I can now speak except to myself or in my sleep. . . . I don't even write verses now; not enough leisure—and when I have got leisure (three days of it on my hands at the moment) then there seems to be no stimulus. . . . I need always the knowledge that people will appreciate what I try to express, else why worry about self-expression at all? And I must have some outside stimulus, provided usually of old by lively interchange of half-formed (and often half-baked) ideas with the sort of people like yourself who would afterwards appreciate an echo of those ideas in verse. . . . Hence I have written nothing in Fiji and am not likely to do so.

Actually, the record shows that a fair number of poems were written during his Fiji period.

Explanations for his lack of productivity at this time, however, are found elsewhere in the letter. Asked for news of himself, he responded:

Said news boils down to: well, it boils down to boils. If I've had one this year I've had fifty—it's living on tinned stuff and native foods that does it. In the intervals between boils it is just hard work: climbing mountains, precipices, boulder-strewn creeks, etc. and working my way through thick forest and undergrowth. Mud, rocks, rain, hills, bush, insects, impassable creeks, uncomfortable camps under just a fly in marshes and up mountain tops; wet boots, clothes, bedclothes; temper; natives, natives, natives, and the eternal moist heat. . . . I enjoy the nátives, good-humored amusing, irresponsible heathens who go every Sunday to the Methodist Church (conducted by a native, of course) because they regard it as a government institution and they have a wholesome fear of the government. They do not, fortunately, practise their Methodism on weekdays; and I love them. I don't really believe I ever want to leave them, though this life-in-death or death-in-life does grow irksome and sometimes I ask myself, "What the hell am I, Robert D. FitzGerald, sometime poet, doing, wasting my golden prime *here?*"

IV *No Wives or Other Extras*

Uncommon in a poet is FitzGerald's trait of gregariousness. No finer line of chat could be heard than his yarns over a half-pint of strong Australian beer. Whenever he was in Suva he fraternized daily with the gang of other surveyors of the Native Lands Commission. He was friendly with almost everyone else he met, despite an occasional Irish outburst when it seemed that some injustice was in the offing. Some of the N.L.C. outfit were to become life-long friends with whom he kept up a correspondence or exchanged visits.

Foremost among these was Henry Stokes, who later passed the examinations for local government engineer and became an official of the Colonial Sugar Refining Company branch at Lautoka, Fiji. After 1932 they have exchanged more than fifty letters which give many sidelights on the author's professional career, as well as glimpses of him as a literary person. Stokes first learned of FitzGerald from a fellow surveyor who said, "From what I hear, this chap seems to be a bit mad. They tell me he would sooner write poetry than eat!" FitzGerald first met Stokes in March or April, 1932. Two years later it became necessary for both of them to ascend Mount Nasorolevu (3,386 feet), the highest part of Vanua Levu. Stokes had gone up the previous year, merely to set a marker; he was the first European to ascend the main peak. The two decided to approach by different sides and meet on the summit for their observations. Fitz set out on May 14, but the tropical growth and undergrowth were so thick that although the next day his men by shouting could talk with Stokes's men at the top, they could not cut a trail fast enough to bring them to the summit until late on the 16th. The weather was so stormy that the men could not leave the tent. For nine days the two surveyors waited, cold and half-starved, for a clear spell, with nothing to do but exchange their life histories. They were not able to finish their observations until the 25th, when Stokes departed. Fitz left the next day, and on the 29th collected enough men to bring down his equipment. This sort of adventure is certainly rare among most men writing poetry even in his generation.

"Misi Ropate," or "Mister Robert," as the Fijians called him, held principles but could adapt to circumstances, as an incident on Sorolevu shows. He was a sincere bird lover. Stokes usually carried a .22 light rifle with him at work and often would bring down a pigeon, which since fresh meat was unobtainable would make, in the form of pigeon and rice soup, a wholesome lunch. "Fitz would have nothing to do with me for shooting the bird but when it was cooked he enjoyed it as much as I did," Stokes recalled in a private memoir. "He later wrote and said that he had taken a page from my book and now carried a gun and often shot pigeons— so he could be practical-minded as well as sincere in his thoughts on bird preservation."[14] The pretty birds were the only fresh meat to be had; tinned food brought on boils.

Although tall and gangling in build, Fitz had a big chest and enjoyed such sports in Fiji as tennis, swimming, and sailing. His long, thin legs were a disadvantage, however, in the tropical bush, where friends with stubbier legs could outwalk him. He always admired the athletic achievements of his brother Desmond Brereton FitzGerald, ten years his elder, who had died in 1928, and for whom he was to name his only son.

FitzGerald's dislike of convention and his assertion of individuality sometimes took the form of carelessness in dress, when his wife was not around. One evening he created a sensation by wandering into the Grand Pacific Hotel—for many years the swankiest place in Suva—without a jacket and with his hair awry. Nor did he endear himself to officialdom by writing, as he did, to the head of his department that "your actions savor of dishonesty." In desperation at Lovo, when he could not go on leave until the district was completely mapped but was unable to get the *buli* to provide labor to do his job there, he wrote to the Commissioner of Lands saying: "Your own actions in the immediate future shall determine, to my mind, whether your government values my services or the *buli's* at the higher rate."

But when he succeeded in his desperate actions to conquer red tape and obtuseness, he was often overcome with repentance. Two weeks after the *buli* was deposed, he wrote to Stokes on July 19, 1934: "I had then to break the news to the poor old blighter, who nearly wept, and I couldn't help pitying him—what is he after all but an old man, a bit soft in the nut, and a native? And this is the man I've had a victory over! It suits me better to lose a fight than to win one; when losing I can at least get a hell of a lot of fun out

of kicking up an unholy fuss. However, the change is a huge success."

Fitz did not win all his battles, but he could take defeat as a howling joke. Once the owner of the house he was renting in Suva requested him to vacate, and Fitz, thinking that an agreement was being broken, threatened legal action. He got a reply couched in prim forensic terms and learned that he had challenged one of the best legal brains in the Crown Colony. Owing to several clashes with the officials and the clerks, Fitz referred to himself as a "bolshevik," but his relations with other surveyors were usually those of warm fellowship, on a personal and professional level. As Stokes says, "We surveyors were not capable of understanding Fitz's poems and politely told him so, but nevertheless we were probably very pleased with the idea that a surveyor could also be a poet."[15]

Soon after his arrival in Fiji, at the native village of Naduri, the young husband began having qualms about the wisdom of bringing his Hunters Hill bride to a bush camp. He felt that he should quit the country as soon as possible, but looked to the day when Manon would arrive, and hired a servant who would help her. She arrived in July and lived with him in the field until the end of the season in December. She then went to Sydney, where their first child, Jennifer Kerry, was born, and named after the county from which her great-grandfather had emigrated. Wife and child joined Fitz in Suva at the end of the 1932 season, and in the following year, after he had finished his Seaqaqa survey and two others left uncompleted in Macuata Province, joined him at Vunimoli, a village in the Sasa District to which he had been assigned. Mrs. FitzGerald and Kerry returned to Sydney before the 1934 field season started, and in that year a second daughter, Rosaleen Moyra, was born.

This was Fitz's worst year in Fiji. He was reassigned to the Wairiki District, where the aforesaid stupid *buli* made it virtually impossible for him to obtain the native labor he required to do his assigned surveys. Lonely and, unknown to himself, coming down with appendicitis, he reached his lowest depths of gloom. When the beer had gone sour and the rum was low he could write to Stokes from Lovo on June 14, 1934: "Trouble is we are a low lot of Colonials: didn't go to Cambridge, don't you know; and all are really only a sort of laborers a bit above themselves and inclined to put on airs. Honestly I wouldn't give two hoots if they did sack me. As you have already remarked, I'm too soft for this country. But not in the head, old boy, not yet though getting that way." But he did finish the Wairiki assignment and departed for Sydney in August on leave. During his leave he underwent a severe operation for removal of the appendix. While convalescing at the suburb of Lane Cove he wrote "The Hidden Bole," which he considered for years to be his most "poetic" poem, containing an idea from which sprang such later speculative works as the prize-winning "Essay on Memory."[16]

Returning, refreshed, in June, 1935, he was curtly assigned to the Veivatuloa District in Namosi Province of Viti Levu, and warned that the employment of most of the surveyors would be terminated at the end of the year, since the main work would be finished. He felt at first that it was the best district he had ever had; from his camp he could see Suva through a telescope. The nickname of "Misi Ropate," he was amused to note, had followed him from Vanua Levu.

But within a few weeks he changed his mind about the district. "This village is built on a swamp," he wrote to Stokes on July 14. "I can only believe that those people of yours are worse than the Wairikians because so are these. I thought them all right at first, but that was this year's unusual optimism. . . . But such a surly, sullen lot of bad-tempered, quarrelsome bastards I never dreamed of. The Seaqaqa people were like another race. I *liked* them." Three villages in the region had petitioned that FitzGerald not be allowed to enter, even though their men had never worked for him. They complained that he worked too slowly and carefully and that his camps were too large to move easily. "Seeing I've cut down to lighter than ever before and cart around no gramophones, wirelesses, stoves, camp-ovens, *wives* or other extras, it is a bit tough."

By then Fitz had learned tactics. He picked the worst bully in the region and made him the head man, who kept the others under control. When Fitz left on November 25, 1935, his Wairiki friends gave him a loud sendoff.

CHAPTER 2

Home to Hunters Hill

F ITZGERALD left the Fiji service in 1936, when the surveying
work was finished. He returned to his family in Sydney by way of
New Zealand, and to support them took work with a private surveyor, engaged in jobs in various parts of New South Wales. He
then joined the surveying staff of the oceanside suburb of Manly.
In 1937 he obtained a similar post as a municipal employee at the
town of Ryde, which was nearer to his home at Hunters Hill.

He was still haunted, in this snug home, by dreams of the rough
years he had endured. As he wrote on April 19, 1937 (the first of his
letters to Stokes to be typewritten): "I had a nightmare last night,
a most realistic dream. I dreamt I was in a Fiji *vale* [thatched shelter]
and that it was the first night out of a new field season. There was
no labor; half my gear hadn't arrived; the natives hadn't come to
light with any *dalo* [taro] and I had only tinned food, and my cook
was mislaid somewhere; I had all my unpacking and sorting yet to
do; worst of all even in my dream I remembered that I had sold my
lamp to that priest from down Serua way (whose name eludes me)
and I found I had omitted to replace it with any sort of lamp at
all. . . . I woke very thankful to find myself a municipal wage-plug—
which I'm getting a bit sick of, by the way." Both his nightmares
about Fiji and his occasional nostalgia for it were natural. As he
wrote to Stokes on April 16, 1965: "I was perfectly conscious that
it would not suit me to go back [to Fiji], and did not really want to."

I   *"The Whole of Australia Could Hear"*

Nights and weekends he exhausted himself studying for examinations that would give him a certificate as local government engineer and a raise in pay. However, his outdoor work in all weathers
was tiring, and he was less interested in memorizing tables and
sewage codes than in writing poetry. The old impetus to put the
world into words was strong, and association with friends in the
literary circles of Australia, which was now expanding with new

writers and experiments, began to assert itself, despite many dis-
couragements. Writing to Stokes on July 16, 1937, he said: "I have
a lot of 'literary' friends in Sydney who, remembering the man-
who-was, plague unduly the man-who-is with bloody stuff to criticize
and so forth and well-meant attempts to get me to put my fingers in
old pies that I thought were chucked to the maggots long ago.
Besides that I've not your interest in engineering and your applica-
tion, so bang goes the study."

The celebrated poems that issued from FitzGerald's pen in these
years did not come from a man living at ease or even in financial
comfort. Depression conditions still obtained, and the family had
to be fed even if literary aspirations were put aside. They had no
car, and there was no chance to go body-surfing during the occasional free weekends. "Carless and no longer at Manly either,"
Fitz wrote to Stokes on September 16, 1937. "*And* broke. Broke.
My gawd, ain't I broke! Never seem to have two browns. Week's
pay mortgaged before I get it. Bills."

Finances did not improve: on the following January 25 he observed: "It becomes increasingly obvious that there are no reasonable jobs for surveyors. I was earning £6 per week wages in 1925.
How I have risen in the world! How I have advanced! In what
other profession would a man have worked as hard, gained as much
experience, learnt as much, and all to so little profit!" After quoting
a poem by A. E. Housman concluding: "And every moon are
older,/And soon we shall be dead," Fitz wryly misquotes Robert
Louis Stevenson's epitaph:

> *Here he lies where he needs must be;*
> *Home is the sailor, home from the sea,*
> *And the Hunter back at Hunters Hill.*

Although in the letter he recalled that *To Meet the Sun* was published in 1928 and that "in 1938 no one will publish anything," he
had been working again at poetry and appearing occasionally in
the *Bulletin*. He was guessing wrong; the year 1938 was to be a good
one for his fame. "My only hope is to win the big prize," he continued; "results not out yet. If I could get my recent stuff published
it would be one millstone untied from round my neck. My literary
career is about at an end; but I don't want it to close with a whole

lot of stuff still lying around unpublished except in periodicals."

The "big prize" was the offering of a sum of £50 for the best poem entered in the celebration of the Australian Sesquicentenary. On this and on shorter verses FitzGerald had been laboring for months, in hours stolen from sleep. Concerning this prize Tom Inglis Moore, Fitz's school chum, recalled: "I ran into Fitz and we had a beer together. He told me he was in a dilemma. He had been asked to serve as a judge for the Sesquicentenary poems, but thought of declining the offer—and the honorarium—in order to take a chance and enter a poem himself. I advised him to have another beer and think it over. After reconsidering, he told me he thought he would decline the sure money and have a go at the prize. That beer cost me £25. He won, of course, and I came in second."

The winning poem was the long, contemplative "Essay on Memory." Moore, then an editorial writer on the Sydney *Morning Herald,* persuaded his boss to print the poem, even though it was quite lengthy for a newspaper's columns, and wrote an unsigned editorial praising the judges' choice. The notoriety resulted in the same year in an offer of publication of the collection *Moonlight Acre,* containing "Essay on Memory" as well as several other long poems or sequences. *Moonlight Acre* was awarded the gold medal of the Australian Literature Society of Melbourne for the best book of the year.

Family duties and World War II almost did end FitzGerald's literary career. In 1939 his only son, Robert Desmond, was born, and in 1942 his third daughter, Phyllida Mary. Children had to be nourished and sent to school. The relief from the threat of war in 1938 had been followed by the outbreak of a global conflict in which Australia was first among the Commonwealth countries to offer support to a threatened Great Britain. But FitzGerald at the time of Munich was receiving only £8/8/7 a week and writing nothing but articles for the *Australian Surveyor* on the use of a new method for computing vertical parabolic curves or on the design of a better form on which to record sun or star observations.

He was not allowed, because of his occupation, to enlist. "Surveyors are in the 'reserved' class," he wrote Stokes on October 13, 1939, "with full restriction, so the government seems determined we shall starve—no work and they won't let us enlist even if unmarried and of military age." Later, when the Japanese were coming over the Owen Stanley Range, FitzGerald—despite his reserved occupation and three children—did enlist, but was rejected because of his age (he was one month over forty).

"I'd like to own a really good coconut plantation and sit back and watch the nuts drop," he had written Stokes on July 26, 1939, just before the war broke out; "this hard work business is over-rated." In October, 1940, as a result of overwork and eyestrain caused by war duties, he had to spend three weeks in bed with iritis, conjunctivitis, and corneal ulcer. On recovering, he changed jobs before the end of the year and joined the Australian Common-wealth Department of the Interior, Property and Survey Branch. This department acted as a sort of surveying firm whose only client was the national government, and during all the war years Fitz was to be engaged in defense tasks.

His labors were classified, but mainly concerned the laying out of airfields in various parts of the country. The work took him to many outlying regions, "from Surry Hills to Broken Hill," and he was separated from his family and friends for months at a time. He failed the engineering examination in May, 1940, through lack of time to study and lack of interest in the usual questions.

He was now a literary figure, even though not a highly paid one, and in October was for the first time asked to appear on radio to give a talk on poetry. "Never again, laddie, never again," he wrote his friend in Lautoka. "It's a ghastly feeling just when you're switched on the air, if you've got any imagination—to know that the whole of Australia could hear every word you're going to say—if it wanted to. Afterward I went to the dentist, which was quite a relief." Later he was to appear further on radio and television, as well as on the lecture platform, and at last overcame his feeling of fearful exposure. While working in various parts of the country during the war he somehow found time to edit the anthology *Australian Poetry, 1942,* designed to represent the best verse published in that year.

II *Lecturer, Editor, and Consultant*

During his war travels FitzGerald found that his home in Hunters Hill had been put up for sale. In alarm, he decided to ensure freedom from landlords by buying a home, in which operation he was aided by a modest inheritance from an elderly uncle. He found a pleasing house—"it's about forty years old but good for forty years more"—at 4, Prince Edward Parade (Hunters Hill, of course). Here the family was living when the last of his children was born, and here the family continued to live, in a charmingly furnished house overlooking a green avenue and neighboring gardens.

FitzGerald's pride in his war work is reflected in a few lines in a letter to Stokes on December 9, 1944, a year of terrible drought: "Earlier in the year I did a complete detail survey of [censored by scissors—actually Garden Island Naval Headquarters and dockyard], picking up everything in sight. That was a real test of patience and meticulousness. It is not the sort of work I like (who does?). All the same *having done it* is one of the high spots of my somewhat undistinguished professional career." The surveyor progressed slowly but steadily in his profession. In 1947 he was made Honorary Secretary of the Institution of Surveyors, New South Wales, and as a representative attended in 1948 the Melbourne meeting at which was founded the Institution of Surveyors (Australia).

Despite the travel and labors of the war years, FitzGerald wrote some of his most notable poems. He kept up his *Bulletin* connection. He was among the first authors to appear in *Southerly,* a leading Australian literary quarterly. He began in 1941 contributing poetry, articles, and reviews to *Meanjin,* later to become the most enduring and influential Australian quarterly dealing with the arts; his correspondence over the years with C. B. Christesen, editor for more than thirty years, is a revealing source of critical materials.

FitzGerald's fine poem "Heemskerck Shoals," which had been printed in the *Bulletin* in 1944, was chosen in 1949 by a master typographer, John Kirtley, to appear as an outstanding example of the art of the private press. The poet wrote to Stokes on June 6: "A bloke down in Melbourne is bringing out a limited edition of my 'Heemskerck Shoals' on handmade paper, about folio size, letters almost half-inch size, I gather, illustrations and what not. You can buy one if you like—one of a signed set of 85—and at the very reasonable price of ten or twelve guineas. . . . Still there are, I am told, enough fools in the world—who call themselves collectors—for there to be quite a little turnover for me at a ten per cent royalty." Purchase of a copy of this limited signed edition, with a map and fifteen drawings by Geoffrey C. Ingleton, would have indeed been a good investment; today most of the copies are guarded in libraries or by "fools of collectors."[1] The book, at Fitz's suggestion, was dedicated to the memory of James Emery, a draftsman friend of *Vision* days who had liked to yarn about music and French literature.

On January 1, 1951, the New Year's Honours List included the name of Robert David FitzGerald, Officer of the British Empire Order, and a medal was later pinned on his chest by the governor-general of Australia as a recognition of his services to literature. Although offhand in speaking to his friends about his O.B.E., the first one given to an Australian author,[2] and a reflection of the personal interest in literature held by the prime minister, Robert Menzies, FitzGerald was proud of this honor. "It seemed to me that there might be much legitimate criticism of myself being the recipient," he wrote on January 20, 1951, to C. B. Christesen, "but that the principle of recognition of this sort being given—at last—to poetry, entirely unmixed with other considerations (for I am in no other sense a public figure of any kind whatever) was so very right that—on behalf of Australian poetry, as it were—I would have done wrong to refuse it. . . . The monarchial system suits me very well."

Between Two Tides, a long poem over which Fitz had been working for a decade, was published in 1952. This volume was based on the adventures of Will Mariner, captain's clerk who survived the massacre of the crew of the British privateer *Port-au-Prince* at Tonga in 1806, and the lad's relations with Finau, chief of those islands. Tonga is a group not far from Fiji, and FitzGerald's five years in Fiji undoubtedly contributed to his interest in this dramatic story and to his handling of the native background. In the following year a collection of shorter poems, also written over the previous ten years and considered by the poet to be his best up to that time, appeared under the title of *This Night's Orbit.* Another lengthy poem, *The Wind at Your Door,* in which the main character is a prison doctor named Martin Mason, one of Fitz's ancestors, was privately published in 1959. *Southmost Twelve,* another volume of verses, was issued in 1962. The appearance in 1965 of *Forty Years' Poems,* a rigidly selected collection, clearly established FitzGerald's right, based on the quality, output, and major achievements of his poetry, to be considered Australia's foremost poet during the previous quarter of a century.

Less widely recognized has been FitzGerald's achievement as a critic. Over all the years since he and Tom Moore at grammar school had commented upon each other's writings, he had been acting as a shrewd judge of his own work as well as commenting on the bundles of manuscript sent him by friends and strangers alike, eager to have the sort of painstaking, line-by-line analysis that required hundreds of hours of the busy man's time and an exhausting use of a brain that refused to be taken in by claptrap. More than thirty book reviews by FitzGerald have been published, but even more voluminous is the amount of commentary in his correspondence and in his reports as an adviser to the Commonwealth Literary Fund.

On May 16, 1959, he wrote to Stokes: "I have, foolishly no doubt, for it means sacrificing my annual holidays and going to Melbourne in July of all months, undertaken to deliver three lectures at Melbourne University in that month under the auspices of the Commonwealth Literary Fund. . . . Am now nearly driving myself and everyone else mad trying (a) to think and (b) write three lectures of an hour each." The result was a successful series of lectures in Melbourne, which were afterward rewritten and delivered to overflow audiences at the University of Queensland in June, 1961. A lecture on Dame Mary Gilmore was given at the Australian National University at Canberra in July, 1960, at the suggestion of Tom Inglis Moore, one of the members of the advisory board of the Commonwealth Literary Fund. The Fund assisted in the publication in 1963 of the three FitzGerald lectures under the title of *The Elements of Poetry*. With Moore's cooperation, FitzGerald in 1948 had edited the *Selected Verse* of Dame Mary Gilmore, beloved poet and worker for social justice. He edited a briefer selection from Dame Mary in 1963, as well as a small volume in the same series in the same year on his own poetry.

III   *Americans—"The Most Helpful, Generous People"*

All his work over his most creative period was done at night in his Hunters Hill home, in any quiet spot he could find—usually a bedroom. As he wrote to Christesen on August 8, 1942: "My own poem [*Between Two Tides*] presses me hard: I work all day at the office, come home, do my chores, have my meal, wash up and go to bed with my clothes on. At 10:30 or so when the house is quiet I get up and revive the fire and write till about 2 a.m.—and lucky if I do three lines. Then to bed and usually fail to sleep trying to straighten out in my mind what I've been trying to write. Why *do* we do it?"

Trying to write great poetry with only a narrow wall separating him from the lively activities of a family of four children and their friends over the years has resulted in at least two stories. One concerns a time when he was attempting to concentrate on a difficult literary task. The family curbed its normal boisterous enjoyment of life and began tiptoeing through the house. The author finally couldn't stand the distraction any longer. "For God's sake, stop tiptoeing!" he yelled. "You make me nervous!"

On another occasion, after an unusually noisy evening during which the father was trying to work, the family retired to sleep. Late at night, when he had finished his stint, he let loose, slammed doors, banged windows, stamped his feet, turned the radio up full blast, and shouted: "All right, you noisemakers, you interrupted me all day and now it's my turn!" The poet's wife calmly considered the carnage with an experienced eye. "I know what to do," she informed the startled children. "We'll pull the main switch." The lights went out, the radio went off, and the entire family settled to sleep.

Fitz was undoubtedly a family man and was proud of his growing children and of his home. When in 1953 he was awarded the Grace Levin Prize for Poetry for *Between Two Tides* he was asked how he would spend the money. He replied that he would use it to fix up the house, where termites had bored into the woodwork. Reminded that the prize had been set up to advance the cause of the arts in Australia, he answered: "It won't advance the cause of the arts if I fall through my kitchen floor!" Readers of his poetry should not forget that FitzGerald is truly a family man with a very practical sense of daily problems.

Best relaxation of all Fitz found in cultivating his garden. Unlike the rest of the family, who specialized in the sort of flowers that make "The Hill" a competitive seed-catalog come alive, Fitz chose the more practical vegetables—especially beets and cabbages.

He delighted on a Sunday morning to visit a neighbor and present her with a sixteen-pound cabbage with the dew still pearling the leaves, saying: "You can't find me a rose more beautiful than this!"

Later he took up lawn bowls at the exclusive club at Hunters Hill, and after a six-month training period could join the blue-jacketed, straw-hatted serious men on Sunday afternoon at their competitions above the riverside. He wrote to Stokes on October 12, 1961: "I've played a lot of games not very well; but none, I think, so damn badly as I play bowls and there's none I have enjoyed more."

The happiest year of the FitzGeralds' life was 1963. He became a teacher in America. (He is, by the way, no relation to the well-known American poet and translator Robert Stuart FitzGerald.) The Australian had accepted an invitation, arranged through Dr. Joseph Jones, former Fulbright fellow to New Zealand, to serve as visiting lecturer for a semester at the University of Texas. "With fear and trembling," Fitz, a man who had never finished college or offered a course in his life, agreed to plunge into academic activity, since there was no other way for him to see America and make a trip around the world.

The FitzGeralds traveled by air to Texas via Hawaii and San Francisco. He was under the impression that his work would involve lecturing on Australian literature and teaching creative writing; but he found himself assigned to two standard courses familiar to thousands of American professors. One was a section of the usual sophomore literature, and Fitz worked in his office from nine to six and then sat up late at night preparing lectures in the hope that he could, after the age of sixty, arouse sparks of enthusiasm in a required course in which veteran professors seldom expect any eager response. The burden was lightened at times when he dealt with *Henry IV, Part I,* on which he had coached his son, and with Montaigne, an old favorite.

The other course, for upper-division and graduate students, dealt with "chief modern poets of England and America"—which included not one from Australia. Here Fitz was, however, on firmer ground, but he still lacked the academic approach. "I told them at the outset I knew very little about English and American poetry," he wrote to Tom Inglis Moore from New York on June 9: "and so they would have to teach me—which they proceeded joyously to do, teaching themselves at the same time. It's a line of action which would never work twice; but *once* situated as I was situated, it had the effect of making them all think, all take an interest. They loved it; and the University authorities were pleased at the outcome. But it was not Australian poetry." Thanks, however, to Dr. Jones, FitzGerald delivered lectures at four other centers and finally was asked to talk on Australian poetry at the University of Texas. He also read poems over the air on Station KASE, Austin.

Slightly disappointed at the lack of facilities for lawn bowls, the poet found compensation in walking. The Texan winter and spring provided much sunshine—quite Australian weather—and Fitz walked from his apartment, about fifteen minutes from the University, to spend the day on the campus and eat lunch from a paper bag beside Waller Creek. In the more wooded regions he was delighted by the mockingbirds, and especially by the squirrels, which he had never seen before. Sometimes he watched the engineering students doing practice surveys and remarked that they were using shockingly antiquated instruments.

He and Marjorie stayed in America for five months, and their travels gave them a view of America that might well have disabused them of the usual stereotypes and be reflected in his future writing. Americans might ponder the candid impressions of an intelligent visitor from an "unimportant" country in the private letter he wrote to his old friend Moore: "We liked the American people. Not nearly as happy about American institutions, such as the insistence on private enterprise versus socialization. We think the private enterpriser (such as the overland buses) push the people around shamefully, and are real exploiters. American democracy is not really as democratic as Australian democracy; American efficiency, that we've heard so much of, is a myth dressed in red tape. And the *United* States of America seem to spend their time most ununitedly fighting the Federal Government. But the Americans are the most helpful, generous people I have ever encountered."

As an honor to the visiting poet, the Humanities Research Center of the University of Texas published in their Tower Series a collection of twenty-seven poems, illustrated by Sister Mary Corita. The title poem, "Of Some Country," based on "The Stranger-Lad" (1931), was rewritten for the occasion on a theme from FitzGerald's early years. Previously he had contributed another poem, "Tocsin," to the summer, 1962, special issue of *Texas Quarterly* devoted to presenting an "image of Australia."

The FitzGeralds continued on their world tour at the end of the term, via New York to Europe. The main goal was to visit the Kerry country from which his ancestors had come, land of the Geraldyns of Desmond. Joined by daughter Rosaleen, they explored with delight the Irish landscape and, by detective work, even identified the exact house in Tralee from which the great-grandfather had departed for Australia. Fitz was enchanted with Ireland; he took photos, collected pictures and local lore, and reviewed local history, reminding himself of the poem he had written in 1951, "Transaction" (110), based on family letters.

London was less interesting than England's quiet shires. Scotland, Sweden, Denmark, and Germany were all new and thrilling lands. Paris was beautiful, and Fitz made a pilgrimage to La Mothe Montravel, near Bordeaux, to visit the home of Montaigne—a visit about which he wrote an essay "A Pilgrimage in the Sudouest." The couple loved Geneva, saw a perfect ballet, and even went up a funicular railway to a mountaintop from which they breathed the air blowing straight across a valley from Mont Blanc. In Rome Fitz gave a lecture. The couple returned to Australia via Istanbul and Hong Kong.

IV *A Poem for "Arts Vietnam"*

Refreshed, FitzGerald returned to commuting to Sydney on weekdays on the Hunters Hill ferry. Supervising surveyor of the New South Wales branch of the Department of the Interior, he sat in his office on the seventeenth floor of a new Commonwealth Building in the heart of Sydney. He was among the leaders of his profession—about which he had, in times of gloom and fatigue, voiced a few harsh words but which he respected as an honorable and necessary vocation. (In a television interview he said that if he had his life over he would again choose to be a surveyor.) He could look up from his desk over the booming city, with skyscrapers overtopping each other from harbor to Haymarket. He could see thirty miles to the westward the Blue Mountains, where in sleet and snow, just back from the tropics, he had tramped with a theodolite over his shoulder. He could finger the tightly packed volume of his latest collection, *Forty Years' Poems*.

This book brought him a tangible reply to envious critics in September, 1965, when a £5,000 Encyclopaedia Britannica Australia Award was equally shared with another poet, Professor A. D. Hope. The chairman of the selection committee said that *Forty Years' Poems* showed that the author was one of the most important and individual Australian poets of the century. "The committee," he added, "has also taken into account his substantial contribution to Australian poetry over many years."[3]

FitzGerald retired from his profession as a surveyor in February, 1966, and concluded his activity by publishing a history of the New South Wales Division of the national society. Saying "Better to wear out than to rust out," he felt free to do things that he had not earlier been free to do.[4] One such task came quickly when the foremost publisher in Australia commissioned him to prepare a volume of selected letters by Hugh McCrae, the elder poet of the *Vision* group. He thereupon began the dismaying task of approaching more than a dozen recipients of the lively letters written by McCrae— often illustrated by clever pen drawings. Hundreds of hours were consumed in correspondence and in reading, selecting, and editing the letters. As he wrote to one donor on February 24, 1967: "McCrae must have spent more than half his time writing letters. I dare say no one in our time has written so many. I have read through over 700 to Norman Lindsay, some of 5 or 6 pages; as many or more to Vance and Nettie Palmer, comparable numbers to Rupert Atkinson, and huge stacks to quite a number of others. I have read nearly 3000 all told. And just after you rang off Gilbert Mant, who also had seen Gellert's article, rang me up to tell me he had two suitcases full." At that time, he had not yet seen the equally large collection contributed by Professor R. G. Howarth. The editor's copies of *The Letters of Hugh McCrae*, with a preface by FitzGerald, were delivered on May 29, 1970—almost four years after acceptance of the assignment.

Meanwhile, FitzGerald's yearning—always keen—for justice in an unjust world had focused upon the conflict in Vietnam, in which he felt that supporting Australian forces should not participate. As early as August, 1967, he began publishing protests. His prestige was so great that his help was strongly solicited by various antiwar groups. After consideration, he agreed to support the idea of a week-long convocation of artists against the Vietnam war, under the sponsorship of the largely leftist Association for International Co-operation and Disarmament (N.S.W.). A committee, with Guy Morrison as chairman, was formed to plan "Arts Vietnam," a program which was given in Sydney during October 3 to 12, 1968. Painters, musicians, actors, folk singers, and even jazz combos offered their talents in the cause. FitzGerald organized the poetry section and also collected funds which in the end exceeded $400 (Australian). Letters and other appeals brought wide support.

On the eve of the poetry presentation, FitzGerald—whose personal efforts had turned him into a "nervous wreck"—prepared his short talk as chairman, introducing the Poetry Evening on October 6. "Poetry, to live," he said in part, "must do more than reflect life, like a mirage in a desert; it must take part in life. So that not only as a duty to civilization but also for the vitality of their craft itself, poets must participate in the world about them." At the meeting over which he presided, a dozen poets were present and read their own poems; more than a dozen others who were not able to attend had poems read for them. FitzGerald participated toward the end of the evening by reading "Lawbreakers."[5]

"My own share in the 'festival,'" FitzGerald wrote much later, ". . . was as organizer of poetry and one of the collectors of funds. . . . Funds were (and are) to go towards bringing some overseas speaker who would carry weight with local audiences beyond that carrier by local speakers. . . . We did not raise enough to do it on our own; but schemes are still afoot."[6] His final opinion expressed to fellow workers ran: "I think the 'feeling of the meeting' and of previous meetings is that Arts Vietnam should conclude. It served its purpose; I believe it did a worthwhile job; but I also believe that if it were to hang on publicly, gradually dwindling, it would not simply cease to be important; it could also dissipate some of the good effect; it could belittle what has been done already."[7]

V *"Produce It, in God's Name"*

As an aftermath of "Arts Vietnam," however, FitzGerald embarked in the spring of 1969 on an antiwar enterprise when approached by Guy Morrison, who asked his support on the principles voiced by Henry David Thoreau in New England in 1849. After some consideration, the poet became a member of the Committee in Defiance of the National Service Act, a satellite of the A.I.C.D. The aims of the committee were clearly stated in a proposed advertisement in a national newspaper: "We believe that no government has the right to force an individual to act contrary to the dictates of his conscience. We therefore believe the National Service Act, as presently constitu'ted, to be an unjust law in its lack of provision for young men whose conscientious beliefs do not allow them to engage in a particular war . . . ."

FitzGerald attended several meetings of the committee and agreed to risk imprisonment by signing a "Statement of Defiance"[8] supporting young men refusing to register under the National Service Act because they would not be coerced into any war they believed to be immoral and unjust. Thirty-seven other signers joined him under summons to the Court of Petty Sessions in Sydney, on September 22, 1969. The charge ran that the defendant "did publish a certain writing the form of which is annexed"—the Statement of Defiance—"which encouraged the commission of the offense of failing to register for the purpose of National Service as provided for by Section 11, National Service Act, 1951–68, the said offense being an offense against the laws of the Commonwealth." Much later, FitzGerald learned that after he left a meeting of the defendants, all agreed during an informal discussion to serve a fourteen-day sentence in jail rather than pay a fine. He decided, for various reasons, that he should pay, and on October 14, 1969, obtained a receipt for $50 (Australian).

The spectacle of a number of prominent people apparently panting to go to prison in an act of civil disobedience aroused varied comments. The committee continued its actions into 1970. They claimed that more than two thousand other citizens had signed the Statement. Several more batches of signers urged that they be prosecuted and even pressed the attorney-general of the Commonwealth to send them off to jail.

A new attorney-general, T. E. F. Hughes, took office in November. He was by chance the husband of FitzGerald's niece, and speculation arose about the possibility that Hughes might have to condemn his uncle. Properly, the lawyer examined the record and found that

FitzGerald had paid the fine. In an interview, the poet was reported as saying: "I was worried that the whole affair was an ineffective waste of time. I didn't know they had all agreed to go to gaol rather than pay, so I paid the money and went fishing. Now I am sorry that I did pay. I feel very much as though I have let the team down."[9]

Other Australians inevitably saw things differently. The use of the law courts for purposes of protest, and the validity of the defense, were discussed by Norman S. Reaburn, lecturer in criminal law at the University of Tasmania, in a letter in which he wrote, in part: "But it does no one any good if people who have not broken the law try to pretend that they have done so and, by means of a carefully stage-managed private prosecution, artificially and unnecessarily restricted the ambit of allowable protests by others." This rendered the action "martyrdom by false pretences."[10]

The committee's program against selective service continued through the launching of a "Don't Register" campaign among young men, mass meetings and propaganda, filing of false registration forms, and threats of strikes if union officials were jailed. By this time FitzGerald felt that he had done enough in that particular effort. He had written to Roland Robinson on October 19, 1969: "We of the first thirty-eight fully believed we might be given gaol without the option of a fine. It was agreed beforehand at a meeting which I attended that if given the option it was a matter for the individual conscience whether we paid the fine or not. . . . I would certainly have paid eventually, for—as you could see—the whole thing was becoming what some have called gimmicky and what I am beginning to call phony." His conclusions were expressed in a letter of January 28, 1970, to Ken McLeod, secretary of the committee: "We want to be as effective as we can in trying to get Australia out of the war (the first consideration) and in getting a repeal of the National Service Act (as a subsidiary consideration to the first). Gestures repeated begin to lose their effect . . . come to think of it, since no one has gone to gaol and only two have paid the fine, we who have paid could begin to say that only we have 'suffered in the cause.'" He had pleaded guilty and had not rescinded his action. From the first, FitzGerald urged that the committee stop short of inciting young men to refuse to register for National Service. He had observed in his own field that a legal conviction, even for a trifling offense, could ruin a man's chances for a career.

After his retirement, the poet's chronic lack of funds lightened somewhat. Desiring to visit their youngest daughter in London, he and his wife sold some family paintings, dipped into savings, and in 1972 made a second trip abroad. They revisited England and France and toured Norway, Germany, and Russia—where Fitz-Gerald was given special recognition by the Writers' Union and swam in the Black Sea. Turned seventy years of age, he was still proudly publishing poems and articles, giving public talks on literature, and bowling on the green lawn of the local club in his ancestral suburb of Hunters Hill. A sheaf of twenty-two type-script poems written since 1963 await publication in a new volume—in his own wry phrase, "probably posthumous." The epigraph of the collection is another expression of FitzGerald's lifelong activism, taken from Thomas Carlyle's *Sartor Resartus:* "Were it but the pitifullest infinitesimal fraction of a Product, produce it, in God's name. 'T is the utmost thou hast in thee: out with it then." At three-score and ten, FitzGerald was still ready to produce.

CHAPTER 3

The Poet Considers Poetry

"NOTHING destroys good poetry so quickly as a theory," Robert D. FitzGerald proclaimed at the age of twenty in his apprentice piece in a national journal. "Remember the horrible example of Wordsworth!"[1]

Despite such disclaimers from time to time, the practicing poet throughout a long life made many comments—in letters, articles, reviews, and lectures—concerning the functions of verse and the aims of the songsmith. Moreover, many of his early ideas were consistent with later views. He may never have launched a poet's manifesto, but certainly his observations over the years are necessary to a better understanding of his intentions, and many of his remarks would be valuable to a beginning poet today. After one sees what FitzGerald hopes poetry can achieve, one may then better judge his progressive achievements.

I *The Wedding of Content and Form*

Dangerously verging on a definition of the indefinable, FitzGerald wrote to his friend Tom Inglis Moore around 1938:

Poetry indefinable but it gives us the shudders in the vitals, yes. But that's only dodging the question. What is it in poetry that gives us the shudders? I take it it is another indefinable, beauty. Not that the subject-matter must be beautiful, that most sentimental and stultifying of notions, but that the completed poem must create beauty—it is beauty which gives us the shudders. That is why a thing can still be poetry although one day it thrills the spine and the next not, though it thrills your spine and not mine; the beauty is in the poetry, the poetry conveys the beauty to the reader who may or may not perceive it. Is then beauty only the same thing as poetry, no. Poetry is beauty in verse and against other forms of beauty.[2]

In the same letter, FitzGerald makes his distinction between "poetry" and "verse":

I brought myself up on a mixture of Henry Lawson and Matthew Arnold and still am unconvinced of any incongruity. Verse and poetry are not

separable, verse and beauty *are;* poetry and beauty are also inseparable
though the kind of beauty which I demand is the beauty of the finished
poem, not the beauty of the subject-matter, and is only recognized by the
hair-raising test. If verse and beauty are *constituents* of poetry and if
you have good verse (like Lawson's) you are a long way towards poetry.
Add a little something more and there you are; and the point is that little
something more is always liable to slip in even in outright comic verse, or
nonsense verse. I have quite a regard for Lawson as a *poet,* quite apart
from his unquestioned other merits.[3]

To a poet, of course, the best way to say anything is always in a
poem. "If one could only talk in poems all the time, how few mis-
understandings there would be in the world. And how splendid all
our legislation would be if it were a rule of parliament that all
speeches must be made in rhyme!"[4]

FitzGerald expanded many of his critical credos in 1953, in a
lengthy review of six volumes of Australian poetry, and dealt especially with the relationship of matter and manner—that is, content and form. Therein he rejected the use of separate standards for
each author and repeated his belief that recognition of what constitutes poetry is a question of instinct and personal taste. The
aspects for analysis "always boil down to three: subject, form, and
the manner in which these two are combined."[5]

The poet again runs perilously near an attempt at definition.
"Manner comes closest to the essential quality of poetry itself; for
poetry is a manner of saying a thing rather than the thing said. Not-
withstanding this emphasis on manner, subject-matter remains a
principal ingredient; otherwise any sort of nonsense becomes ad-
missible. While theoretically any subject-matter provides a fit
material for verse, its contribution to the verse considered as poetry
must be an emotional or imaginative contribution, or what I should
call a moral contribution—an attitude to life; never a purely intellectual contribution."[6] FitzGerald concludes this essay with the
belief that too much modern poetry attempts to produce what will
be remembered for some statement, character, or anecdote, "rather
than for haunting lines, lingering music, or the hypnotic quality of
architectural construction—the flow of thought and image. But it
is these qualities—of manner rather than matter—which make
poetry."[7] Further discussion of FitzGerald's opinions on
manner—or poetic technique—appears in Chapter 4.

A review of FitzGerald's other critical writings reveals a number
of deeply held opinions. His championship of free verse—such as
that of Ezra Pound—in 1922 was followed a year later by "A
Defence of Slang." In it he wrote: "There is no doubt that the new
slang terms of today become absorbed into the spoken language
of tomorrow and into the written language of the day after."[8] He
felt also that slang performs the minor duty of absorbing and finally
rejecting words that the language has decided to discard. The use of
dialect, he thought, had done little to change speech. Although the
earlier Australian literature had abounded in provincialisms—often
bold and sharp—FitzGerald was to eschew in his poetry the colorful localisms of such groups as the bush balladists and many versi-
fiers of the Sydney *Bulletin* stable.

FitzGerald's first appearance in the beloved *Bulletin*—on
May 21, 1925—revealed an appreciation of the sea chanteys and
songs collected by John Masefield, later to be one of England's poets
laureate. The following year the young writer again made the
columns of the "Bully" with an analysis of the experiments of the
current laureate, Robert Bridges. In still another *Bulletin* piece
FitzGerald averred that Henry Lawson, the laureate of the Australian
back-blocks, had been unfairly classed with the bush balladists,
but that his work at its best "displays thought and vision, and has
an admirable simplicity too often mistaken for crudeness. . . . Actually, within its narrow limits Lawson's technique was a splendid
example; his powers of conception and construction were uncom-
monly good, and his sense of form was sound. . . . His is the song of
dawn breaking on unexplored plains."[9] Lawson's work certainly
does have more form than was generally appreciated in 1930.

FitzGerald had embarked even while an undergraduate upon a
lifelong career as reviewer of the work of his fellow poets. His first
topic was a little book by Winifred Shaw, a fourteen-year-old girl.
His first regular assignment, however, came in October, 1937,
when he began a stint of a year and a half for the *Australian
National Review,* covering such varied volumes as those by
Kenneth Mackenzie, a sensual member of the Lindsay circle; by
Douglas Stewart, a venturesome New Zealander who became
editor of the famed "Red Page" of the *Bulletin,* presiding for
years over this literary section and becoming one of FitzGerald's
closest friends; by Shaw Neilson, a Scottish singer whom FitzGerald

admired highly; and by Samuel Hoffenstein, a brash American versifier who wrote *Poems in Praise of Practically Nothing.* In this period the developing critic hammered out many a firm opinion.

Perhaps FitzGerald's most revealing early review was his lengthy treatment of "Three Australian Poets" at the end of 1939. Here the reviewer was able to extend his comments when dealing with current volumes by prominent contemporaries—Hugh McCrae, Mary Gilmore, and Kenneth Slessor. His friendship with the two men in *Vision* days quite qualified him as a commentator, and he felt willing to make an exacting analysis especially of McCrae, who had been "a star in his firmament." Commenting upon McCrae's *Satyrs and Sunlight,* FitzGerald confessed that the satyrs left him cold and the sunlight did not warm him in the least; but he took the occasion to remark that he was always fascinated by the more mature work of any poet. "Superficially sometimes earlier work is fresher, more exuberant, richer in color and imagination, more varied, more moving" he said in a rare generalization; "but a poet who cannot carry over into later years the excitement and energy of his first enthusiasm, to become a controlled fire, a directed force in his more developed and characteristic work, will usually be found on close examination to have lacked, even in youth, something essential to that fire, some quality of endurance. Where on the other hand energy has not failed there is growth and progress."[10] FitzGerald's own desire that his earliest poems be forgotten reflects his hope that maturity would bring richness.

Although FitzGerald later edited the work and lauded the art of Mary Gilmore—who was created in 1937 a Dame of the British Empire order for her services to literature and to Australia—he noted in 1939 that "Subject-matter is always vitally important to her, and literary effect only a means to an end. She is, indeed, a skilled craftswoman and knows well how to use literary effect for this, its proper purpose; but above all she is a crusader."[11] That he does not minimize clarity in meaning is shown in his conclusion that "Poetry oftenest lies . . . not so much in what is said as what is unsaid, and in indirect statement. But confusion and distortion invariably arise when the surface-statement is not perfectly clear and direct."[12]

Turning to Kenneth Slessor, the reviewer felt that form must be given close attention but recognized that Slessor used certain styles and methods not for the sake of novelty but for that of suitability. Here there is thus a return to FitzGerald's concern in 1922 for the wedding of content and form. He admired the unexpectedness of each fresh Slessor poem and found "nothing that is not alive with Slessor's acute perceptions, charged with his imaginative force, rocked with his rhythm."[13] His high praise of Slessor's "Five Bells" as a "really lordly elegy" is extended in a separate note seven years later.[14]

II   *Poetry and Sam Johnson's Toe*

In the same year that he published "Three Australian Poets," FitzGerald wrote a strongly revealing contribution to a proposed volume that was abandoned because of the outbreak of World War II. This essay, "An Attitude to Modern Poetry," did not appear in print for almost a decade. The "attitude" was a strong attack on European modernism of the 1920s, best exemplified by T. S. Eliot's *The Waste Land* (1922). FitzGerald felt that the intention of such writers was to produce quite different mental effects from those which poets had produced in the past—in short, to change poetry itself. Denying the possibility of "pure poetry," FitzGerald felt that traditional verse had tried to embody "the finer, the more intense, thoughts, realizations, and emotions of mankind" and that "to destroy the old standards of sound craftsmanship, sanity, beauty, music, clarity, urgency, nobility, was plain vandalism."[15] The kind of obscurity indulged in by Eliot projected, he felt, a philosophy of "hatred of life, and passion, and desire."[16] This intense essay, written as another world war loomed, violently voiced FitzGerald's fear that the most highly lauded verse in English was truly glorifying a world of fragmentary, bewildered, discontinuous subjectivity. The European wasteland was for him a land of wasted talent.

Several reviews and articles published in the 1940s reveal a continuing interest in the power of poetry. Analyzing the verse-drama *Shipwreck* by Douglas Stewart, FitzGerald remarks of such plays that "when truly moved, characters speak in poetry because it is the natural way to speak. . . . The movement goes forward dramatically; but it also goes forward lyrically." And he concludes, with further attention to the need for form: "Certainly, on the technical side, a short lyric, like a full-length play, should obey a simple rule, the neglect of which accounts for many poetic failures: it should evolve consecutively from impulse to conclusion: it should have a beginning, a middle, and an end."[17]

An article on the little-known poet Peter Hopegood in 1948 deals with obscurity, allusiveness, and the use of verse for propaganda. Of his friend's bewildering lyrics, FitzGerald remarks that "Clearly we may accept propaganda (or incantation) as legitimate where the matter constitutes poetry. . . . One can undoubtedly concede work to be poetry without fully understanding it, for no one fully understands what, in fact, poetry itself is."[18] He continues: "Anyway, it is open to question how much a writer is to be taken to task for obscurity due not to his manner of expressing himself but to ignorance in the reader."[19] He feels that too much allusiveness, especially of a private kind, is always an artistic defect, and that Hopegood's "mumbo-jumbo" may arouse a suspicion of leg-pulling. Strongly anti-mystic, FitzGerald here anticipates a later lecture on "Poetry's Approach to Reality." He concludes: "While all matters can be subject-matters for poetry, poetry is not an agent or a tool."[20]

The following year, FitzGerald published a piece that asserted: "Poetry is a natural language for anything that requires to be conveyed from mind to mind a little more movingly, a little more nakedly than by the ordinary medium of speech. . . . What does not gain such ready acceptance is that poetry is a living language whose syllables fall naturally into verse. . . . Any really prolonged and heartfelt profanity may lack originality but its imagery is elaborately fantastic and it invariably scans."[21]

Perhaps FitzGerald's most important formal statement of his general views on poetry is found in a small volume containing the texts of three lectures first delivered at the University of Melbourne in July, 1959, and, after being rewritten, delivered again at the University of Queensland in June, 1961. Collected under the title of *The Elements of Poetry,* they deal respectively with "Motif, Theme, and Method," "Motif in the Work of Douglas Stewart," and "Poetry's Approach to Reality." Modesty personified, he does not even mention the title of a single poem of his own composition.

The poet begins the first lecture by refuting A. E. Housman's remark that poetry "is not the thing said but a way of saying it."

Poetry is by no means concerned with manner and nothing else, says FitzGerald: "I do not see how you can have poetry without subject-matter," for he feels that "pure poetry" does not and cannot exist. Poetry, he proclaims, "springs from the interrelationships between motif, theme, and method." "Motif" he defines as the underlying purpose of a poem, as in the didactic, lyric, dramatic, or epic modes. He rejects his dictionary's listing of theme and motif as synonymous; to him, "theme" is "the central subject-matter of the poem."

The technique of verse is handled—tongue in cheek—by referring solely to the authority of George Gascoigne, whose "Certayne Notes of Instruction," written in the 1570s, were presumably quite valid in 1959. Mention of the roles of intellect, the restrictiveness of theories, the cult of "Australianity," and the poet's intentions leads to a final pronouncement on the role of meaning: "There are more meanings than surface meaning. . . . But an intelligible surface meaning is still an essential. . . . Other meanings too must be taken into account: the meaning which is form, and the meaning which is music. . . . They are the unifying agent, the cement of the edifice of poetry. Without them . . . there just could not be poetry at all."[22]

In his second lecture, FitzGerald extends his definition of "motif" to distinguish it from theme. Motif is a difficult and abstract idea, yet of great importance, since it determines what direction theme shall take, or even what theme is chosen. He exemplifies this idea by showing motif—the impulse behind theme, the directive force that develops the thought in a poem—in the various and diverse works of his friend Douglas Stewart. In its broadest sense, motif implies the whole character of an author, his moral stance, his philosophy. Always, however, "if they are to achieve anything at all, art and poetry must give pleasure."[23]

The final lecture in the series, "Poetry's Approach to Reality," is a testament to the author's conviction that the task of poetry is to disprove the view of common sense that the so-called material universe is illusory: "It is a function of poetry to show that in one special sense, anyway, it is not illusory at all. . . . Nevertheless, in a world of illusion, illusions are all-important; they become, in fact, our reality."[24] This paradox is developed lovingly. "The attitudes of Science, Philosophy, Religion, and Common Sense are each in their own way correct; but poetry is less concerned with their findings or assumptions than with the things themselves on which these findings or assumptions are based."[25] FitzGerald would agree that poetry, like Samuel Johnson's toe, refutes Bishop Berkeley's idealism by stubbing itself against the hard wall of reality that is there.

II *"Hell Take Freak Poetries!"*

FitzGerald returned to Mary Gilmore and to his basic concern with form and content in an essay in 1960. "Values in poetry balance between the thing said and the manner of saying it. One must therefore be careful to remember that poetry is created by the correct amalgamation of the two. Primarily any estimate of the work of any poet"—and here the poet-critic verges again on a definition—"must be concerned with its attainment as poetry even though some uncertainty must always exist as to what poetry in essence really is."[26] He distinguishes here between "verse" and "poetry" and says that Dame Mary wrote much verse, but *good* verse. Three years later, in the introduction to his collection of Dame Mary's poetry, he states his aim as selecting from her extensive range in verse "those pieces which make the most complete fusion of distinctive material and satisfying form."[27]

A lengthy address in 1962 still can say much to any teacher of poetry in any country. "Modern Poetry and Its Interpretation in the Classroom" is a charming combination of critical remarks and vivid reminiscence, as well as a *vade mecum* for the teacher of poetry. Although repeating that "there has never been an acceptable definition of poetry," FitzGerald limits its scope for his purpose to "any writing in verse whose primary appeal is not to any craze for novelty—though it can be as new as one likes—but to the emotions or imagination, yet verse that can stand up to the test of reason; conversely, it can appeal to reason but only by virtue of an exercise of imaginative powers."[28]

The lecturer makes the usual and correct distinction between "modern" and "modernist" poetry, and gives a history of the latter—which might be synonymous with his term "Eliotism"—from T. E. Hulme, the Imagists (including Ezra Pound, whose later work such as the "Cantos" FitzGerald found "a self-deluding monstrosity"), the Sitwells, the Eliot of *The Waste Land* and *Four Quartets,* to Dylan Thomas, "who was modernist in his obscurities and his distortion of language to new ends, but otherwise was the beginning of a departure from modernism."[29] Along the way he inveighs against Gerard Manley Hopkins for commencing "a breaking up of all the old accepted rules and rhythms of prosody."[30] The Hopkins revival, he feels, can be blamed because "a great deal of the rhythm and music of poetry has gone out of even the best of modern work, especially the more obvious kinds of rhythm and music which truly are by no means to be despised."[31] Beauty, a much misused term, was still regarded by his own generation, the poets of the 1920s, as the chief good.

After listing the four attitudes of concern toward poetry—those of the writer, the critic, the teacher, and the student or common reader—FitzGerald offers his own experiences in reading poetry and his suggestions for teaching it. He feels that he loves poetry because he was made to learn many good poems by heart at school and that good poetry is not ruined by forcing children to analyze it and then put the parts together again. Indeed, "a love of poetry can be induced by a close textual examination of poems, provided they are interesting enough poems in the first place." He concludes that the way he taught himself to appreciate poetry was very satisfactory, and if such a method would not work in our day with modern poetry, "it may be modern poetry that is at fault, not the method or any other method."[32]

FitzGerald gave a lecture in 1966 on "Narrative Poetry" in a series delivered by contributors to a collection, *Voyager Poems,* edited by Douglas Stewart. Two of the six long poems were the work of FitzGerald: *Heemskerck Shoals* and *The Wind at Your Door.* The lecture opened by the statement that, considered as belonging to the strict narrative genre, not one of the six selections is really satisfactory. The student audience was asked to consider the possibility that all poems that tell a story evolved as action song, epic, ballad, unheroic direct narrative, and, finally, "various kinds of indirect narrative." Distinctions among these depend mainly upon structure, and only to a lesser degree upon subject matter. The lecturer felt that his experience in Fiji had qualified him to believe that action songs and dances are the beginning from which all narrative poetry has developed. Discussion of the Australian "voyager poems" included references to "The Song of Roland,"

"Piers Plowman," Chaucer, "Sohrab and Rustum," *The Ring and the Book,* Tennyson's "Maud," Masefield's "Dauber," *Paradise Lost,* "The Rape of the Lock," and "The Rime of the Ancient Mariner." FitzGerald naturally insisted that this form, to be successful, must be both good narrative and good poetry. He concluded: "I have confined myself to technical matters. But any of these poems is worth your reading for what it says as well as for how it says it."[33] Again FitzGerald appears as a scholarly expounder of types of verse and verse techniques.

A recent essay on a baffling contemporary well sums up FitzGerald's views on meaning and obscurity in verse.

It is no use upbraiding the reader if he finds nothing where the poet cannot, or will not, show what he holds in his hand. It is not good enough for the poet, uncertain of what he really wishes to say, to hint that he perceives a mystery too vast or too subtle to be conceived, let alone disclosed. . . . One should not quarrel, however, too stubbornly with more meaning being put into words than they will normally carry. This can be legitimate enough, provided the overloading does not develop into a private mysticism. These are areas of consciousness within the province of poetry which can only be explored by an extension of language to the edge of meaningless. A poem does not always have to stand up to rational analysis.[34]

Finally, FitzGerald's disillusion with recent poetry is well expressed when he considers the present

an age when poetry, or rather verdicts upon it, have become very much the preserve of coteries whether academic, political, religious, regional, or in other ways narrowly partisan. A poet who writes comprehensively in recognizable verse, and who, above all, finds something to say, would surely reach a wider audience than [Martin] Haley has as yet, were it not that the section of the public—small at best of times—which might be expected to appreciate poetry has been largely estranged from it by the contempt in which its taste in verse is held by self-appointed experts. Fashion prevails. The accent today is so heavily on "prose rhythms," or freakish techniques, that many of the newer poets overlook one great requirement of even free verse itself: that the subject-matter must find its appropriate rhytnm or cadence, however varying. But matter also seems greatly ignored today—perhaps behind some pretense at symbolic or inferred meanings too deep for the ordinary reader to dive for. There is vast emptiness behind the lines of mutilated prose.[35]

The conclusion of an unpublished sonnet, "Just Once," puts the point even more tersely:

> *. . . And, one final curse:*
> *Hell take freak poetries; I like good verse.*

CHAPTER 4

The Poet Considers His Craft

A poet must be concerned not only with theory, intentions, and meanings, but with the hard necessity of hammering out lines of verse that, with luck, might also be poetry. Technique in any art requires mastery of the medium. As the painter deals with pigments and canvas, so the poet deals with words—their sounds, histories, connotations, associations, contexts, arrangements, implications, echoes.

Robert D. FitzGerald, despite his various disclaimers of expertise in traditional versification, has from school days been aware of the need for craftsmanship—which properly includes everything about a poem remaining after the meanings and imagery have been absorbed by the reader. Many critics, indeed, consider that an additional meaning can be gained from studying a poem's prosody and that this meaning is itself an experience. Further, the appreciation of prosodic skill is one of the many rewards of study, and the knowledgeable listener can enjoy this aspect just as an amateur pianist can get additional satisfaction from observing the virtuosity of the professional. As has been said, "A master is one whose practice persuades us that his general metrical choice is the only thinkable one for his poem."[1]

Usually, readers accept the fact that the technical form of a poem (including rhyme, meter, stress, sound color, tempo, line length, and stanza form) complements its semantic form. The present chapter will attempt to show that FitzGerald's interest in poetic technique matches his interest in the functions and aims of the poet. From his boyhood through the biblical age of three score and ten, he has expressed an expert's concern with technique and has used both traditional and experimental schemes of versification in his poems.

I *A Question of "Quantity"*

"It has been said or inferred quite often of myself," FitzGerald wrote in the introduction in 1963 to a selection of his poems that he edited, "that I am little concerned with technique so long as my verse makes its required statement. I trust that this selection will refute the charge by showing how technique has had attention from the outset. Techniques are at the foundation, and composition and construction are of the very essence, of every work of art."[2]

The critics have, indeed, almost uniformly overlooked the technique of FitzGerald's verse. They apparently agree with Judith Wright's brief comments that "'The Face of the Waters' . . . is in free rhythms, and it is unrhymed, where FitzGerald usually prefers more or less conventional forms,"[3] as well as her conclusion that "he has little of Slessor's obsessive interest in technical accomplishment. He early worked out a pleasant straightforward prosody, with few fireworks but capable of expressing his often involved and qualified thought processes; and from the beginning he has elevated content to a higher place than form in his verse."[4] A lengthier treatment of the poems since "Essay on Memory" given by H. M. Green[5] apparently sums up the feeling that little more need be said about the form, in contrast to the content, of this poet's body of work. Moreover, FitzGerald's own attitude, seemingly deprecating his concern for form, has discouraged much investigation of his early, broad, underlying, and continuing fascination with prosody. Actually, he has spent many hours reviewing volumes of poetry with technical appeals and has even offered line-by-line comment on the metrics and diction of poems submitted to him by friends.

As an undergraduate, FitzGerald published in the University of Sydney literary magazine a "Ballade: A Lecture on the Differential Calculus." He was certainly aware thus early of the variety of such French stanza forms as the ballade and rondeau, available to poets in English. He even attempted the most challenging metrical form, and was represented in a 1926 volume, *The Sonnet in Australia*.[6] As should be noted, most of his mature work appears in freer forms, but as late as 1945 he published "In Personal Vein," a Petrarchan sonnet with the Miltonic variation. A long 1966 poem, "One Such Morning," uses the rhyme royal stanza favored by Chaucer, Shakespeare, and Masefield. Even the late, compassionate "protest poems" are couched in orthodox sonnet form.[7]

At the age of twenty, FitzGerald published a thoughtful essay on free verse, then considered a new movement. He notes that

earlier masterpieces had been written in *vers libre,* "and despite
the fact that the modern variety has frequently made more radical
departures from set forms than have these . . . masterpieces, it,
none the less, still uses rhyme, rhythm, meter, vowel tones, and
consonant values—all the old tools. It also uses cadence and balance
much more than they have previously been used in verse, some of
the new poetry depending for its music upon these last to a greater
extent than upon all the others."[8] In the same place he proclaims: "There is always form where there is poetry. That is a natural
law, physically impossible to break. . . . Always for the work to be
great the music must 'fit' the subject, and accompany it, and make
it more vivid, more beautiful." In conclusion, he quotes Ezra
Pound as "the most consistently successful writer in the more advanced school" at a time when many professors had not even
heard the name of Pound.

Young FitzGerald published in 1926 another article on technique, commenting on the experiments of poet laureate Robert
Bridges. Aimed at refuting an article by Hilary Lofting appearing
in the *Bulletin* several weeks earlier, this piece contains an extended
exercise in scansion. Of Bridges, FitzGerald wrote: "He is an ex-
perimenter, perhaps more so than any other English poet. He was
one of the first writers to appreciate fully that the stress rather
than the foot is the principal factor in English prosody. He has
closely examined the values of time and quantity and has given
these items particular prominence in his verse, preserving nevertheless an even balance with the rhythms of ordinary syllabic verse.
He has made a careful analysis of stress and accent and has examined the distribution of forced stresses, giving consideration to
the natural rhythms of prose."[9] This early interest belies remarks
by FitzGerald that he has had little concern with traditional prosody.

Such remarks, for example, appear in private letters, like the one
that FitzGerald wrote to his poet friend Tom Inglis Moore on
April 27, 1938:

I think you worry unnecessarily about stresses. Personally I never count
them. I go by the length of line or "weight" of same. Your "scansion"
exercises are quite above my head. I never got more than 2/10 for scansion
at school. I *think,* though I don't really know, I allow three beats to the
line, not five as a rule, though it varies up to as many as six. It stands to
reason a six-stress line has less or lighter weak syllables than a three-stress

one. The three-stress line must fill up with a number of unstressed or weak-stressed syllables. But I do not work it out mathematically. Also I allow a bit of run-over from one line to the next to make 'em harmonize one with another ... by ear ... by my ear, that is to say, for I can't account for my neighbor's ear. ... As it so happens the lines you quote as out of scansion do not come into the "unavoidable" category. Some of them seem to be four-beat, some six as you say, but all seem to carry the correct "weight," so pass.

FitzGerald's years in the crown colony of Fiji, as will be shown, exposed him not only to a new language but to new rhythms in song that appeared in much of his later verse. Back in 1931 he used the terminology of traditional prosody to describe in his diary (April 29) his impressions of the primitive chanting of the Fijians living near his field camp: "Most of the songs have a trochaic rhythm, 4, 4, 6 beats, then 4, 4, 5, or roughly that with 'lengthening out' variations applied both to the couplet and to the individual 4 or 5 beat line—which usually ended in an accented syllable or an unaccented syllable strengthened. The trochee occasionally or frequently had an extra light syllable." This passage is not a bad description of the metrics of some of FitzGerald's own poems.

FitzGerald's references to "verbal music" show his awareness of the kinship of poetry and instrumental melody, although he felt that, with him, sound was subordinate to sense. "Also I have always liked the sound of words rather than meters or even rhythms," he wrote to Tom Inglis Moore on December 30, 1938. "What little music my stuff does possess comes from happy juxtapositions of the right vowels and consonants rather than from pure verse-effects, with the result that when the subject-matter (always rightly or wrongly my main preoccupation) forced the syllable-music out of place, there was no verse-music to carry the sound along. Hence frequent horrible harshness."[10] Shortly afterward, in discussing the prosody of his friend Hugh McCrae, he wrote: "His verse is metrical rather than rhythmic, and within the compass of strict meter he achieves amazing music. ... But close adherence to rigid rule lends itself most admirably to the lighter measures and most fanciful themes of which, in his more developed phase, he is supreme overlord."[11]

FitzGerald in 1948 expressed the idea that Australian poets should try in their rhyming to make up for the comparative deficiency in the English language of rhyming pairs. Many of the most useful pairs, he felt, have become well known—and well worn. "The problem has become to make use of the richness of rhyme-sounds," he wrote, "and so to avoid hackneyed couplings and at the same time achieve gains in musical effect."[12] His nimble use of near-rhymes in later poems testifies to his search for varied verse melody.

The publication by R. G. Howarth in 1949 of his small volume entitled *Notes on Modern Poetic Technique, English and Australian,* deriving from a series of lectures by the author, encouraged his friend FitzGerald to read the chapters critically, from the point of view of a practicing poet. His six-page typescript of comments concludes: "I agree with nearly everything you say."[13] However, a number of queries and comments are offered that illuminate FitzGerald's own ideas of technique. For instance, "The term 'false stress' is not explained as I'd like," he writes; "does it differ from artificial stress? A stress is not necessarily false if it falls *by position* on a syllable not usually stressed. The converse applies; sometimes, by position, a stress is lifted off a syllable normally stressed. This without forcing at all. A stress by position is usually weak. You don't mention weak and strong stress." Here FitzGerald reveals that he has firm opinions on the use of "accentual-syllabic verse (or accentual verse with a high degree of syllabic regularity)," which has been called the "one great tradition" of English prosodic history.[14]

In a long comment on the term "quantity"—which in classical verse is merely the relative brevity or length of sounds, usually vowels—FitzGerald makes his own definition, terming quantity the equating of a number of short syllables with heavy unstressed syllables, to balance a line (he considers the line to be the main unit of rhythm). The whole passage is important to an understanding of FitzGerald's attempts to please the ear by delicately adjusting line weights.

Quantity. There is quantity that is not classical. A bunching of short syllables can add to the weight of a line of verse and be balanced by heavy unstressed syllables. But the unit of quantity is the line of verse; and the only measure that I know of is the ear. Verse need not be strictly metrical at all—and I am not speaking of free verse—so long as each line weighs the same as the other lines near it. A line which scans readily enough to the ear in one place in a poem can, if transferred to another part—all in the same meter basically—be found quite out of scansion. I don't think my own verses really scan at all; I was always told they didn't by blokes like Tom Moore who understood the subject, and long since ceased to care. My aim is to make the lines as a whole weigh right against the equivalent lines. I think I know a bit about rhythm on the practical side, though I am so out of my depth discussing it with an expert like you, who can understand the theoretical side too, and is familiar with the historical side as well. But knowing nothing of classical quantities, I feel that the line not the foot is the unit of English verse; and that if you write by ear, rather than rule, it comes out that equivalent lines in neighboring parts of a poem tend to *weigh* the same. You breathe the same amount of air speaking them, as it were.... You can even have too few or too many stresses in a line and it will weigh correctly.

II   *No Good Poet Has a Bad Ear*

FitzGerald's use of near-rhyme is rather well explained by his comments on Howarth's divisions of this topic. He felt that the author of the handbook made, for practical purposes, too many distinctions between the classes of rhyme, although "there are variations within those classes, of course—as many variations as there are rhymes." He notes in detail:

There is true rhyme, both vowels and consonants. Then there is rhyming on vowels alone and rhyming on consonants alone. Both true and consonant rhymes may be full: "fair-fare," "mystery-mastery." True full rhymes are usually unpleasant. Vowel rhyming is apt to be too primitive altogether—like Fijian verse:

> *Ni mai rogoca na gone tagane*
> *Na talanoa sa duri tale.*

There are also off-accent rhymes like "had-ballad." These and vowel rhymes have their uses, but are generally unimpressive. That would almost cover all classes of rhymes—except one you mention, near-rhyme: I recently rhymed "to-now" myself and probably got away with it. . . .

You say there is no vowel-music. The whole idea of rhyming is dependent on vowel-music. Though certainly it must vary. The trouble about any true rhyme is the internal vowels in the line, or internal consonants. You keep hearing extra, atrocious rhymes, that the poet never intended. I excepted true rhyming from this fault. I should not have done so; but the danger is less great. But you do get bad vowel clashes between internal vowels and rhyme-vowels. Worse—not always avoidable or even necessary to be avoided—are vowel clashes from one rhyme pair to another.

Continuing, in his correspondence with Howarth, a discussion (December 14, 1949) of the complexity of rhyming, FitzGerald wrote: "Naturally if one is using, say, two or even three different ways of rhyming (normal, consonant, and vowel), then you introduce two—or as the case may be, three—different ways in which you may get internal clashes. You ask the ear to expect queer rhymes—and it obliges by hearing more than were intended. When using anything but pure normal rhymes anything in the way of a *deliberate* internal rhyme can be almost fatal."

Commenting on a friend's remark that some passages in Fitz-Gerald's long poem "Between Two Tides" might be taken as prose if written without line breaks, the poet wrote to Howarth (November 22, 1952):

It may be quite true that some pieces of blank- or free-verse written straight out without breaks become indistinguishable from prose; *but the author did not write them so.* He put in the line-breaks and he intended them to mean something; not necessarily a heavy pause at the end of each line, but nevertheless some break there in the continuity. In other words, the actual division into lines is as much a technical device as rhyme or meter 'em-selves. I doubt if that point has ever been clearly made. As a nearly parallel case you might rewrite a sonnet, say Keats' "Chapman's Homer," putting in sufficient synonyms for rhyme-words to deprive it of rhyme and then ask: "How now do you distinguish a sonnet from blank verse?"

Again in a letter to Howarth of August 16, 1953, FitzGerald concluded his running observations concerning his use of rhyme by discussing internal rhyming:

The whole problem of internal effects is very tricky; there seem to be no rules. Sometimes what would be expected to be distressing turns out to be pleasing; and indeed the most musical lines of verse are almost always lines in which there are subtle internal effects of rhyme and half rhyme. So what are you to do? The answer is that an effect deliberately sought and carefully weighed by the ear *or* a lucky hit instantly approved by the ear can be musical; but that a careless or unwitting repetition internally of the vowel-sound of the end rhyme *frequently* (not more can be urged than that) grates. Personally I don't find consonant effects nearly so difficult provided I can eliminate actual tongue-twisters.

In his 1962 lecture on the teaching of modern poetry, FitzGerald complained that Gerard Manley Hopkins "commenced a breaking up of all the old accepted rules and rhythms of prosody."[15] Such a remark would indicate that FitzGerald held some respect for these "old rules."

Finally, a few quotations from a long letter to the present author, written by FitzGerald on April 18, 1960, will show the poet's continued concern with traditional prosody and its twentieth-century modifications:

We had a few lessons on prosody at Sydney Grammar School and I always got full marks; but at the same time developed a contempt for the subject and decided I could do without it. Although I could reproduce what was asked and get good marks, I could not see that there was really such a thing as a "foot," and certainly could not concede that there is any distinction between an iambic foot and a trochaic foot. . . . There are no such separate things as trochees and iambs: there is only a certain rhythm dependent on alternate stressed and unstressed syllables . . .

I came to the conclusion that the science of prosody was simply nonsense; there was only rhythm; and I would have nothing more to do with prosody once I had added up my good marks. I have not *entirely* stuck to that good resolution; but I have never had any reason to alter my opinion.

To label prosody as "nonsense" might be considered a disingenuous act by a man who, in his published work, has utilized many of the devices of traditional English versification.

The most extensive study of FitzGerald's technical accomplishments is that made by Miss Maureen Cassidy.[16] Agreeing with the handbook view that "a vital relationship exists between a poem's vision and its versification: the latter is in some way always made to work actively in the former's service"[17] and that in a particular poem "a poet's intention always is to shape a prosodic form that is perfectly suited to the point he wants to make,"[18] Miss Cassidy evaluated the techniques of *Forty Years' Poems* by examining meter and rhythm, rhyme, and the other physical aspects of the poems, as they help or hinder the presentation of the poet's ideas and feelings.

Miss Cassidy's study of the suitability of the sounds in each poem, to accord with its evident theme or intention, is painstaking and valuable. For example, the brief poem "Calm" (6)[19] shows the pattern of having each stanza begin with the words "A sole star." Alliteration appears four times in the second stanza, in addition to the opening line:

> ... *Poseidon,* Sh*aker of* Sh*ips,* ...
> *from this* jogging *and* jigging ...
> *the* fl*ip* fl*ap of the rigging,*
> *a helm* d*ead and* d*ull*

"'Jogging and jigging' and 'flip flap' communicate also a sense of onomatopoeia by producing an imitative effect. In the third stanza, in addition to the opening line, the phrase 'Shaker of Ships,' which occurs in the previous stanza, is repeated as the final phrase of the poem. . . . The versification pattern of 'Calm' is quite appropriate to the theme evoked by the title and carried through into the poet's desire for 'peace at last.'"[20]

Concerning euphony, Miss Cassidy continues her analysis:

An examination of the first stanza of "Calm" reveals a number of long vowels which lengthen the sound value of the words. These, together with several liquid consonants, *l, m, n,* and *r,* and the nasal *ng,* produce a lingering and tranquil effect which is particularly noticeable in the first and second stanzas and is particularly appropriate to the poem. . . . A word that is especially successful in this [second] stanza is "lull," with its prolonged and full sound and its prominent position at the end of the sixth line. Although quantity or duration of sound is quite difficult to assess, it is apparent that it takes more time to say "lull" than to say other single syllables in this stanza. Its presence is effective, too, after the quick tempos of "jogging" and "jigging" in the preceding line, and its sound is quite appropriate to its meaning.

The third stanza contains fewer long vowels and liquid consonants. . . . The most striking jarring note of the poem occurs in this last stanza, where the placing of "giddily" temporarily destroys the peaceful atmosphere evoked thus far in the poem. In sound and rhythm it is out of place, but it almost certainly marks a change in the poet's attitude from uneasy searching and dissatisfaction to something closer to calm.[21]

Similar close evaluations by Miss Cassidy of the role of vowels and consonants in the poems show again and again that the choice of words—usually quite compatible with the other main aspects of the poem, such as theme, images, allusions, tone, intensity, pace— does not come by chance, but is planned by the poet to enhance his total effect. Much leeway, of course, is allowed him in taste and in feeling for the best diction available, but no good poet has a bad ear, nor does he often spoil his result by unplanned clashes or discordances.

III *A Half-Century as a Critic*

After studying the entire collection of FitzGerald's work of "forty years," the conviction comes that he is a master of traditional prosody. For instance, Miss Cassidy notes, concerning the poem "Meeting" (5): "This poem is an early (1924) example of unrhymed free verse. With two notable exceptions, 'The Face of the Waters' and 'Between Two Tides,' FitzGerald has preferred for most of his poems the strengths and restrictions of rhyme and regular meter."[22] A few early examples of traditional forms will now be selected.

The difficulties of trying to apply methods of scansion—the analysis of a rhythmic structure—are properly noted by Miss Cassidy: "Two people rarely scan a poem in exactly the same fashion, nor do they see or hear the same sound colors or tempos, nor do they arrive at the same decisions as to the meanings of those prosodic devices in terms of the whole poem."[23] Nevertheless, the following of any standard method reveals many enlightening clues to the art of such a technician as Robert D. FitzGerald.

The main value of having a more or less fixed prosodic scheme of rhyme and rhythm is that the broad framework or stanza provides a background pattern, and substitutions or variations in the standard line lend an emphasis that could not be obtained in unstructured verse. This clash between the expected regularity or the background and the occasional variation creates a tension that keeps monotony at bay. Everyone knows, for example, that a trochee replacing the first foot of an iambic line arouses the reader in a bold way. Although FitzGerald may deny in practice the existence of standard terms like "iamb" and "foot," his various references to strong stresses in the line justify a scrutiny of his frequent resort to traditional rhymes and rhythms.

A look at the prosody of a few of the items in *Forty Years' Poems,* following Miss Cassidy's survey but using a much simpler marking method, reveals a continuing preoccupation with regularity and tradition. Beginning with the earliest poem in the volume, "I Too . . ." (4), appearing in the University of Sydney magazine in 1922, one notes that the poem contains three quatrains, rhyming *abba*. The rhythm is predominantly iambic pentameter, but there are many substitutions in the distribution of stresses, as well as the addition of syllables to the line. The first three lines of each stanza contain eleven syllables with five stresses. The last line of each stanza contains six stresses, but varies in number of syllables.

"Pursuit" (3), the first item in the first section of the collected poems, has one stanza of eleven lines, rhyming but not following any predictable scheme: *abbacdedcde*. The predominant feeling is dactylic, but the exuberance of the varied unstressed syllables gives an appropriate lightness and speed to the vision of a heavenly fox hunt. "It would seem, therefore, that the various verse techniques employed in this poem—freedom from restraining rhyme and rhythmic patterns, effective use of appropriate consonants, parallelism in structure—are particularly suitable to the theme and subject-matter of 'Pursuit.'"[24]

On the other hand, in "Passer-by" (3), appearing in 1929, FitzGerald offers a poem in two quatrains, with a regular *abab* rhyme scheme. The first stanza is almost perfect iambic pentameter:

> The wín/dows póur/ing góld/ into/ the dárk
> have wátched/me év/ery níght/and séen/me páss
> beyónd/ the lít/tle próv/ince thát/ they márk
> with dwínd/ling ráys/ fánned óut/ acróss/ the gráss.

However, one can read a pyrrhic substitution into the fourth foot of the first line, and a spondaic substitution into the third foot of the fourth line. "Thus, it is apparent that this is an example of the heroic quatrain in which all four lines are iambic pentameter rhyming *abab*—a fairly common type of quatrain which is the favorite English verse form."[25]

In "Well-wishers" (4), the two quatrains, rhyming *abba*, have a predominantly iambic hexameter rhythm, with some substitution of anapests. "The Wall" (7) is a single twelve-line stanza rhyming *aabbccddeeff*, primarily in iambic pentameter.

The first section of "The Greater Apollo" (7–8) has four stanzas of five lines, rhyming *aabba*. This is the scheme of the comic limerick, but the iambic tetrameter of the poem is far removed from the light anapests of the limerick. The second part of this series has four stanzas of six lines, rhyming *ababab,* alternately iambic tetrameter and iambic trimeter. The third consists of five quatrains rhyming *abab,* primarily in iambic pentameter. The fourth presents four stanzas of ten lines, rhyming *abbabcdcdc,* almost always in iambic tetrameter. The fifth consists of three stanzas of nine lines each; the rhyme scheme is *ababxcddc,* but it should be noted that the *x* line rhymes with the fourth and fifth syllables of the following line—"proudly/loudly," "twitter/glitter," "cheated/undefeated." Furthermore, the "twitter/glitter" rhyme of the second stanza is picked up again in "litter" in the last line of this stanza; and the "cheated/undefeated" rhyme of the third stanza is picked up again in "uncompleted" in the last line of this stanza. Other internal rhymes prove this to be prosodically the most complex of "The Greater Apollo" series. The sixth part is a single stanza rhyming irregularly, as in the English ode, usually with three stresses to the line. "The number of enjambed [run-over] lines adds to the feeling of time flowing on relentlessly; only eight of the twenty-one lines are end-stopped."[26] The seventh and final part returns to the quatrain form, rhyming *abab,* with an iambic tetrameter rhythm with trochaic substitutions that emphasize the first word in three of the lines. As Miss Cassidy concludes, the success of the prosody in this quite early sequence (1926) is considerable: "Almost all the technical devices employed—length of line, rhythm, rhyme, alliteration, assonance, general combinations of sounds—become an integral part of the total effect of this poem."[27]

The three eight-line stanzas of "Sobriety" (14–15) rhyme *ababcdcd.* The first seven lines of each stanza are mainly in regular iambic tetrameter. The eighth line in each stanza is in iambic trimeter, "a slightly surprising alteration in the rhythm which may indicate a mild reversion to the old dreams."[28]

A final note here on the prosody of a revealing early poem deals with "Michael Eyquem de Montaigne" (15–16), about FitzGerald's favorite author. The poem is a single stanza of thirty-two lines, in predominantly iambic pentameter. The rhyme scheme looks impossibly complex unless it is divided thus into quatrains: *abab bcbc cdcd dede efef fgfg ghgh hihi.* Moreover, the final rhyme of each "quatrain" marks the initial rhyme of the following one. "So, in its rhyme scheme, the poem pays tribute to the ordered and disciplined world of Michel de Montaigne."[29]

Reading similar analyses of the prosody of these few early poems should convince anyone that the technical aspects of FitzGerald's art are indeed impressive. While seeming to minimize technique, he has pondered it early and late, and skillfully practiced the craft of versification. Further interesting prosodic achievements in FitzGerald's poems will be noted in the general comments on the various items, to be given in the next four chapters.

The survey in Chapters 3 and 4 of FitzGerald's prose—mainly as it pertains to his ideas of the functions and techniques of poetry— should prepare the reader for estimating his success in achieving his ideals. Perhaps it is not fair to question whether a critic practices what he has preached. Yet in many ways these pronouncements of the poet might justly be used as measures of his growth in reaching his goals. The present review of FitzGerald's observations between 1922 and 1972 concerning the function and craft of the poet indicates that he has spent half a century as a critic, whose collected prose might well be published as a revealing volume.

The reader may now approach, in the next chapter, the commentaries on FitzGerald's collected poems, as well as those pieces appearing since the publication of this collection.

CHAPTER 5

Salvage of the Early Years

W HAT influences, after his student years, were most potent in determining the sort of verse the young poet would cast upon the waters of the Australian publishing scene? To begin an examination of the most revealing poems in a career extending over half a century, one should first understand some of the poet's backgrounds. Moreover, since it is impossible to quote extensively from all his collected works, to have at hand a copy of his collection, *Forty Years' Poems,* is indispensable (numbers in parenthesis hereinafter refer to pages in that volume).

I Vision *and Other Early Outlets*

Although examining FitzGerald's juvenilia might be unfair— "like poking sticks at something dragged out of the river," in his own simile—he did serve his apprenticeship in undergraduate days; the earliest piece included in *Forty Years' Poems,* "I Too . . ." (4), first appeared in the Sydney University literary magazine in 1922.[1] While still at the university, he first proudly received an acceptance from the Sydney *Bulletin* for a poem, "The Savage" (December 11, 1920), which was chosen in 1922 for a collegiate collection.[2] Publication of one of his poems in the first volume of the magazine *Vision* marked him as a member of the most *avant-garde* group in the metropolis of Sydney.

Again it may seem like poking sticks by the riverside, but quoting the first of FitzGerald's poems in *Vision* might convey not only some feeling about the poet but about the magazine:

WITCHCRAFT

Ah! Sorceress, and was it not enough
That all night long across the dark there flocked
Unbidden shapes that taunted me and mocked
And tempted with their presence and called my name?
Poor Sleep was driven by the riot thereof

To stand apart watching his kingdom's rue
As near my side a thousand times they came,
Each separate wanton a wild thought of you.

So fled the unquiet hours across the void,
Yet still a white confusion crowded in
About my heart, and still I strove to win
One shadowy kiss from clutched-at emptiness.
Truly it were enough had day destroyed
These conjurings or proved you for a dream;
But I was awake when dawn came, Sorceress,
And lo, the sunlight on your breast a-gleam![3]

Actually, FitzGerald published only two poems in the short-lived quarterly, but his acquaintance with other members of the circle formed his first strong professional influence.

Vision was founded chiefly to publish the accumulated earthy illustrations of Norman Lindsay and the joyous, pagan verses of Hugh McCrae. The "foreword" of the first issue (May, 1923) brashly proclaimed: "The object of this quarterly is primarily to provide an outlet for good poetry, or for any prose that liberates the imagination by gaiety or fantasy. Unless gaiety is added to realism, the pestilence of Zola or the locomotor ataxia of Flaubert must finally attack the mind. We would vindicate the youthfulness of Australia, not by being modern, but by being alive. . . ." The tone of the magazine was reminiscent of the English 1890s, Oscar Wilde and the *Yellow Book*. "Several of the poems contributed to *Vision* could well have been written in England during the 1890s," notes John Tregenza,[4] who compares FitzGerald's poem "The Dark Rose"[5] with the work of Ernest Dowson. "They [the contributors] did not write then like their contemporary T. S. Eliot because they did not know his world."

Jack Lindsay, who had earlier claimed that FitzGerald and Kenneth Slessor, a *Vision* editor and contributor, had been "sucked in" by the magazine's manifesto,[6] later stated: "FitzGerald and Slessor were the poets who were to carry on in their own ways the impetus begotten by *Vision* and in the 1930s to dominate Australian poetry, lifting it definitely to a new level of intellectual responsibility and ending once and for all the reign of the slipshod, the pedestrian, and the emotionally inchoate."[7] Slessor went on to become the foremost "modernist" poet of Australia, but Fitz-Gerald clung for years to his early allegiance. He asserted again and again, often in romantic terms, the *Vision* idea that modern man is starved for adventure and gaiety and passion.[8]

II *Recollecting Emotion in Viti Levu*

The *Vision* experience was reinforced by FitzGerald's five-year sojourn—from 1931 to 1936—in Fiji.[9] Both in supplying subjects for verse and in determining the development of his distinctive style, this Fijian period was highly determinative of his career. His labors in that crown colony had a strong effect upon his literary output—"an effect," wrote FitzGerald to Henry Stokes on April 16, 1965, "which Fiji undoubtedly had and which, I acknowledge, has been of inestimable value to me." Many of the other fine poets of Australia's recent past might well have benefited by such a violent, though ultimately enriching, initiation into an exotic land.

As one of the surveyors of the Native Lands Commission, Fitz, as he was usually called, began his field work in mid-April, 1931, to spend most of the year living in native houses but often sheltering under nothing more than a tent-fly beside a stream. He soon began to wonder whether he had made a mistake in coming to this country and in planning to bring his bride of a few months to share his camps. An entry on May 24 shows his mind running on making poetry: "I've thought out the beginning of a scheme for a long poem, 'A Song of Exile.'" An early verse, "A Date" (46), was inspired by the poet's waiting for his wife to journey over the Pacific and join him.

Despite many handicaps, and puzzled that he, a sometime poet, was "wasting his golden prime in Fiji," FitzGerald did produce a fair quantity of verse during his five years there. In that period the following poems of his appeared in the Sydney *Bulletin:* "Chaos," February 19, 1932 (52–53); "Predecessors," May 11; "A Date," July 4, 1934 (46); "Long Since," September 5 (36–37); "Rest House Verandah," January 23, 1935 (retitled "Rebirth," 39);[10] "Task," March 6; "At Least," March 20 (58); "Defenders," March 27 ("Departure," 31); "High Tide," April 10; "The Wolf," April 24; "Reality," May 22 ("Return," 34–36); "Ransom," September 18 (55); "Contest," December 11 ("The Traveller," 51–52); "Rewards,"

December 18; "Paid Off," February 12, 1936 ("Coiled Wire," 37–38); and "Side Street," May 6 (54). Not all of these poems present the Fijian scene. "Predecessors" and "Rewards" were probably drafted before FitzGerald's arrival in Suva. "Contest," which may have been written in Fiji, derives from a lonely journey from Kurrajong to Singleton in New South Wales. On the other hand, the list contains a number of poems that do deal with Fiji; of them, about a dozen were considered by the author to be sufficiently durable to reprint in *Forty Years' Poems* (as indicated by the parentheses above).

To examine the seven sweat-stained diaries of Fitz the surveyor, written by the light of a Coleman lamp and toted through drenched jungle trails to swampy insect-shrouded fly-camps, is an exciting experience for the biographer. Among the memoranda pages of the "Fiji Civil Service Diary, 1936," for example, surrounded by notes on "office system," "plots," and "coördinates," one is struck by the words: "The rooster that crowed up this dawn contemplates the first rooster in the east and the last in the west, deciding they must be the same, concludes the earth is round." Here is the genesis of the poem "Copernicus" (57), a surveyor's pragmatic (and animistic) refutation of Ptolemy. On another page is a reminder: "Make 'Paid Off' clear by starting it as follows," with the addition of half a dozen lines to the poem that would appear in the *Bulletin*. Some pages later one comes upon an eight-line description of the exact impact upon the poet's ear of the noise made by a cricket that banished sleep. In the journal entry of January 31, 1935, are scrawled the concluding lines of "Ransom" (55). As the author was to note in his selections in the Australian Poets Series, "The scene is the Suva waterfront, but could be any waterfront." On March 8, 1936, while in Suva, the poet made the entry: "Wrote 'Back from the paved way'" ("Side Street," 54).

Other entries are equally revealing. Nostalgia may account for the fact that in the middle of a Fijian village, FitzGerald, according to the entry for June 24, 1933, "wrote poem about Mary Ann Bell" ("Legend," 40–42) and his grandfather's courtship in Dublin. The entry for June 29, 1935, runs: "Wrote a Red Page *[Bulletin]* article 'Credo'—hope they take it. Unlikely." On July 6 is the note: "Wrote 'Atavism'" ("Ransom"). On August 1: "Wrote a section of 'Spoil'" ("Chaos," 52–53). On August 3: "Wrote R[ed] P[age] art. reply to

C[ecil] M[ann]." All in all, the time-scarred diaries reveal that, especially after he got settled in the colony and began making his family fairly comfortable, FitzGerald did have more time to recollect emotion in comparative tranquility and produce as well as ponder verses.

III   *A Heap of Letters from Fiji*

The diaries also are a decisive document for the germ of Fitz-Gerald's only published short story. Mention is made on June 25, 1931, of his surveying the tomb of Kobukobu and seeing extensive fortifications at Korosaiwaka with ten-foot-deep trenches. On September 21 he saw the grave of Salovodranikai, a chief whose body was buried on top of the corpses of a hundred slain followers. The entry for September 23, 1932, runs: "Heard stories at Vuya told of *gauna makawa* by Aisakataletu. Taito was at Calalevu inside the fence and helped build the oven and prepare the fire. His uncle cut up the *bokolas* [corpses for eating] into sections. Taito being young (about 12 he says, says he is now 43) did not eat but smelt and says it smelt good like pig. Aisaka told of the respectful *bokola* at Macuata." Just a month later, on October 21, FitzGerald noted: "Sent off 'His Blameless Youth.'"

This story, printed in the *Bulletin* (February 8, 1933), makes full use of the local color of the old cannibal country. The respectful *bokola* is there along with the all-powerful chief. Middle-aged Taito is there also, as narrator, recalling for the listening surveyor the wicked old days of "long pig," and denying any youthful complicity, but winding up his story with the words: "Yes, the old days were very bad. These days are good days and the government is a good government. . . . But the food is not so good." This successful venture into *Bulletin* fiction arouses wonder that it was never followed up.

Fiji allowed FitzGerald time now and again to do some reading. Books that might have influenced his later writings are mentioned in diaries and letters. Items include Longfellow, Boswell and the *Rambler,* Borrow's *Lavengro,* and *The Mysterious Universe* by Sir James Jeans, an early and exciting popular book on modern physics. This title also appears on the flyleaf of the 1933 diary as part of a list of book purchases, a baker's dozen which also includes

Arthur Eddington's *The Expanding Universe* and *The Nature of the Physical World,* A. N. Whitehead's *Science and the Modern World* (highly influential upon FitzGerald's philosophy), "an English grammar," and *Rotunda* and *Music at Night* by Aldous Huxley. Among the rest is *The Name and Nature of Poetry* by A. E. Housman, with whose definition FitzGerald was to take issue in the first paragraph of his critical volume, *The Elements of Poetry.*

After returning to Australia and to the life of a municipal surveyor, FitzGerald could not forget Fiji. As had been noted, he described to Stokes on April 19, 1937, a vivid nightmare when everything went wrong on the first night in the bush during a new field season. On March 8, 1941, he wrote to his friend: "Funny thing, I don't know whether it's a belated form of homesickness or what, but I've been taking a great interest in things pertaining to Fiji lately: have been getting books from the library and reading up history and that sort of thing. . . . It adds to the interest of the reading to remember the language. I find I have forgotten nothing of what I knew."

"Essay on Memory" (71–82), FitzGerald's best-known poem, a major achievement that won him first prize in a nationwide contest in 1938, goes back to his last surveying season in the islands. The ideas, as the poet says in his Australian Poets note, were "conceived under canvas in unceasing heavy rain in the mountains of Veivatuloa (Namosi Province, Fiji), 1935, . . . carried about for some time, [and] materialized eventually in this manner." "Rain" is the first word in the poem, and rain is a symbol throughout. The work, however, is mainly concerned with the meaning of memory. Here again a study of the Fiji documents is helpful. As early as July 5, 1934, during a spell of enforced idleness at his Lovo camp, FitzGerald wrote a long letter to Stokes in which several pages are devoted to an analytical discussion of two systems of memory training, weighing the merits of Pelmanism against the scheme delineated in Kitson's *How to Train Your Mind,* which FitzGerald had been reading. His conclusions in "Essay on Memory" go back at least to such speculations beside a creek on Vanua Levu.

The Fijian influence is quite strong in "Heemskerck Shoals" (94–100), and almost overhelming in what is FitzGerald's most impressive major poem, "Between Two Tides" (117–94). Many things can be said about "Heemskerck Shoals." The first point to be noted, how-

ever, about a poem that bears the subtitle "Fiji, 6 February, 1643,"
is that it concerns the first European ships ever to sail the waters of
the Fiji group.

An entire essay could be written on the effect of FitzGerald's
residence in Fiji upon "Between Two Tides." Although the setting
for this fine poem is Tonga and Tonga is not Fiji, the two groups
are not far separated, and a great deal of culture-swapping has always
gone on. As FitzGerald says in the final note to "Between Two
Tides": "Tongans have very likely become Fijians." Undoubtedly
his knowledge of the psychology of the native people among whom
he lived, and whose unspoiled humanity he loved, provided him
with much of the power that produced this poem, of which Douglas
Stewart wrote in his introduction to *Voyager Poems:*[11] "The nearest
we have to a true epic poem in Australia is probably FitzGerald's
'Between Two Tides,' a poem which, though it embodies much
of the best of his writing and is his most impressive feat of construction, probably misses full epic significance simply because its
theme is not Australian. Perhaps it will become an epic in Tonga."
It is certainly a memorial to FitzGerald's epic thoughts while in
Fiji.

Even a poem apparently far removed from the South Pacific, such
as "Fifth Day" (104-9), had its roots in the Fiji period. As early as
May 5, 1935, an entry appears in the diary in shorthand. FitzGerald
taught himself this skill from the eighteenth edition of an eighteenth-
century manual by Joseph Gurney and ever after used this rare form
of stenography. An explication of the poem will not be given in this
chapter; but one can remark that the upshot of this apparently
critical point in the trial of Warren Hastings was that it gave a
day's honest employment to Joseph Gurney, a hard-working, res-
pectable court reporter.

"This Between Us" (228-29) is a direct recollection of camping
beside the stream at Lovo in 1934. An early reference in the poem
to "Tagi-na-sola" (meaning the-stranger-weeps met by this pass
as enemy) is enriched by some lines in the poet's letter to Stokes
of February 11, 1951: "Toward Satulaki it got a bit rough as you
will recall, for you visited me there, and that's where I took over.
Beyond Satulaki before you get to my old camp at Lovo—which
we both visited on a day's descent from Sorolevu—there is a *really*
rough bit called Taginasola, which I believe means in local dialect:

'The stranger weeps.' I was the stranger; it was enough to make anyone weep. Just about there all my survey party deserted me—really remembering what it was like I can hardly blame them.''

Even after more than a quarter of a century, the memory of an incident—the viewing of a chief's grave on top of an isolated ridge—could, through the obscure process of poetic germination, eventuate into verse. FitzGerald once wrote: "The poem 'Relic at Strength-Fled' [229–33] is the result of pondering over a period of thirty years, in order to resolve an experience that once happened in the field in Fiji." "Embarkation" (233–34) also has a Fijian setting. Such a recent poem as "Invocation of Joseph Asasela" (*Meanjin,* XXVII [No. 2, 1968], 146–49) glorifies a wandering native of Kandavu who died alone in the Arctic.

Looking back, it is surprising that FitzGerald, with his intimate knowledge of the Fijian people and language, never wrote any nonfiction accounts of the natives. Once Stokes asked him why he did not, and the reply was: "*Poetry* is my life." However, years later he regretted that his daily duties and preoccupations had kept him from using this material. While reading *A Fijian Village*[12] by Buell Halvor Quain, FitzGerald wrote to his old teammate, Monty Miller, on February 11, 1952, and commented on the book in part: "The place is only about twenty miles from my beloved Seaqaqa: the natives seem all tremendously familiar to me as he tells about them in minutest detail. Once again I am thoroughly ashamed of us all, of myself in particular, that with our great advantage we did not collect a lot of this perishing material and set it down." It is still possible, however, that readers may obtain impressions from those vanished days. The poet wrote frequently to a beloved sister in Sydney; and these letters, heaped in a chest in his Hunters Hill home, would make a unique volume if edited and printed.

The influence of FitzGerald's knowledge of the Fijian language and chants upon his verse style is quite evident. Soon after his arrival in the field, Fitz, in company with Murray, studied the language from a battered copy of David Hazlewood's *A Fijian and English Dictionary.* The surveyor, required to do his job solely with the aid of drafted local laborers who had to be threatened or cajoled into unpaid hard work, quickly mastered a practical command of spoken Fijian. When he left, according to Stokes, he knew "more about the grammar and syntax than the best of the old hands."

During his last evening in a Fijian village, when the populace was staging an all-night sendoff in his honor, he wrote in his diary on November 25, 1935: "How well I understand the language, though, now; speeches, sermons, conversations all one. I even to a large extent know what they say to each other provided dialect isn't laid on too thick. All for nought seems a waste, never to use it again." His knowledge was not really lost; it was incorporated into his future writing as a subtle undercurrent.

The lad who published an essay at the age of twenty on free verse was not likely to overlook the percussive rhythms of the Fijian *meke* ceremonies at which, night after echoing night, he was the honored guest. In a lecture in 1966 he said, concerning his Fiji nights of listening: "It is generally conceded that dramatic poetry and the drama itself sprang from action-song; but I see action-song such as I know and have even partly translated as the source of straight narrative also."[13] (None of these translations has been published.) Speaking to the present writer about "Relic at Strength-Fled" (229–33), he agreed: "I did try to give it a bit of a Fijian beat."

The influence of five years in Fiji, it seems clear, has had a strong effect upon FitzGerald's choice of subjects and upon his prosody. It has even affected his personality. All his life his zestful enjoyment of the humor of existence on our planet has been expressed by an uproarious laugh that involves his whole being. During his island period he added to it a typical Melanesian clapping of the hands that flabbergasts any bystander within range. FitzGerald's friends have learned never to tell him a funny story in public. He was never more Homeric in his laughter than when he was telling a tale at his own expense.

IV   *"A Drift of Blown Smoke"*

It is impossible in this examination to comment at length, in four chapters, on all of FitzGerald's poems over the past half-century. The remarks in the following chronological commentary, therefore, will usually be limited to observations on themes, forms, settings, and comments by critics, and only occasionally will go further afield. Fuller explanation should be a most enjoyable task for any concerned reader.[14] However, every poem in *Forty Years' Poems* will receive some mention, along with a few published since that date.

The large body of criticism by other commentators deals almost altogether with FitzGerald's longer poems, although, paradoxically, the critics usually praise his lyrical gift. Since the Bibliography can refer the reader to critiques of "Essay on Memory," "Between Two Tides," "The Face of the Waters," and "The Wind at Your Door," the present reviews will devote more space than usual to the shorter pieces. Some commentaries may properly exceed greatly the length of the poem.

The first section of *Forty Years' Poems* is entitled "Salvage (1922–1930)," and contains such poems as the author wishes "to rescue from my first two books, *The Greater Apollo* and *To Meet the Sun,* together with a few pieces, written a little later, but at much the same stage of development, and omitted, chiefly for that reason, from my succeeding volume, *Moonlight Acre*. It contains all I wish to preserve of my poems of that period, now that I have done what I can for them by quite recent revision."[15] The section contains two dozen poems, presumably written over this eight-year period. Most were published in the latter 1920s.

The section opens, suitably, with a clarion call to join a celestial hunt, in which the speaker utters a view-hallo to guide the Riders of Air in pursuit of their quarry, the wild weather, flying over the night "like a fox on the heath." Most of the salvaged songs, however, deal with the twin themes, first, of the alienation of the artist, and second, of romantic love. The loneliness of the poet is acute in "Passer-by" (3), in which the man beneath the lighted, threatening windows is aloof because he seeks "old kinships" unknown to dwellers under leaden roofs. The early rebel that was Bob FitzGerald reveals in "Well-wishers" (4) his hidden allegiance to "the knaves and the pitiless" and ironically thanks his "kindly-speaking friends" for the folly of their good word. In "I Too . . ." (4)—revised after its appearance in the university magazine in 1922—the bohemian confesses an animal envy of the joys and frolics of the throng in which he is an alien. "Meeting" (5), in spirit as Whitmanesque as in its free-verse form, implies a cosmic coincidence in the encounter of two strangers who do not even glance at each other in passing. "Calm" (6) is a controlled cry by a young man beset by the doldrums of existence. Few poets, or none, have so perfectly melded this anguish of forced inaction with the image of a sailing vessel in the "great lull," until all life seems frozen in a "jogging and jigging" under a sole star. As his work shows, life to FitzGerald is usually synonymous with action.

The romantic strain is evident in the youthful disdain of booklearning in "The Old Cities" (5). Like the European poets a hundred years earlier, who felt guilty because their enjoyment of reading sometimes led them to neglect "nature" and "real life," FitzGerald inveighs against the ivory-tower inhabitants who allow themselves to be imprisoned by a pile of books. He admits the attraction of the scholar's career but in such alienation sees "the grey peace of death."

Few Australian poets have written love poems, and none have written major ones. FitzGerald is among the few. The love motif is broached in "The Wall" (7). "Sobriety" (14–15) reconciles the dreamer, who hoped to create a dazzling mosaic of his life, to the "placid and dull" design of routine, forsaking the flowered valleys of adventure. (Renunciation of adventure, however, seems premature for a twenty-four-year-old romanticist.)

The somewhat artificial "Song" (18) of love was included in FitzGerald's selection of his poems in 1963 as an example of "technical trickery."[16] It is indeed an echo gallery that overpowers its cavalier message.[17]

> *Dear Girl, I did not mean to part*
> *with all my heart so suddenly soon,*
> *but walk what careless road I willed*
> *to years of afternoon.*
> *Alas, how poorly I succeed*
> *in such an undecreed design!*
> *Was ever in all the sane world*
> *so wild a love as mine?*
>
> *Now go your way and get you gone—*
> *what has been done is past repairing.*
> *Though you have changed my life, my scope,*
> *I'd have you leave uncaring.*
> *I wait, disturbed and mind amiss,*
> *till other days than this come after,*
> *a prisoner in the future's keep,*
> *the captive of your laughter.*

In eight lines, "Sculpture" (18) presents an ironic reversal. The poet calls the image he conjures up of his beloved a "sculpture of the pliable air." This vision as a work of art is implicit in words such as "images," "paint," "art," and "copies." Nevertheless, the vision is shattered by the reality of the loved one's appearance in the flesh. A similar use of metaphor is found in "The Cup" (19), in which the lover is likened to a cup once full of the "wine-flood of adventurous youth," but now emptied in sudden wisdom and poured out in a toast to Imogen. An almost metaphysical imagery is conveyed in three quatrains with overtones of fullness, emptiness, and liquidity, coupled with such words as "spilt," "wine-flood," "poured," and "toast."

"Blown Smoke" (19–20) is the confession of a lover who, tired and overwrought, might find surcease and an antidote for the bloodless vision of his mistress—a "drift of blown smoke"—in the more earthly arms of a warm girl. The prosodic complexity of this lyric compensates for its repetitive length.

V *Farewell to Gods and Fays*

"Tradition" (20–23) is an extended exercise in evoking the heritage of courtly love. The pleading aspirant asks: "Grant I be not unworthy of that company." The six sections, in their variety of rhymes and stresses, constitute a tapestry of lost gallantry. H. M. Green[18] charges that the first stanza is an excellent example of FitzGerald's inability to discriminate between prose and poetry. The offending stanza does, however, have a rhyme scheme—*abcabcdefdef*—and a generally iambic pentameter beat, and compresses in its lines a portrait of the ideal knight who still should not be chosen as the lover's rival.

The earlier title of "Release" (23–24) was "Alchemy Unavailing," but the imagery throughout deals with necromancy rather than alchemy. The face of the beloved in memory's crystal ball is crowded out by later, inferior portraits. There are references in the three quatrains to a spell and a magic wand, and there is the suggestion of a séance, willing an image to appear.

"Economy" (24), which was first published in 1927, is truly an expression of a lover's thrift, prizing "as gold largesse/her light caress." The form is economical, making use of short, terse lines.

The last three of the four quatrains constitute a single sentence, opening with two clauses. The diction well suits the meaning: business terms like "thrift" (used twice), "valued at nought," "store," "stock-in-trade," "weighed," "cheap," and "gold" contrast roughly with love words like "favors," "careless kiss," and "light caress."

The unobtrusive form of "Her Hands" (25), with a regular eight-line rhyme scheme and basic iambic trimeter rhythm, does not distract from the theme. The soft hands of the first stanza might, the speaker fears, become at the end more like claws and beaks, merciless against the "night-borne" victim. "The number of sibilant *s* sounds in the two stanzas," notes Maureen Cassidy, "together with the intent of the words used, creates soft rustling movements such as hands might make.... In the second stanza there is a definite note of harshness both in meaning and in sound."[19]

"Of Some Country" (25–26) originally appeared in the *Bulletin* early in 1931 as "The Stranger-Lad," and was markedly revised for later printing (as in the volume *Of Some Country* in 1963). It consists of two stanzas, each welded from three standard quatrains. The rhythm is generally iambic trimeter, eight syllables to the line. A. E. Housman, whom FitzGerald admired, would not have disdained its authorship. The wayward young man, "unresting as torn flame" and "fretful for no cause," must forsake the girl with his love half-told and follow burnt roads of sand and gravel. The diction suitably arouses restlessness in the reader.

The section on "Salvage" fittingly ends with "Black Words" (26–27), in which compliments penned for the lost love might be salvaged for future courtship, and with the brief and metrically loose "Regret" (27). Here the poet perversely regrets not the errors of the past but rather the possible "follies not committed yet/and songs not put in rhyme." This message invites the reader to look ahead to the coming, more mature selections in the volume.

Several poems in "Salvage," however, do not fit the two categories of loneliness or love. "Michael Eyquem de Montaigne" (15–16) is a tribute to an older man who did not bemoan the passing days or call young people fools. Young FitzGerald also pays homage to Montaigne's celebrated book of essays. Three years after the poem appeared he was still keeping company with that book; in a letter to Tom Inglis Moore from Seaqaqa, Fiji, on November 16, 1932, FitzGerald wrote: "My reading has been limited to Shake-

speare, Montaigne, and *Na Mata,* the latter being a monthly publication in Fijian." It is pleasant to note that thirty years later he
realized his dream and made a pilgrimage to Montaigne's baronial
home in France and, in the very room where the *Essays* were written,
touched with one reverent finger the essayist's own chair.[20] The
complexity of the Montaigne poem's form, as noted in Chapter
4, well suits the complexity of the essayist's mind.

"At Arica" (16–17)—possibly reflecting the Lindsayian joy in
pirates and other rogues—was FitzGerald's first and last attempt
to write a poem to illustrate a drawing. It was composed at the
request of a friend, Unk White, to "poemestrate" a picture of pirates
that White had made and vainly hoped to sell. The poem was rejected by the editor of the *Bulletin* page, presumably because Death
was termed "a starveling sort of whore." It finally appeared in the
second (and last) number of *Australian Outline.* This poem was
written too late to be included in *To Meet the Sun* and was too out
of keeping to go in any later collection before 1965.

William Dampier (1651?–1715), protagonist of "At Arica," was
indeed a buccaneer, as well as the finest Pacific navigator before
the time of James Cook. When an attack on the town of Arica, on
the Pacific coast of South America, failed badly, the buccaneers
lost their leader and withdrew. "The poem has two things against
it very obviously," FitzGerald wrote to Douglas Stewart on April
6, 1960. "One is that 'Arica' is wrongly accented. . . . The other
obvious thing wrong is that I don't think by any possible stretch
of imagination the character depicted either by Unk or by me is
Dampier."

Finally, FitzGerald's long, contemplative poem "The Greater
Apollo" (7–13) foreshadows such sequences as "The Hidden Bole"
and "Essay on Memory." The seven "metaphysical songs," as
the early collection was subtitled, were privately distributed to friends
in 1927 as a memorial to the poet's mother. The metrics of the
sequence have been mentioned in Chapter 4.

The meditations echo the main idea that man is alienated from
nature by his perception of the passage of time. Change and decay
are the lot of mankind, and even nature is mutable: "the scored sea-
cliff," year after year, has "fallen back." Seasons recur, however,
and the pattern of nature is continuous. And "Time is a fool if he
thinks to have ended/one single splendid thing that has been."

An individual may die, but the human type will survive. The fourth section accuses the speaker of presumption in seeking to understand the intent of the Greater Apollo, "embodiment of all that is." Comprehending whatever Creator that exists is beyond human powers.

The poet's friend Phil Lindsay, writing under a pseudonym,[21] placed FitzGerald first among the current poets of Australia, but quite properly pointed out that the pieces in *The Greater Apollo* are not truly "metaphysical"; they are not abstract arguments but rather declarations of faith, expressing a simple philosophy of delight in the material world. Much of the meaning of the sequence is crammed into these lines:

> *The valley path is calm and cool*
> *as I walk here between green walls—*
> *and those are diamond waterfalls;*
> *this is a bird; and that's a pool.*
> *I heard their far insistent calls*
> *and gladly have returned to these.*
> *What is revealed to me and known*
> *beyond material things alone?*
> *It is enough that trees are trees,*
> *that earth is earth and stone is stone.*

Thus early the future lecturer on "Poetry's Approach to Reality" attained a canny view of the physical world.

Hugh McCrae, darling of the *Vision* coterie, claiming to have read *The Greater Apollo* twice seven times to ponder its "bright, yet difficult, language," in a review launched an opinion that was picked up and parroted by later critics—the notion that FitzGerald's poetry appealed mainly to the head and not to the heart. Labeled by such a sin against Romanticism, FitzGerald was to find it hard to earn freedom from easy dismissal as a "philosophical poet." "FitzGerald opens like an old book rather than like a flower" wrote McCrae; "the acrid flavor goes to the head, with little immediate effect upon the heart; but his emotional approach is camouflaged and gradual, and, once it has been made, is never forgotten. . . . FitzGerald is an individual writer, and a strong thinker; but, at present, he is working too hard at poetry to be, naturally, a poet."[22]

The fourth section of *The Greater Apollo* has likewise been taken as a vow to renounce FitzGerald's close association with the *Vision* group. Proclaims the young poet: "I look no more for gods among/ the lace-like ferns and twisted boughs" of Norman Lindsay's arbors at his Springwood estate. FitzGerald has done with "fays/ dancing light-foot down leafy ways, or Pan. . . ." From now on, he will view the visible world with his own clear, but not cynical, eyes.

CHAPTER 6

Harvest of the Thirties

W HAT was FitzGerald's contribution to the increasing self-
awareness of Australian poetry in the 1930s? Beginning in
that decade, the verse of the period broke away from its bondage
to imported ideas and, avoiding a blatant nationalism, began to
express personal feelings freely and sincerely. Leaving the nymphs
and satyrs behind, the *Vision* graduates took the lead in encouraging
natural expression in lyric form. "In poetry [Kenneth] Slessor and
FitzGerald in the thirties led the development of a mature, independent treatment of Australian themes with individual wisdom and
contemporary idiom. Today there is virtually no trace of colonialism
or any cultural clash of the poets."[1] The slow but eventual decline
of the "cultural cringe" had begun.[2]

I *A Mental Amulet Against Dejection*

FitzGerald's *Moonlight Acre* (1938, with a second edition in
1944) appeared nine years after *To Meet the Sun*. The poems included those in *Forty Years' Poems* headed not only "Moonlight
Acre (1930–1938)" but also "Copernicus (1931–1936)," "The Hidden
Bole (1934)," and "Essay on Memory (1937)." More than half
the years between the two collections of 1929 and 1938 were spent
in Fiji, and the verses often use this setting. The poet's ideas matured
but did not greatly change their direction. His style became less
outwardly lyrical and more meditative, although phrases shining
with imagery were not lacking.

The arrangement of the section dated 1932–38 brings out a lifelong attitude of the poet—the need for action to implement belief,
accompanied by the irritations of inaction to a vigorous constitu-
tion. FitzGerald does not imply that the highest good is action for
action's sake—the world has seen too much evil resulting from such
dynamic creeds. His urgings to be up and doing often sound,
however, like the reproachful expressions of a man of ideas who
fears that Hamletlike loss of the name of action stultifies the will.

"It is significant," Tom Inglis Moore wrote recently, "of the importance of the activist of our earth-vigor in our writing that Fitz-Gerald's book [*Forty Years' Poems*] as a whole is a testimony to its philosophy."[3]

The "Moonlight Acre" section opens, appropriately, with "Departure" (31). In moonlight the speaker makes ready to leave his beloved and returned to "the lonely stars, the forsaken sun." A rather commonplace six-line verse, rhyming *abccab*, is broken by the blunt interjection: "Put my armor on." A new, perhaps dangerous adventure must be faced.

"Exile" (31-32), although it was apparently not printed until it was included in the 1938 volume, probably expresses FitzGerald's feelings when he decided to leave for Fiji in order to earn a living. The burden of the poem is clear. Had Caesar banished him, there would still be hope of a reprieve. But "Caesar is now a purse," and with his own hand the speaker signed his writ of exile, under the rule of the new royalty of traders, from whom there is no appeal. The merchant and clerk are the new masters—"O brave King Harrys!" (The epithet recalls Kipling's portrayal, in "The Wrong Thing" in *Rewards and Fairies*, of Henry VII as a penny-pinching builder.) This poem was considered by F. M. Todd to be a good example of FitzGerald's success in the new poetry. "For while he is now dealing with ideas, with abstractions, with states of mind, with mental events, his meticulous storing of the fruits of experience in the world of sense does stand him in good stead. His imagination is vivid and concrete, so that his abstractions are objectified powerfully and strikingly, in imagery whose boldness is matched by its success. The cerebration is active, the thought and its expression never flaccid."[4]

"Moonlight acre" is the key phrase in the opening line of "Invasion" (32). In two quintains, delicately rhyming *abaab,* an imagistic scene is revealed. The dark trees overpower the unwatchful sentry, the wind, and silently invade the "white lands," "Tom Tiddler's ground," open to the first comer.

"Rewards" (33-34) is a violent expression of regret that the road to romance is now closed—the "musk of Ind," the "Courtyards of the Khan," the "tides of Venice" are now beyond the range of one who has grown taut with longing and is like a stretched wire, tense with inaction. "But better surely that a note should stir/the pulse of consciousness, the action of breath,/rather than beauty have no life, no death. . . ." The "rot of peace" should be combated by riding out in the lost cause of "some frenzied Lancelot." But the stay-at-home, the "poor fugitive behind stout bars," can never know the most fatal appeal to halt the seeker of truth: the cry of the hearths of little homes at dusk. FitzGerald's passion for beauty is now revealed as a passion for the beauty of action. The form of this longer lyric comprises eleven quatrains, rhyming *abba;* the rhythm is five-stress, with a marked iambic beat.

"Return" (34–36), originally called "Reality," pictures a turning away from the imprisonment of the senses and from recollections of a perishable, violent past: "a clashing of arms" and "unperishing hunger-cries/of flesh that dies." Again, the answer seems to be to launch into the unknowable, and the conclusion runs: "So I pass outward, and beyond/thought's reckoning, where time's a pond/unrippled by any stone/knowledge has thrown."

The nine stanzas of "Return" rhyme *aabb,* making it properly a couplet poem. The first pair are usually tetrameter and the second pair trimeter, lending variety. The imagery of the opening has been deprecated. "In three tiny verses we have at least five images to indicate one thing. 'The darkness,' 'somnambulist life-in-a-mist,' 'masonry caging-in the mind,' 'ashlar of sense,' and 'dream-woven filmy veil,' all refer (or seem to refer) to the tyranny of the senses. And when they are brought together in such a short space, they must appear a most incongruous collection of generalized images. The very syntax is disturbed by the overcrowding, and becomes an additional agent of confusion."[5] Enjoyment of variety in imagery, however, could be a matter of taste.

The rhymes in the eighth stanza contain the same vowel sound. FitzGerald, in a rare comment on one of his own poems, wrote to R. G. Howarth on December 15, 1949, concerning this stanza:

I have known successive rhymes on one vowel (usually a deplorable weakness) to be successful even when not deliberate, or peculiarly fitting as in this case. It is easy to let them slip by unnoticed in reading; for when that happens it really means that there is for some reason no real defect. In writing, too, one sometimes fails to notice one has done it. Then one gets used to it and cannot hear the grate. There's a stanza like that in my *Moonlight Acre* series in the set commencing "Boring the darkness these eyes burn"; I am so used to it and it was so long before I noticed it at all that my ear has acquired a tolerance for it; but it must set most readers' ears completely on edge.

"Long Since" (36-37) combines melodic beauty with forced in-action, frustrated aspiration. "The scene is a village on the Macuata coast of Vanua Levu, Fiji; but the poem was written in Suva."[6] The comparison is between the remembered "muttered anger of the reef" beside "the old sea" far away from waters stifled in the Fijian lagoon and the softer sound of waters in "so dulled a clime." The recollected "alert, masterful waves summoning beach and palm/to be up and about and moving ever upon quest" contrast with the speaker's lassitude as he wonders "what weakness took toll/that thus I must go scurrying ratwise to my hole" in a thatched Fijian dwelling. The beauty of the poem has been recognized. Evan Jones notes of the author that, in his opinion, "The most graceful poetry he ever wrote was in the best lyrics of *Moonlight Acre*," and quotes the opening lines of "Long Since."[7]

In the short lyric "The Toss" (37) may be found a touchstone to separate two kinds of readers. Eight lines of haphazard stresses suggest the risks and rewards of playing the gambling game of tossing a coin, and in the larger sense the game of living.

> *Life, toss up your florin;*
> *"Heads," I call.*
> *Regret be far and foreign*
> *whichever fall,*
> *whether for losing or winning*
> *the stake scarce to be won—*
> *it's a fine flash of silver, spinning*
> *in the gay sun.*

The same critic who admired "Long Since" declares that "FitzGerald was affected by the Lindsayian demand for Gaiety, and the en-thusiasm for Life; he is at his worst in ['The Toss']. . . . He never gave over this vitalist and Lindsayian insistence on the delight of the present moment, on clamorous and more or less roistering action."[8] (One wonders whether it is better for a poet to be lan-guorous and morose!) On the other side, Nancy Keesing, herself a poet, refers to "The Toss" as one of her "mental amulets against dejection."[9]

II *"Ransomed" in Two Senses*

Returned to "the jail of town," the activist in "Coiled Wire" (37–38) frets at the "atavistic twitch/of muscles" that urges him to pace his cell, for "those times are overpast/when one gave chase if fortune fled too fast." Out of employment—"the hands are all paid off ashore"—he advises himself to "preserve his bootsoles,/ moved no more by any tremor of coiled wire that mocks/the physical Jack, jumped clean out of the box." The "atavistic twitch" is the coiled spring that activates a Jack-in-the-box. Those who know this toy recall that its chief value is surprise; and the series of images ends in this surprising twist. Within the images are sardonic pieces of self-counsel to a man chafing at inactivity. The form of "Coiled Wire" also is a surprise; although the rhythm is not iambic pentameter, the rhyme scheme resembles a variant of the English or Shakespearean sonnet.

The action theme is reinforced by inclusion next of a quite early poem, "Accomplishment" (38–39), first appearing in 1927.[10] Using one of FitzGerald's favorite symbols, the sun,[11] the young poet proclaims that anything is possible for the aspirant; one might as well reach for the sun as for a straw. Dreams are more precious than the fungoid race of men. "Fell the tree to pluck a leaf;/mow with swords a mangled sheaf:/Life itself were cheaply spent/for the frail accomplishment."

A woman critic finds in these lines a masculine tone recalling the tradition of the Australian balladists of the backblocks. "This is perhaps a more unchristian and inhuman statement than FitzGerald would care to stand by now; but it does point to a certain strain which has persisted in his poetry. This blunt-mindedness—which, to do FitzGerald justice, seems to stem rather from an uncritical enthusiasm for action as such, than from lack of sympathy for slaves and underdogs—is allied to that quality in him which links him to the bush balladists and the tough-masculine strain in Australian development. He is, as it were, the poetic apotheosis of the balladists."[12]

This early poem, by the way, is a prosodic tour de force. Again the stanzas rhyme *aabb;* there are regularly seven syllables to a line; and the meter is the rare trochaic tetrameter. The steady beat is full of energy and emphasis, urging its strong feeling on the reader; assonance and alliteration reinforce the bold rhymes.

"Rebirth" (39–40), originally titled "Rest House Verandah," has a Fijian setting, with its mention of "the tropic light over the sugarcane," "palm tops," "ukulele playing," and "island airs." The evening coolness brings some return of energy, but it is easier to be possessed by vague longings than to obey the urge to "take up again the dropped threads of our youth." Action here is inhibited by ambience. The opening line has a parallel structure: "The fall of evening is the rebirth of knowing." Paradoxically, a "fall" is at one and the same time a "rebirth." The beauty of this poem is subtly enhanced throughout by its structure. "After a single line opens the poem, there are three-line stanzas of interlocking rhyme called tercets. The rhyme scheme is, in full, *a bca dce dfe gfh gih jik jlk*. Only two lines are without matching rhyme. Since the rhyme scheme is fulfilled only as one moves from stanza to stanza, the reader's attention is pulled continuously forward in anticipation of the following sound."[13]

In a Fijian village, FitzGerald wrote "Legend" (40–42), an evocation of one of FitzGerald's ancestors, the Mary Ann Bell who was courted and won in Dublin by the poet's great-grandfather, and came with him to Australia. Here is action in God's plenty, but in an earlier generation. The quirky tone reminds one of "My Aunt" by Oliver Wendell Holmes. "Legend" foreshadows the choice of an ancestor for a subject in "The Wind at Your Door" and the unpublished "Verse for a Friend." The main charm of the poem lies in its graceful narrative and use of references to Irish places and objects, as well as in its Irish flavor of speech. It was published fifteen years before FitzGerald set foot on Irish soil.[14] The structure of "Legend" suggests the timing of an Irish jig. The predominant rhythm is anapestic, producing comic and exuberant effects heightened by a number of feminine rhymes, double and triple.[15]

"Versatility" (42–43) declares that the speaker might have specialized in science, foppery, or—worse still—commerce, but instead he had "found happiness, without looking for it,/time and again on entering new glades/where life forgot I had committed this wrong/and was itself a feckless Jack-of-all trades." An introductory stanza is omitted in reprintings.

A springtime siege of illness must have inspired "Entreaty" (43), in which the poet pleads for the summer to bring release. The irregularity of the prosody reflects the disorder brought to the household by illness, creeping in like an unwanted stray animal. This plight is emphasized by many sounds with unpleasant meanings. Again, healthy action is repressed by climate.

In "Crescent," the moon—subject of the verses—is contrasted with the sun and personified oddly as a body-surfer through the clouds. Perhaps this metaphor could have been given in briefer space.

This section of *Forty Years' Poems* ends with disillusion. The aspirations of the opening pieces have been frustrated in "The Blue Thought of the Hills" (47). As ridge after ridge appears ahead of the weary climber, so does attainment of the quest vanish in the distance. "Although your way might aspire/from the peak to the further peak,/vision and blue retire;/beyond even desire/they are still to seek."

The lyric impulse is not repressed, however, in the new section labeled "Copernicus (1931–1936)." The opening poem, "The Traveller" (51–52)—published earlier under the titles "Contest" and "Conflict"—derives, in the author's words, "from my lonely trip from Kurrajong to Singleton" along the Great Dividing Range of New South Wales. The poem opens with a clarion call to the "traveller on the barren roof of this high country," who is challenged to a contest with raw nature. Surely "The Traveller" is one of the best poems to have been written about the landscape of the Blue Mountains. As elsewhere, FitzGerald shows his study of geology in such lines as "Conflict of shaggy rams of stone. . . ./Savage great ridges, jarring, test/strength upon strength, crest reared at crest,/spur jolting spur's flint forehead-bone. . . ." There are five stanzas of seven lines rhyming *abbaacc*. The meter varies pleasantly to enrich the statement of the poem.

"Chaos" (52–53) is a poem of amateur ethical speculation, in which the paradox is presented that life is ruled not by the scales of Justice but by the scales of Chaos. The tone is dejected: "what can we hope to gain with our best toil?/with life itself?/what wring from this bleak place?" But in a reverse paradox, FitzGerald went on living and hoping that Justice would rule in the end. The poem would serve as an example of the prosiness of which the author is occasionally accused, except for its complex metrical pattern, an interlinking similar to the sort used in "Rebirth" and "Quayside Meditation."

Written in the capital of Fiji, "Side Street" (54) speculates on
the future of the Melanesian populace, faced with racial competi-
tion. Both rhythm and rhyme are irregular, giving the effect of
free verse. Local color is prominent throughout.[16]

"Ransom" (55) presents the Suva waterfront, which could be
any waterfront. The prosody is again irregular. The coming of
night awakens in the watcher a memory of man's primitive past.
What was in our primordial forefathers a "howl to the moon" is
nowadays a surrender to the wonder of nature. We are "ransomed"
in two senses: we have paid a debt by becoming more civilized,
and also we are redeemed from civilization by sharing the pristine
ecstasy of the blood. The "lit doors" of the final line repeat this
double sense; they may signify the warmth of the modern home,
or else the mouths of caves lit by primitive campfires.

III *A Poem, or a Debater's Brief?*

Not evening but tidal return is the topic of "Tide's Will" (55–56).
The atavistic pull of the moon-powered ocean tide brings lovers
again together: "being tryst, renewal, of tides felt before/dragging
upon those depths which are our world's truest core." The form
of the poem, apparently casual, repays analysis. Three eleven-line
stanzas rhyme *aabccbddeee*. Each stanza easily breaks into two
parts of six and five lines. The stronger stresses in each line of
each stanza run 3, 3, 5, 3, 3, 5; 4, 4, 5, 5, 6. The undertone of varied
rhythms, like the incoming lapping of the tide, well suits the thought
that "even as through abysmal ages earth/has grappled under the
stars with surge of death and birth."

The title poem of this section, "Copernicus" (57), appeared in
1938, but its germ idea is found, as has been noted, in the surveyor's
diary for 1936. From the point of view of a rooster, the sun's passage around the earth depends upon the crowing at dawn from bird
to bird. The title, drawn from the name of the man who first out-
lined the various orbits of the sun's system, is ironically transferred to the pondering cock who reasons, delighted in his discovery: "The world's egg-round!" Those who forget FitzGerald's
joy in playful humor should not overlook "Copernicus."

The opening lines in "At Least" (58) urge that life is justified
because of the occasional rewards offered by the keen senses: "If

I should die tonight—/should death strip the festoon/twisted for brief delight/ . . . at least I have seen the moon."

The final selections in *Moonlight Acre* are two poems of speculation, "The Hidden Bole" (61–66) and "Essay on Memory" (71–82). These confirmed the critics in labeling FitzGerald a "philosophical poet," and he did not disclaim the title if applied to him in the broadest sense.

These two lengthy poems, along with others such as "The Face of the Waters" (102–104), differ markedly in style and intention from the shorter lyrics. They are well characterized by T. L. Sturm, who attributes their thought content in large measure to the philosopher A. N. Whitehead, whose volume *Science and the Modern World* formed part of FitzGerald's small library in the Fijian bush in 1933.

There is a curious mixture of rhetorical and meditative tones, of rhythmically smooth, almost lyrical, cadences, and lines in which the rhythm is abrupt, halting, or awkward. The texture of the verse contains what appears to be a peculiarly uncompromising blend of discursive generalization and a dense, tangled undergrowth of metaphor and imagery that often turns out, on close inspection, to be operating in paradoxical ways. The poems appear to be offering meanings primarily of a philosophical nature, yet because of the dense texture of the verse these meanings constantly evade ready formulation. . . . Yet what is fascinating about them is the stubborn movement of mind which they project, as we follow its oscillations, under the pressure of some emotional experience, some interaction of the personality with its immediate environment, between poles of belief and rejection, rhetorical assertion and counter-assertion. . . . It is primarily an intellectual mode, but it allows for a surprisingly wide variety of emotive effects, ranging from the low-keyed detachment of purely expository passages to climactic moments of intense rhetorical involvement.[17]

"The Hidden Bole" was written at Lane Cove, a Sydney suburb, while the poet was convalescing from an appendicitis operation in 1935. The occasion for the work was the death in 1931 of the great ballerina Pavlova, but the theme is the essence of Beauty, especially in its relationship to Time. Opinions on "The Hidden Bole" appear to be polarized. One critic confesses that it "hardly seems to me to be a poem at all. It is in poetic form, an exceedingly intricate form; but its meaning has not been conceived as poetry."[18]

FitzGerald himself wrote: "It is, I feel, perhaps my one claim to being considered as a poet."[19] Its value, of course, lies between these extremes.

The dominant images in the poem are the dancer and the banyan tree.[20] The opening stanza presents a stage floodlighted by the sun, with a backdrop of seasons and stars; but the dancer has been stilled by death. Questions arise about the survival of Beauty in a universe outside of experience—"the Nothing (contracted to some blackened point)/where wakes the dream, the brooding Ultimate." Is Beauty "some shadow on this dream which dreams the world"? Or is it a melody that listens to itself? Or "the risen cream upon man's milk of thought" (an almost metaphysical image)? Or a treacherous spell of magic? Other possibilities—such as that Beauty is a Platonic ideal—are carefully omitted from speculation.

Nature is bluntly ruled out as the origin of Beauty, whose home is "the cliffs of intellect," where savages never come. "Nature is your alembic"; in it Beauty distils her potion to attract the senses of mankind and thereby arouse within the artist, unaware, the power to express his vision of Beauty. This process seems vain, however, for "All perishes; all passes," and "nothing attains some loveliness but mars/century-toil of stars..../time will fell the tower as death the dancer." The storms of vicissitude sweep on. European man, offspring of the Ice Age, may be replaced by other races "now lagging long in the sun." Moreover, "quake or plague/ might well supplant us with the developed bat,/give bees inheritance of our masque of sorrow..../nature could tip her balance with a gnat."

Humbly, mankind, and especially the artist, accepts the vulnerability of Beauty to the operations of Time, because permanence is rigidity, and art loves to reflect change. "We ask no more than let our joy be frail,/since its whole wisdom is its passing hence;/ nor would we stamp on you the permanence/which, only, is death."

The banyan-tree image now appears as the manifestation of the poet's exemplar of a primordial core of survival deep within the jungle of life. The quality of the banyan is that the original sapling puts out aerial roots that reinforce the bole, and eventually the single tree becomes a widening mass of trunks that intertwine their leaves and flowers. The blossoms last but a day and may vainly seek reasons for their evanescence, "ignorant that no cause need

be, its falling/being what spun hours have worked for and last aim/
of evolution—old, gnarled, twisted tree. . . . Who knows/where its
true nucleus grows/when every shoot of progress makes the claim?"
The main line of descent is the invisible core—"the hidden bole."
And the search for purpose is meaningless; it suffices the poet that
he can view "fresh fronds, bright berries."[21]

Beauty, in sum, is a dancing light, a song heard between gusts
of storm. Beauty does not last, but the artist may briefly capture
his vision of "eyes that speak, flung shoulders and feet fleeing."
The dancer of "Giselle" survives death because the memory of
her survives in the minds of those who have viewed her. Transience,
paradoxically, triumphs over Time, and as twilight dims the stage
the poem can fall into a serene closure.

Although admiring the "appropriately steady rhythm" and
"interesting and beautiful if somewhat contorted imagery" of "The
Hidden Bole," H. J. Oliver felt that it is "full of non sequiturs."[22]
On the other hand, Leonie Kramer stated that "In 'The Hidden
Bole' argument—and the poem must be praised for its logic—
blends perfectly with image to define the meaning of abstract con-
cepts."[23] The poem is a poem, not a debater's brief. T. L. Sturm
concluded:

The critic who complains of non sequiturs in "The Hidden Bole" is beside
the point; the poem is not a logical disquisition on the Immortality of Beauty,
and the last lines are in no sense a "resolution" of conflicting arguments:

> *I praise your triumph for its transience,*
> *that the notes pass and fair dies into fair.*

It is simply the way in which the poet makes meaningful to himself an
experience which has deeply moved him. It is a meditative rather than
an argumentative poem; the movement of thought is circular rather than
linear, and its interest for the reader lies in the conflict, the ebb and flow,
of the emotions which prompt the "argument." . . . [FitzGerald's] best
poems are those in which meditation is cast in a dramatic form. The obvious
comparison is with . . . the Browning of the dramatic monologues. "The
Hidden Bole" is finally a successful poem because the poet is able to
distance himself from it; he is present only as a persona, as an actor in a
miniature drama.[24]

IV   *The Flame of Individual Survival*

The technique of "The Hidden Bole" is complex, reflecting the complexity of the thought. The sixteen stanzas are each twelve lines long. The rhyme scheme is *abbcaddcefef,* and the endings are an agreeable mingling of exact and near-rhymes. Five good stresses are found in each line, except for the seventh line, where there are three. Again, a short line in midstanza gives a break that comes to be anticipated. The long stanza offers appropriate scope for the serious tone of discussion in the poem.

FitzGerald was pleased when Tom Inglis Moore gave "reasonable attention" and appreciation to "The Hidden Bole" when other critics ignored it. Moore had written that the poem

is one of the highest peaks of the national literature. In fact, I prefer it to the "Essay on Memory," for, although it has not the amplitude and weight, the brilliance and the vigor, of its fellow-poem, it flows more spontaneously. It has a cleaner, purer line as well as a melody which is wanting from the "Essay." It has caught some of the exquisite grace of the ballerina, so that the thought, ever present and subtle, sings itself into expression. "The Hidden Bole," inspired by emotion, is—despite some lines of metaphysics—almost all pure poetry. The "Essay on Memory," dominated by the working out of an intellectual concept, is often rhetoric rather than poetry, even if the rhetoric is a *tour de force* of brilliancy, and is continually being swept into poetry by a dynamic imagination. In the tribute to Pavlova, moreover, FitzGerald finds a fervor rare in his work, for one of his characteristics as a poet is a lack of passionate utterance.... Yet the beauty of Pavlova, that embodies in her dancing all the line and movement he loves, in its most consummate form, has stirred him into creating a loveliness of answering song.[25]

Previously, FitzGerald had written about the mutability of Beauty and—notably in "The Greater Apollo"—of its possible survival after death. He was to write further on the subject of permanence through recollection in his next work, the long poem "Essay on Memory."

The ideas in "Essay on Memory" were "conceived under canvas in unceasing heavy rain in the mountains of Veivatuloa (Namosi Province), 1935, and, carried about for some time, materialized eventually in this manner."[26] The poem was written in stolen hours during many months in 1937 and first appeared in the Sydney *Morning Herald* on April 9, 1938. Although FitzGerald felt that his literary career was "about at an end," he hoped to "win the big prize," and this long poem would be his admission ticket. His hopes were fulfilled when he did gain the £50 award for the best poem entered in the celebration of the sesquicentenary of the first settlement of Australia in 1778. The poem deals with universal human feelings, but does conclude with a testimony of belief in the future of the southern nation. "We'll make fabulous," he proclaims, "this world,/ in honor of them who gave it us,/not just the Nelsons, Newtons, of our race,/the Phillips grounding at a landing-place/continent-wide," but all others who share his lust for creative action.

The length of the "essay" (350 lines) has worked against its popularity, although it might be argued that a good long poem is even better than a good short one. The "obscurity" of the thought, sometimes censured, is probably a result of the length. As FitzGerald concluded many years later, "The 'Essay on Memory' was actually about the first poem of any length written by an Australian this century; even Chris Brennan's very closely integrated work is in the form of a series of short lyrics; and what I think people *really* found hard was the need to concentrate on trying to read a poem that was a little bit longer than a sonnet."[27]

To give the argument of the poem line by line would lengthen this chapter intolerably. The metaphysics was early examined by A. R. Chisholm, whose essay is still worth study; it was commended by the poet himself, with slight reservations.[28] Two recent analyses note some sources of ideas and expand the philosophical analysis.[29] A brief sketch of the main points may, however, lead each reader to experience this adventure in ideas for himself.

Rain opens the poem and is a unifying image throughout. The rain is the bony hand of Memory, knocking at the vaults of the dead, persistently stirring up the carrion and mocking the "mild dream, half guess, half lies" of History. Memory is not precisely a faded old photograph, nor the story of archaeology, nor the composite "mind of the race." Memory may have something of all this, but in addition is a frightening ghost as old as the earth. Memory is "the wind's voice in the crevice"; both the rain and the wind are cosmic forces greatly predating mankind. Memory is the whole past. It is necessity, process, the chain of cause and effect, the life stream. The buried dead, who lived so merrily, were not "dupes of the dawn," for they are "loot of Memory" and their actions continue to affect the actions of the living today.

The sixth stanza considers the problem of the individual conscience and suggests that the past is required to activate individual efforts in the present. The imagery is complex.

> ... No comfort could we claim
> except from that one wavering inward flame
> unquenched through change and time, which though it wrought
> in intricate iron the twisted chain of thought,
> link by link stretching, vagrantly designed,
> back past first hammerings of conscious mind,
> is yet so fine, for all its intense white core,
> stretched fingers freeze which were but chilled before.

The difficulty here is what the "wavering inward flame" might be, why the chain of thought should be twisted, and why the chilled fingers stretching out as if toward a flame will freeze the more they approach the "intense white core."

Although surprised that certain ideas in his poem should be unclear, FitzGerald discussed this stanza with T. M. Cantrell and explained that the "wavering inward flame" is intended to refer to the self as influenced by ancestral memory.

All present effort is made by virtue of the effort or thought of the past, of which our present effort is necessarily a continuation. The idea is that the self, by its very creativity through self-expression, creates the "chain of thought," "twisted" and "vagrantly designed" because it is the product of the effort of so many ancestors, and seen as stretching "back past first hammerings of conscious mind," back, that is, even prior to geological pre-history.

Having asserted the age-old and enduring nature of the chain of thought, gradually but surely produced by countless individual efforts, the poet then urges his concept of the necessity of basing present efforts on an awareness of the past. The flame (of mind) is so *insubstantial* ("is yet so fine") without the reinforcements that memory gives, that any attempt ("stretched fingers") made by the individual to gain something for himself, an attempt that must necessarily involve his efforts to define the self *as* self, will be futile unless it is based on the memory's awareness and acknowledgment of the past. The contention is that it is only when we see the self in the perspective of memory that we can achieve anything at all.[30]

This flame of individual survival burns on, but would perish except that "we clasp about us cast-off rags/and robes of dead kings."

V   *The Action Is a Mind at Work*

The multitude of the dead is like the myriad raindrops at the beginning of "Essay on Memory," falling minute after minute all over the world. They are all about us, the dead—in the dust, in blades of grass. Each person's arms are "so trussed/in thongs of old inheritance they can/but move in those accustomed tasks of man/allotted, limited, by the flesh they wear/ancestrally." Stanza 10 states that we are but the substance of the thoughts of the dead, "forms worked over/in one huge bulk ere each is lost forever." To balance this apparently overwhelming influence of the dead, the poet in stanzas 8 and 9 points out an attitude that prevents us from feeling like mere "inert, plastic material" into which Memory kneads itself. Again Cantrell's conversation with FitzGerald is helpful.

If, with this perspective of ourselves as the mere products of memory, we probe into the past which increases ("spores") as we probe, then we begin to fade out of existence altogether. We increasingly lose our distinctive individuality insofar as it is the activity of the past, rather than the individuals who comprised it, that impresses itself upon us. The individual existence becomes submerged in and ultimately undifferentiated from the stream of events of the past. The phenomena of the past seem not to be substantial realities, but to partake of existence only as fleeting phases within a process. They are not *things* but patterns in water, purely expressive of their origin. Everything is seen in terms of what is done: the bird's flight *as* the bird. All things appear "not as existence, but as forms worked over/in one huge bulk ere each is lost forever," not, that is, as sundry particular and individual existences but as physical forms. This couplet simply expresses the scientific law of the indestructability of matter and of physical energy, the concept that everything is absorbed into the earth and reissued in another form.

The position reached is that if we see ourselves merely as the products of memory, then we tend to reduce the importance of our individual existence. FitzGerald is here presenting polarities and working towards their synthesis.[31]

Paradoxically, we are not "shadow-thralls" of the dead; we are

ourselves Memory, and our vitality conditions the very survival
of the dead. Again the idea of action as the *summum bonum* is
typical of FitzGerald's body of verse. He brings together in this
long poem in the "grand style" the polarities of necessity, chance,
and free will, just as does Herman Melville in prose in "The Mat-
Maker" chapter of *Moby Dick*.

The following stanza contains one of FitzGerald's most striking
metaphors.

> *Argument is the blade-bright window-pane*
> *which shears off cleanly the slant sheaf of rain,*
> *and in the room heart's dream and life's desire*
> *are radiance and curled, unfolding fire.*
> *Here thought may ponder in peace or work at will*
> *or take down book from shelf and read his fill;*
> *but though among men's assets he bides long*
> *always his ears are turned on that same song*
> *of rain outside; for that's the force he knew*
> *which drenched his hands that battled it, breaking through*
> *while yet he was homeless in the world, unsafe,*
> *wandering in mindless marches the wind's waif,*
> *and had not learned to build up words and fix*
> *a house for himself in speech's bonded bricks.*
> *Hearing it he remembers: though large walls*
> *shelter him now, hold out the rain, rain falls.*

Within the shelter of the windowed room, Thought may work at
ease; but the pane is not impervious, and always his ears are tuned
to the rain, representing the forces against which he fought while
wandering, "the wind's waif," through primordial marshes before
he learned to build shelters of words. Thought remembers that,
despite the walls, rain still exists and persists.

The earth, like the rain, also possesses wisdom that Thought
cannot fathom. In realization, Thought becomes "a trifle impatient
of philosophies" and soliloquizes: "Put aside the reading-glass
and trust your eyes, which see that things are not as they purely
exist, but as they act. Go among men, see how they 'command
the future, and the past obey,/their present only a footing on some
height/that fronts new dawn forever.'"

The poet then turns to the days to come and urges adventure,

even if we risk danger, as William Dampier did when he surveyed
unknown coasts where future settlers of Australia would sow wheat
and dig for gold. The present is soon spent, but its decisions may
give birth to other presents that are equally uncertain. Yet our
present is someone else's past, and this generation should act in
such a way that it will be honored in its turn. There may come wars
(the time was 1939, the uneasy eve of World War II). There may
come a future of Satanic mills, a smoky city operated underground
by "strange engines and strange customs and strange men!" Hor-
rors may rise that will force a father to ask himself "doubt-drunken-
ly," "What have I done?" in breeding children to face such di-
sasters. But rain will once more wash the air, and Memory will
mint bright faith that shames us for ingratitude to our own forefathers. We must adventure still. In a burst of Lindsayian vitalism,
the poet predicts: "We'll slit gloom's gullet, oracling defeat,/
and crack great barrels of song in open street,/free for the drinking."
We must imitate the founders of the nation, make the present a rope
ladder of change by which to ascend, struggling, to achieve beyond.
"Wherefore all good is effort, and all truth/encounter and over-
coming." For

> *. . . We whose scope*
> *clasps the tremendous leagues of summer-south,*
> *thunder-oppressive with curbed energies,*
> *least of all folk need question our day's worth*
> *or think its turmoil twitchings of spent earth.*

Australians, least of all people, should despair. "Essay on Memory," a great patriotic affirmation, can still be read with optimism
even two centuries after the discovery of the eastern side of the
Australian continent by Captain James Cook in 1770. "Not yet the
impetus flags whose course began/when at the blank mouth of
our stinking lair/we saw night's infinite curtain shake with grey/and
so went forth determined to be Man." Memory, the "one live link/
of gone with all-to-come," will sustain bold venture as it has done
"in older abyss where time slept stirless yet."
   The structure of "Essay on Memory" is quite logical, then, and
its imagery is torrential.[32] The stanzas of the poem function as
paragraphs of varying length, without loss of continuity of statement. The rhythm is loose pentameter. The rhymes come mainly
in couplets, varied by an occasional quatrain. The prosody is

relaxed—perhaps because the tightness of the argument forces concentration on subject matter. Moreover, the many runover lines break up the beat and create a controlled looseness free from methodically end-stopped lines. Sometimes a stanza is entirely composed of couplets with exact or near-rhymes, as is the first stanza. The versification is polished and sustained throughout. As one otherwise dissenting critic remarks: "The *poetry* of the 'Essay' never lets one down."[33] If the broad theme of this long poem is an evocation of the core of continuous meaning in the universe, then the rhythmic flow of the verse reflects this theme. In manner as well as matter, "Essay on Memory" is an outstandingly successful long poem, a high peak in the range of Australian literature.

The main quality of all the essay poems is, perhaps, not their contribution to metaphysics but the achievement of a melding of thought and poetry. The action in each poem consists of the working of a sensitive mind grappling with broad questions that all of us must face or be forever craven. The thinking progresses, finds images, negates and affirms, leaps to speculations, comes to tentative judgments, on a mental platform around which echoes a verbal symphony. The effect has immediacy, for the thinking is happening *now*.

Having stated, in such achievements as "The Greater Apollo," "The Hidden Bole," and "Essay on Memory" his metaphysical ideas, FitzGerald was willing to go ahead and exemplify these ideas in further lyrics and, especially, in narrative verse, in which characters other than his own persona will voice their reveries in historic situations. The Browningesque pieces of the 1940s, like "Heemskerck Shoals," "Fifth Day," and the epic "Between Two Tides" are logical sequels to the long poems of personal speculation.[34]

CHAPTER 7

The Forties: Short Poems and Long

THE wartime and postwar decade of the 1940s revealed in FitzGerald's work a more serious vein, adventuring into longer forms although not neglecting the short lyric. "The tone of the poems in FitzGerald's third phase," says H. M. Green, "is soberer, the analyst more in evidence as such. The enthusiasm which is perhaps his most marked characteristic is evident enough, but is now comparatively restrained and runs often beneath the surface; youthful exuberance has given way to a conservation of the energy of which there is, however, no lack."[1]

Fifteen years passed between the *Moonlight Acre* volume (1938) and *This Night's Orbit* (1953), but the poet had not slackened in periodical publication betweenwhiles and, moreover, had published in 1952 his epic *Between Two Tides*. All but a few of the nineteen items in *This Night's Orbit* came out in the 1940s. The earliest piece, "Duped Though We Were," in the section of *Forty Year's Poems* headed "This Night's Orbit (1939–1952)" appeared in 1940; the latest, "Transaction," was published in the *Bulletin* on March 7, 1951.

I   *Snap the Snake by the Tail*

"This Night's Orbit" (85), title poem of this section, originally called "Turn and Fall," was termed by the author a "rehabilitation poem," comparable to "Long Since," and "an example, too, of a special technique for a special purpose."[2] It repeats the poet's hopeful view of life as he strolls in the moonlight beside sea dunes, unwilling to be bound by memories or old routines or wasted hours. "But always I have met,/and shall meet, the fresh hour. . . . The turn and fall/of living brings me," he remarks, "into the employ/of wars, business, events, to run/new errands"—he had been doing essential surveying to aid the war effort—but he hopes he can still follow successfully the path he has been trained to follow. "This Night's Orbit" is composed of a single stanza of six quatrains.

107

The rhythm is irregular, with line stresses varying from four to six, giving a turning-and-falling effect.

Optimism is still stronger in "Duped Though We Were" (86). The hopeful walker now finds himself laden "with swags of sober sense that balk/leaping at easy stiles"; but the far hills beckon still and "defiance flouts, anew,/found fact," and fooled eyes "shall stare down, outwit,/curt logic of dismay." For when "time, the sharper, reaches to thieve/last rags from limbs and back" the cunning victim is also able to use trickery; the fifth ace in his pack is hope. Published in 1940, the poem, without hinting at war, suggests a realization that dreams of peaceful existence have been shattered. The five quatrains again have an irregular rhythm, but are mainly alternating iambic trimeter and tetrameter.

The interest of the four-line poem "Experience" (86) lies in its brief statement about the clumsiness resulting when a new task is faced "not scribed to a template, squared or planned,/and never drafted at the desk." The terms, of course, refer to the tools and blueprints of the poet's own profession of surveying. Experience in one area seldom transfers to another.

The key word in "Wonder" (87) is "epicycle"—in astronomy, a cycle in which a planet moves and which has a center that is itself carried around at the same time on the circumference of a larger circle. The cosmic line drawn in the void is contrasted at the end with the deceptively irregular paths of bright comets. Except for the opening quatrain of the four, the rhythm is suitably regular. It is noteworthy that all the rhymes are exact rhymes, "obedient to strict law."

"Individuality" (87–88) invites the poet's friend to exchange skins, thoughts, minds, instincts, courage. Few basic differences will be found in human reactions, except for personal memories. Even these might not be too different: "Exchange our memories last. Remains/to each the bower-bird Me./Old consciousness now wears new brains; but who is Tweedledee?" The reference is to the Australian bird that builds a "bower"—a playground structure of interwoven sticks, decorated with bleached bones, pieces of stone or glass and other bright objects, and bunches of berries. The seven quatrains of "Individuality" have a regular rhyme scheme and a certain regularity in rhythm, but use other devices to avoid monotony in versification. The regularity, however, suggests the lack of strong individuality between person and person.

The poem "1918-1941" (89) is a strong reminder that the lessons at the end of World War I have been forgotten when once more, in 1941, the stern schoolmaster War proclaims that, for a young man, no other calling is suitable except battle. The speaker foresees that the distant guns will eventually summon the youth of Australia to play their former role, and he wanders "shamed before beholders" in the tattered garment of bewilderment. Here is a highly personal poem, raising a question with no clear answer. The five stanzas each have five lines with the unusual rhyme scheme *xaabb*. However, the first line rhymes with a word in the second line ("unheeded/ impeded," "talking/chalking," "yonder/under," "veering/hearing," and "shoulders/beholders"). The lines vary in length from as few as nine syllables to as many as fourteen, and the number of stresses per line varies from four to seven, but the total effect is of an inevitable march into probable disaster.

"Roly-Poly" (90) is in one sense a nature poem about the Australian equivalent of the American tumbleweed. "The weed is well enough known on the western plains," notes the poet. "It grows in a roughly spherical shape about two feet in diameter, and when it dies it dries and blows off as a springy mass."[3] Apparently it gets no water from the earth or from a river: "drink/not at some Darling but sky's brink." Yet FitzGerald utilizes this plant as a symbol; in wartime even the vagrant and apparently useless object must be harnessed to the grim emergencies of 1942. "Wars now and work: the moment's need/stings, grits the wind." The six quatrains are generally in tetrameter, and occasionally there are rolling vowel sounds matching the motion of the whirling dried weed.

"In Personal Vein" (91) is indeed a highly personal, and compassionate, view of the later progress of the war. "Speaking from the heart," the poet feels that even in 1945 there is need to remember "that men bleed/much the same blood, attackers and assailed;/that shattered dams pour death; that those discs nailed/flush to the earth were cities." Consideration of the moral rights or wrongs of massive bombing night be deferred for years; but "in personal vein/it is well that the heart sees and still speaks out." In this poem FitzGerald forsakes for a while the quatrain and shapes two sentences into a rhyme form resembling the Petrarchan—or rather, the Miltonic— sonnet. The scheme is *abbaabbacdeced*. The turn of the thought begins in the middle of the ninth line. Although the poem contains only two pentameter lines, this fact does not deny it the label of sonnet; G. M. Hopkins and W. H. Auden, among others, have broken away from the iambic meter. Traditionally, the sonnet has been used to express feelings "in personal vein." Remarkable it is, though, that such an outburst of compassion for enemies could be confined within this rigid frame, in which the argument overwhelms almost every vestige of melody or imagery.

Action is once more stressed in another nature poem, "Week-End Miracle" (91–92), which reveals the sudden blooming of tea-trees in an apparently barren landscape, bringing hope to "a world which is not sick but fears it is." The postwar world can recover by remembering that "health is not healing" but "outthrust of renewal from within" and "scarcity's not sickness." Of this verse Judith Wright remarks: "FitzGerald seems a poet for the man-of-action in need of a faith for everyday use."[4]

"The Scavenger" (92–93) depicts Time as a thief who gets the leavings of a past life. The most grievous loss, however, is the theft of possible future achievement: "He takes—but all he'll not allow/is bitterest to remember." The poem has three eight-line stanzas; each is end-stopped after the fourth line, giving the effect of two joined quatrains. The regular meter makes Time move ahead inexorably, thus reinforcing the main image. The tone, however, is far from bitter; the poet celebrates loss in a rollicking, ironic mood.

In "Favour" (93) the speaker boasts that he despises superstition but receives the benisons of fortune because he flouts the rowdy "Lady Luck," who is no lady at all. His advice is to be bold:

> But snap time's tail up: that hour's woes
> will not snake round at now, bite back
> where a game grip jerks a summons—
> Luck loves him longest who can crack
> this kind of lash on omens.

The figure here is that of a possible victim who seizes a snake by the tail and snaps the body like a whip, preventing the head from inflicting a bite. A harsh tone, suitable for this bold attitude, is reinforced by a plethora of monosyllables. The unusual rhyme scheme (three stanzas rhyming *aabcbc*), some alliteration, and tense diction do much to reflect the poet's feeling about unearned "favor."

II   *How to Avoid Civil Conflict*

"Heemskerck Shoals" (94–100), a long dramatic monologue, is one of FitzGerald's most popular poems. It is patriotic in tone, appearing in the Sydney *Bulletin* on March 8, 1944, during World War II. It fits in well with the poet's interest in causal events of history and with his affection for Fiji—for Tasman's ships were the first from the European world to penetrate a part of that region. Indeed, *"Heemskerck droch"* is marked on the celebrated Tasman map of 1644, reproduced in glowing mosaic on the floor of the main lobby of the Library of New South Wales. The poem satisfies the desire for a true tale with a prophetic motif. The reader overhears the meditations of a voyager who has just escaped wrecking his two ships, and from these thoughts he himself realizes the dangers to be found in "thousands of miles of trafficable seas."

Abel Tasman was sent out from Batavia in the Dutch East Indies on his most important voyage in 1642 in command of the small war-yacht *Heemskerck* and the flute *Zeehaen*. FitzGerald feels that it is hardly fair to say of the expedition that it sailed right around Australia without finding it. By 1642 the Dutch already knew of the existence of the west coast of "New Holland," as it was called. As the poets comments: "The voyagers were seeking discoveries further removed. It is clear that on the sound advice of the experienced Visscher"—the pilot-major—"they chose a course that would avoid the continent and keep them in open sea till beyond it. . . . After several important discoveries including Van Diemen's Land (Tasmania) and Staten—or States—Land (New Zealand), Tasman found himself caught (6th Feb. 1643) in a strong wind with a horseshoe-shaped reef [now called Nanuku Island] to leeward and half-surrounding the ships. He escaped by daringly shooting his ships across this reef (which he afterwards named Heemskerck Shoals) where the water seemed deepest."[5]

Tasman's meditations just after missing death by inches begin with irritation at the need to follow committee orders from stingy Dutch officials and to convene councils aboard ship before any important change is made by the leader—"that was no way to run an expedition." The orders even require that one must keep his face indifferent to avoid betraying excitement if a native brings gold to show him. How would the officials back in Batavia like "the faces held on a vessel trapped between wind and a half-circle reef"? Even though some new land has been found, he can predict the reactions of the directors when no gold is brought to fatten their balance sheets. "The gain," in Tasman's opinion, "was in learning what not to expect"—that the chance to sack new Mexicos or Perus has passed, but that even to plot "wide, open, landless ocean" is to increase man's knowledge.

FitzGerald's personal dislike of officialdom and red tape is echoed in Tasman's ponderings. "More could have been done but for such tight instructions." Tasmania and New Zealand should have been charted and not left to be exploited by others—"there were these Englishmen everywhere." The poet thus reminds us that Captain Cook, unlike Tasman, did not sail away from New Zealand after a single brush with murderous Maoris but spent six months mapping the islands, so that today New Zealand, Dutch in name, is British in population.

Tasman, "as a practical man," dislikes dreams of the future, but none the less can picture the unexplored southern land as a country of farms and cities and shipyards in what is reputed to be a desert. He has, indeed, a strange love for this country he has not seen and a feeling for its future greatness:

> ... the place which lay, unleased
> beneath its empty centuries and stars turning,
> was waking under his love and would call those
> fired with the same unreasonable yearning
> who'd take it for their own.

It will not matter too much if the future settlers are not Dutch, just so they are Europeans, escaping from lands of hatred where men suffer "squeezed penury at best, consoled by wars." Then the poet touches squarely upon race and introduces anachronism by contrasting the Negro problem in the United States with the "White Australia" policy. This passage will be discussed more fully later.

> And lately he had feared the Atlantic's west
> where much fresh hope was pivoted, could drown
> in a black stream it drunkenly gulped down—
> slaves who might not stay slaves. There was one place—
> only the south was left—where spread clear floors
> for feet of the Europeans. He'd have it the test

> *of southern citizenship how much the need*
> *to preserve it so by battle and vigilant doors*
> *was sacred in men's bone, immutable creed.*

The thoughts of Tasman, the sailor, now shift to the question of navigation. Where on the earth are these shoals? The poor charts show no islands hereabouts. Are they part of the Solomons, which Mendaña had found in 1568 and no man had ever sighted again? The captain will have to call a ship's council after all, to vote on their location. But until some better instruments can be devised, it will still be possible for a ship to be twenty degrees astray among Pacific waves.

Here the mind of FitzGerald the surveyor transmutes computations into literature. Tasman anticipates the need of calculating longitude by using a sextant to determine time by the sun, and comparing this local time whith the time at another, fixed longitude of the earth.

> *Some new breed*
> *of cross-staff should be thought of (none too soon);*
> *though unless you carried time round in your pocket*
> *you still would miss your easting. . . .*
> *How could you carry time?*

Tasman's question was not answered for some while. A practical chronometer, for whose invention a £20,000 prize was offered by the British Admiralty, was proved feasible only after Cook returned to London in 1776 from his second voyage—his chronometer having lost, after sailing around the globe for three years, only seven minutes. Tasman, not being able to invent the chronometer, gives up the dream of settlement, establishing depots and bases for Dutch expansion, and possibly founding a free nation in Australasia; because "no one would take longitudes at sea,/and after all one was a practical man."

How much does a poet have to know about a historical character before he is qualified to write about him? FitzGerald has valuable comments to make on this question. In an undated letter from Newcastle addressed to Douglas Stewart, presumably when asked for some notes on poems to be included in Stewart's anthology, *Voyager Poems* (1960), the author of "Heemskerck Shoals" wrote:

Anyway you know as well as I—or better—that though everyone thinks because you have written a poem or a play or a story about—say Henry Parkes,

since we don't like to say Ned Kelly or Tasman or even Cunninghamskink—
that the idea gets around that you're an authority on the subject. Actually
you have dug up just the amount you needed (call that literal truth), invented
a bit (call that imaginative truth), and added the two together with technique as
glue and have created poetic truth, which is a higher kind of truth. That is
Browning's parable of his "Ring" in the Prologue to *The Ring and the Book*.
Anything beyond what you needed you have deliberately tried to shut out
from consciousness as irrelevant—even, for the purposes of poetic truth,
untrue.[6]

   The main theme of "Heemskerck Shoals" seems thus to be: "Discovery of future nations should not be a penny-pinching endeavor
wrapped in regulations and directed by clerks far from the scene;
exploration is 'practical' only when pains are taken to do the job
thoroughly on the spot and when cautious considerations are ironically replaced by daring venture, based on use of the best instruments known." While thinking of Tasman's "failure," one has once
more in mind a comparison with the boldness of James Cook, who
in 1770 drove eastward from New Zealand into the unknown sea
now named after Tasman and finally bumped into the eastern coast
of what was to be called Australia. One is reminded too of Kenneth
Slessor's use of the same need for decision in a passage from another
great voyager narrative, "Five Visions of Captain Cook":

> *"Choose now!" the trades*
> *Cried once to Tasman . . . and the Dutchman chose*
> *The wind's way, turning north. . . .*
> *So Cook made choice, so Cook sailed westabout,*
> *So men write poems in Australia.*[7]

   If we accept some such statement of theme, we must still face the
stress that FitzGerald places in this poem on the importance of race.
The purpose or "motif," to use his term, is frankly to support the ex-
clusion as settlers in his native continent of people of non-European
stock. Two decades before the civil-rights riots in the United States,
FitzGerald made plain his hope that Australia would not be swamp-
ed with folk of other colors and cultures than the predominantly
North European stock of the Australian populace. He would probably
agree with the remark made by an important British ship's officer:
"I consider it madness deliberately to introduce into any country a

minority group that is doomed sooner or later to arouse civil conflict."

A form of "White Australia" policy prevailed until recently as at least an unofficial program. It allows non-Europeans to live in the country for special purposes, such as to study under the Colombo Plan, but encourages settlement only by those who would not lower economic standards and who would fit into the majority group. The name of the policy has aroused criticism by many in other lands, and a few years ago the Australian Labour Party decided to erase the term from its platform.

III   *The Pinpoint Bursts into Reality*

FitzGerald lived for five years among Melanesians and East Indians. He had found in his heart great affection for the Fijians. But he had also watched the growing clash between these two groups—the Fijians and the more acquisitive Indians, former immigrants who are now the economic masters of the islands and who outnumber all others in the population. FitzGerald felt called upon as late as 1953 to protest an apparent weakening of the White Australia policy. In reply to an editorial in the *Nation* (Australia) of February 14 of that year entitled "The Politics of Mrs. Tompkins' Nose," he rebutted the conclusion that the consequences of the maintenance of the policy in future would be "outright hostility" and that it was continued merely because of the snobbishness of "Mrs. Tompkins," whose prejudice is to look down her nose at neighbors who are unlike her. He wrote:

> What you overlook is that there are 73 Mrs. Tompkinses in every Australian street and at least 873 in every street in Asia. . . . Not the mixture of bloods should concern us, but the "social" immiscibility of ideas, ways of thought, traditions, customs, religions, civilization, cultures. Mrs. Tompkins, in short, cannot so readily be pushed aside. Neither can Mr. Tompkins, who—genuinely—is not in the least interested in questions of racial superiority, but has old-fashioned ideas that colored competition for his job might lower his living conditions or perhaps eliminate him from the labor-market. . . . Unhappily the barriers are already down. The Liberal Party has abolished the Dictation Test: and I am not aware that it has set up any effective substitute.[8]

Like most Australians still, FitzGerald stresses the fact that the policy is based on economic considerations and that a tide of

Asian migrants would destroy Australia and not appreciably help Asia. Perhaps the fact that the poet was the father of three daughters might also have affected his outlook on racial interloping.

This commentary may sound far astray from Tasman on a shoal in 1643, but that FitzGerald's poem does emphasize the color of Australia's future cannot be overlooked. Evidence is available in a letter to Henry Stokes of December 9, 1944: "The verses you referred to were not about Fiji, but about the White Australian Policy of which (perhaps because I've seen the Indian problem in Fiji) I remain a religious supporter." The reader may decide that this motif in "Heemskerck Shoals" is discriminatory, but he should be aware that it exists.

The poem's chief defect is a coolness that results from FitzGerald's determination to rein in his inherent Romanticism. Tasman, we feel, is just a bit too calm and rational for a man whose two ships have almost had their hulls sheered off by a razorlike reef. Although the type of the poem comes from Browning's monologues, Tasman's thoughts lack the blurting revelation of a Fra Lippo Lippi, caught off guard by torches at his face and hands at his throat. As FitzGerald's mentor, Norman Lindsay, wrote, "'Heemskerck Shoals' is another vital experiment in Browning's method of projecting a character by merging an almost colloquial idiom with pure poetic imagery," but is "lacking the half-dozen lines of description that would bring the sea, the ship, and Tasman fully to life."[9]

The form of this long poem is a rough five-stress line which rhymes with a pleasant irregularity: *ababcbbcdedecfgfhgiih,* and so on, reminiscent of rhymes in English odes or Wordsworth's "Tintern Abbey." This slow and not too even cadence reinforces the feel of a ship riding the South Pacific swell and the running of waves of thought inside Tasman's skull.

On most counts, "Heemskerck Shoals" deserves its high repute, which caused it to be chosen by a renowned typographer to appear in a beautifully illustrated, limited folio edition so tall that one collector had to build a special high shelf for his treasured copy.[10]

"Traditional Tune" (101) gives a contemplation of Sydney Harbor and the city under moonlight. Its main interest is, perhaps, technical. The three stanzas, each eight lines long, rhyme *abacdbdc.* Each holds the same number of syllables per line and the same

number of stresses. This regularity in rhythm fulfills one's expectations
of a tune that is truly "traditional."[11]

In "The Face of the Waters" (102–4), FitzGerald achieves a more
vivid, if more cryptic, attainment of metaphysical expression than in
"The Hidden Bole" and "Essay on Memory." As the poet reports,
"The Face of the Waters" is in one sense a footnote to lines in "The
Hidden Bole": "the Nothing (contracted to some blackened point)/
where wakes the dream, the brooding Ultimate," and gives his own
interpretation of the attitude embodied in the striking imagery.[12]
This brief but culminating philosophical poem has been called "a
daring raid on the inarticulate"[13] and "perhaps the most unexpected poem by any Australian poet."[14]

"The Face of the Waters" is not an attempt to rewrite Genesis I.
It is, rather, an effort to justify an apocalyptic vision of life emerging
from nothingness. The poem opens with a surrealistic nightmare
that calls for an explanation which, despite wrestlings with speculation, remains beyond explanation. It is a brave attempt to conceive
the inconceivable.

> *Once again the scurry of feet—those myriads*
> *crossing the black granite; and again*
> *laughter cruelly in pursuit; and then*
> *the twang like a harpstring or the spring of a trap,*
> *and the swerve on the polished surface: the soft little pads*
> *sliding and skidding and avoiding; but soon caught up*
> *in the hand of laughter and put back. . . .*

The cruel laughter has been misinterpreted as that of a malign,
Hardyesque creator delighting in thwarting its creations.[15]
However, the laughter is defined in the fourth stanza as the "agony
of not being."

The second stanza adds a "denser black" background under
"the imminence of huge pylons—the deeper nought," and the
twanging of a string "which is not a string but silence/plucked
at the heart of silence." The third stanza uses the symbol of a diver
who cannot fathom the bottomless. Then, in the fourth, out of the
tension of silence (the twanged string) and out of the agony of not-
being (the terrible laughter tortured by darkness), comes once again
the "tentative migration" of "feet running fearfully out of nothing,"

a "universe on the edge of being born." This sporadic effort of life
to emerge from nothingness is, however, not Darwinian, for
FitzGerald's universe is that of modern science. Eternity, as stated
in the fifth stanza, is not endless space; time is not endless duration;
infinity is not a circle. Not-being is inconceivable, except as "a
placeless dot enclosing nothing, the pre-time pinpoint of impossible
beginning." This doorway between nonexistence and emergence
into everyday life—"your hand stretched out to touch your neighbor's"—is comparable to T. S. Eliot's "still point of the turning
world," the axis that does not move but about which the universe
circles ("Burnt Norton," II). This fifth stanza is "the crux of the
poem," according to T. L. Sturm, who interprets it at length in terms
of the works of A. N. Whitehead.[16] Sturm goes on, however, to
point out that in the sixth stanza there are certain limitations to the
apparently boundless range of possibilities of existence: "What
FitzGerald seems to be saying (as his somewhat cryptic note that
this dualism is 'somehow integral' with the 'pantheistic view of the
universe' suggests) is that forces and laws (both in the scientific
and socio-historical sense) are explanations for phenomena which
point to and are themselves part of the evolving pattern of the
universe. Ideas and thoughts bear the same relationship to actuality
and potentiality as objects."[17] As the poem says, a hill is neither
animate nor inanimate, but a part of the universal "flowing"—Fitz-
Gerald must have known his Heraclitus—differing little from the
winding of thoughts in the mind.

The final stanza has been condemned for its confusing metaphor:
"The egg-shell collapses/in the fist of the eternal instant; all is what
it was before." Judith Wright sees this image, along with the "hand
of laughter" in the first stanza, as one of the two defects of the poem.[18]
On the other hand, T. J. Kelly, a meticulous explicator, concludes
that "The moment of possible beginning is, however, finely realized
(finely, that is, within the limitations of a poetry where imagination
is the instrument of, not one thing with, structuring intelligence)
when the dot, the pinpoint of nothing bursting into reality, becomes
an 'egg-shell,' held in intolerable suspension between the buckling
force of impossibility, crushing beginning back into nothingness,
and the thrusting force of possibility, pushing outwards towards
'magpie-morning and all life's clamor and lust.'"[19] The eternal
instant of the eggshell's collapse, when the pinpoint bursts into

reality, is linked with "the feet scurrying on the floor." And at the end of the struggle, when the shell buckles under, "light and the clear day" break through, implying an idealistic finale.

IV *Importance of a Twist of the Head*

"The Face of the Waters" has aroused more varied interpretations than any of FitzGerald's other poems. It goes far beyond the acceptance of the view in "The Greater Apollo," in which "trees are trees, earth is earth and stone is stone." The poet's friend and fellow poet Douglas Stewart recalls: "FitzGerald has explained this poem to me a dozen times, carefully, in words of one syllable suited to my understanding. Sometimes, for an instant, I have it. Then it goes again, darting off into the outer darkness like an azimuth. All I know for certain is that it is indeed a most haunting poem. It makes me feel, as D. H. Lawrence said of the quantum theory, that space is alive, 'like a goose.' It makes me feel that FitzGerald was personally present at the creation of the universe."[20] A brace of critics opines:

Although (the poem seems to argue) the mind may strain back to where matter becomes nothing, life itself becomes non-being, this state is unrecognizable except at the point where matter becomes actuality again, non-being becomes being: what ultimately exists is energy—motiveless perhaps, but as far as we can tell, inexhaustible. Life is a supply that has not yet run out, and there is no evidence that it ever need do so. Representing perhaps the utmost stretch of FitzGerald's thinking, "The Face of the Waters" accounts for the facts that demand to be accounted for, but without abandoning the world of "tangibles and actualities" for some transcendent order.[21]

H. M. Green calls the poem "the expression of what cannot except symbolically be expressed,"[22] and Judith Wright marvels: "We wonder if the poem can rescue itself, as it were, and return to the upper levels on which alone poems can properly function; and when it does so there is a sense of relief as though some trapeze act were safely over."[23]

The prosody of "The Face of the Waters" is complex, in tune with the theme. Seventy-five lines are arranged in seven stanzas which vary in length from seven to fifteen lines. It may properly be termed free verse, but in several stanzas a rhyme scheme is in evidence. The diction reflects the energetic tone of the whole poem, giving an effect of strenuous effort.

This last of the personal, speculative poems is probably an enigma because the symbols came before the theme, and the theme is an attempt to find meaning in an intense dream. The modern pylons are not congruent with the primordial scurrying of feet on black granite, caught up in the hand of cosmic laughter; the images are not chosen but given by the subconscious and defy ultimate rationalization. If successful with the reader, the poem is valued as an intense poetic experience rather than as a capstone of FitzGerald's metaphysics.

The meaning of the long courtroom poem "Fifth Day" is much less perplexing. The poet himself has given a lengthy footnote on its origin. He had taught himself in Fiji to write shorthand from a book on the Gurney system. In it was reproduced a page of Joseph Gurney's actual notes, which the poet transcribed, headed: "Trial of W Hastings 5th Monday 18th Feb/88 The proclamation for silence Warren Hastings called to come in:—(Wants a quarter of twelve a clock)."

This fifth day opened with a speech by Edmund Burke, leader of the prosecution.

The prosecution at the impeachment of Warren Hastings (1788) was led by the great liberal statesman Edmund Burke. The trial was a failure for Burke in that after seven years' intermittent hearing it ended in acquittal for Hastings; and a failure too in that Burke's violent detestation of Hastings somewhat clouded his judgment and proportions; but a triumph in that it resulted indirectly in the destruction of the worst features of British exploitation in India under the system which Hastings had represented. Part of Burke's intemperate attitude is probably attributable to his being misled in many matters by Sir Phillip Francis, the bitter personal enemy of Hastings and almost certainly the author of the notorious "Letters of Junius."

"Another hour" refers to Burke's effective opposition to any kind of compromise with the revolutionaries of France—no small factor in the later determined resistance to Napoleon.[24]

Neither Hastings nor Burke, however, takes up the entire foreground of the action in the poem. Rather, the camera roves around the courtroom and focuses in the end on the lowly recorder Gurney, who earns a day's pay by adding to history's pages—and inspiring one of FitzGerald's best poems.

"Fifth Day" opens with a description of the court, whose galleries serve as "a roost for lords." This is the place where fashion gathers; Mrs. Fitzherbert, illegal wife of the Prince of Wales, is in the royal box. The scene is like a historical canvas, but will survive only through the writing hand of Gurney. The trial will run for seven years and end in an acquittal. "Britain was built/round India and on Hastings— prove his guilt!" If proved, share the charges of misdemeanors and high crimes! The defendant is an insignificant figure—"infirm, staggering a little, undersized, spare, licked dry by tropic heat, a plain man in a plain suit." But "the eye strays from the center. The axle's part/is just to endure the play and spin of the spokes." Yet "it concerns all men that what they do/remains significant unbroken threads/of the fabric of our living. . . . Attitude matters; bearing. Action in the end/goes down the stream as motion, merges as such/ with the whole of life and time. . . . It matters for man's private respect that still/face differs from face and will from will." This is the chief message in "Fifth Day," reminiscent of other editorial comments on action in FitzGerald's verses.

Other characters in the drama are presented: Edmund Burke, who will inveterately pursue Hastings for years, urged on by Sir Phillip Francis, follower of Charles James Fox, who sits in the court near William Pitt. Toward the end of the day, Burke the orator falls ill, Fox replaces him, and the court is adjourned early. But in future, Burke will speak out to protect England from following the excesses of the French Revolution and inspire his country, almost alone among nations, to resist the imperialism of Napoleon.

Yet there are really no great men who sway history. "Results mean little." "The common work" outweighs the results of their acts. "What indeed/of that old struggle matters or would be left/but for an ordinary fellow's simple need?" Gurney wipes his pen; he has earned his fee and for once can go home early. "Though Hastings bent/that frown, there remained but shorthand."

After putting down the free lines in "The Face of the Waters," FitzGerald in "Fifth Day" reverts to tightness—here, in fact, to the rigid form of the rhyme royal made celebrated by Chaucer. The twenty-one stanzas have seven lines each and rhyme *ababbcc*. Not all the lines, however, are regular iambic pentameter. The fifth line in each stanza consistently has four stresses, breaking up the rigidity of pattern. In choosing this form for this narrative, FitzGerald could hardly have done better. All the critics acclaim its form as well as its storytelling power.[25] FitzGerald's use of rhyme royal and other prosodic devices enhances the memorability of this venture into historical verse. The poet's few thoughts are almost lost behind descriptions of the colorful cast of characters in an eventful setting. He here achieves a distance from his mouthpieces that will succeed even more in later narrative poems such as "Between Two Tides" and "Relic at Strength-Fled."

"Transaction" (110–12), like the earlier "Legend," is a personal poem with a round Irish flavor. It is the story of the sale, at far distance by correspondence, of the home of FitzGerald's great-grandfather in County Kerry to one "Pat Donovan of the Square." It was written in 1951, twelve years before the poet visited Ireland. Of that visit he published an account which details his discovery of the "Strand Street house," which his grandfather had sold after his own father died in Balmain, a Sydney suburb. In Strand Street the poet "sat in my great-grandfather's living-room and drank Irish whisky before a turf fire in my great-grandfather's great fireplace— the highlight of my travels."[26]

Unlike "Legend," "Transaction" lacks exuberance and joy in living. It is the record of breaking ties with the old country. For the settler, "life was a quest." "England, Ireland, Europe are clatter/of tongues and hatreds none understands." "We sever worn threads." The narrative of an early "New Australian" ends:

> The choice made and the new land entered,
> not for a day but for days to be,
> what next but to grasp this life that centered
> in the south? The north had been sunk at sea.
> Ireland, the last of it, passed from view
> to another's trust. I cede my share,
> and hope he died as rich as a Jew—
> Pat Donovan of the Square.

"Transaction" is composed of eight stanzas of eight lines, rhyming *ababcdcd*, a joining of two quatrains. The fourth line, with one exception, is marked by terminal punctuation. An Australian critic goes astray, however, in referring to this poem as having "a strict metrical pattern."[27] Rather, it has an irregularity or variety that is quite well suited both to the discursive parts and the meditative. This lends a more natural form of expression, since very few people think or speak in measured cadences. Thus the prosody of the poem matches quite well its content and intent.

"Glad World" (112–14) contains three lyrics, each giving a different point of view in a different meter. The first reports that "toughness of hide" can keep off ills, whereas wholesome happiness is still vulnerable. The second deals with the idea that efficiency does not suit living people; "Death will be tidy enough." The third observes that a man needs nine lives in which to explore all the roads open to him; it contains a few lines parallel to the thought in Robert Frost's "The Road Not Taken." Yet the fact that man has only one life puts a God-given urgency on the need to "press on towards breakfast."

Part I of "Glad World" is the only one that is metrically regular; it is composed of two five-line stanzas rhyming *ababb*. Part II contains three stanzas of six lines rhyming *ababab;* the calm tone of the first is forsaken and irregular rhythms lend a rough restlessness. Part III has five quatrains rhyming *aabb,* but the rhythm varies from two to six beats; even a directionless activity, it implies, is better than apathy.

"The Bend" (114), last poem in "This Night's Orbit," was called "Importance" when it appeared in 1943. It reveals the significance of walking beyond the concealing trees and discovering that the river bends to the right rather than to the left. The mind then can deal with what has become a 180° shift in theory, and put in their places "old aims like cash or bread or fighting." "Living," the poet concludes, "needs more this twist of the head/looking upstream then down." The poem is calm metrically, composed of five quatrains rhyming *abab;* all the rhymes are exact. This whole section of *Forty Years' Poems* thus closes on a thoughtful, controlled note.

CHAPTER 8

The Later Decades

T HE scope of FitzGerald's poetry after 1950 ranged widely, from
an epic of the Tongan Islands to an unpublished sheaf of recent
lyrics. The poet spent eight years (1944–52) writing a narrative poem
of some twenty-five hundred lines, based on the story of Will
Mariner, the London lad who survived the massacre of a British
privateer's crew and became a chief in the Tongan Islands of mid-
Pacific. He drew acclaim when *Between Two Tides* (115–94) appeared as a book in 1952, but a review in *Meanjin* that mixed some
laudation with some harshness caused him for a while to vow
he would never publish again. Fortunately, he did not end his career
then, but filled the next two decades with further significant verse.

I   *A Book Going for Two Guineas*

To anyone who has read deeply into the bulky volume of small
print entitled *An Account of the Natives of the Tonga Islands,*
compiled and arranged by Dr. John Martin and published in 1817,
the possibility that an epic poem could be made from such an origin
is fascinating. A brief account of the facts will show how closely
the poet stuck to his sources.[1] Dr. Martin had become acquainted
in London with an intelligent, somewhat taciturn young sailor
named Will Mariner, who told him an amazing tale. As a boy of
thirteen Will had gone to sea as clerk under Captain Isaac Duck
on a voyage to the Pacific Ocean that combined whaling with pri-
vateering. The crew preyed on Spanish shipping off the western
coast of South America and at the town of Ilo sacked and burned
the place, plundering the church of silver candlesticks and crucifixes.
At Tola, another little town, the governor, a man of the world who
knew how to put his enemies at ease so far away from Spain, bar-
gained with the pirates. His pretty daughter of sixteen (FitzGerald
calls her Micaela) spoke enough English so that Will could chat
with her. Horrified by his story of the sacrilege in the church at

Ilo, she predicted, truly, that his ship would never see England again. Later he presented her with a fine cheese, and she gave him a gold shoe-buckle.

Captain Duck died and was buried at Cedros Island off Lower California. He was succeeded by the first mate, James Brown, probably the most stupid and obstinate officer ever to command a ship in the Pacific. In need of repairs after two years at sea, the *Port-au-Prince* put in, toward the end of November, 1806, at Lifuka, one of the Tongan Islands. Captain James Cook, who had been the first European to find this region, had been well treated by the Polynesian people there and had christened them the "Friendly Islanders." Brown took this label literally and, as Fitz-Gerald dramatically describes the event, trustingly lost his ship and his life when the vessel was captured, looted, and burned.

Young Will—whose behavior had been noted by Finau II, an ambitious high chief who thought the lad was the captain's son—was spared and taken into Finau's household. Will's knowledge of firearms and his bravery in war qualified him to serve as a chief under the name of Toki Ukamea, the Iron Ax. He became aware of the complicated politics of the time, when Finau was striving—like Kamehameha I in the Hawaiian Islands at the same period—for primacy over the entire Tongan archipelago.

The "Friendly Islands"—today an independent kingdom—run north and south for almost two hundred miles. They consist of three groups: Vavau to the north, Tongatapu to the south, and Hapai—Finau's headquarters—in the middle. To gain his ends, Finau could be cruel and treacherous. Much earlier, in 1797, he had encouraged his half-brother, the high-minded Tubou Niua, to assassinate the hereditary ruler of Tongatapu, a vicious tyrant. For years the men of Hapai had carried on a ritual warfare against the bamboo fortress on the hill above Nukualofa at Tongatapu. This year, with the aid of Will Mariner and other survivors of the *Port-au-Prince,* the fortress was destroyed in less than an hour, and several hundred defenders were killed by cannon balls.

Finau was called back to Hapai toward the end of July, 1807, to take part in the lifting of the tabu which had been in force for eight months after the death of the Tui Tonga, supreme hereditary ruler of all the island group. Finau then craftily sought to clear his way to winning the high title of Hau, or military ruler of all Tonga.

He could not tolerate a rival—not even his loyal and honorable half-brother Tubou Niua. His instrument was a lowborn son of Tui named Tubou Toa. The murder of Tubou Niua, and the self-justifying oration by Finau after the event, inspired a lengthy scene in "Between Two Tides" in which young Toki is forced to decide what his future should be.

Early in 1810 the news came that the ruler of Tongatapu, weary of strife, offered to come to Hapai and acknowledge Finau as Hau. But Finau's joy at winning leadership was turned to despair within a few weeks when one of his daughters, a child of six, fell ill. In desperation, the father dragged the ailing girl from one shrine to another, begging for help from the priesthood he had despised. His final sacrilege was so great that the old gods of Tonga exacted a fearful revenge. In horrible convulsions he died, and his son Moenga, Will Mariner's fellow chief and closest friend, became a wise ruler under the title of Finau III.

Mariner—that is, Toki—had lands, wives, and high honor, but he still yearned to go back to his homeland. One evening in November, 1810, while returning in his canoe to his estate at Vavau, he sighted an Australian ship, the brig *Favourite*. After a farewell party aboard, attended by Finau III—who had to be dissuaded from accompanying Will to England—young Mariner left the islands where he had spent four years and worked his passage back to London. There he became an accountant in the office of a merchant, married the daughter of a Welsh banker, fathered a dozen children, and became a respected stockbroker. Ironically, the Mariner whose adventures had filled Dr. Martin's big book drowned when his little skiff overturned one day on the river Thames.

The poet actually opens his long narrative with a depiction of the accidental death of Mariner, middle-aged voyager on the very waters on which he had embarked in 1805 for the Pacific. With Conradian calm, FitzGerald kills suspense and avoids a climax that would magnify Mariner's role in the poem—for, as will be seen, the Mariner story is not the story of Mariner alone.

The printed sources of "Between Two Tides," in addition to the Martin book, are acknowledged in a note by the author. His five years in Fiji, as has been said, supplied him with much background and characterization. The origin of FitzGerald's interest in putting this Pacific adventure into verse is complex. In a letter of

April 23, 1950, to Douglas Stewart—to whom "Between Two Tides" was to be dedicated—FitzGerald wrote: *"You* started this with an article on the Red Page which said that it was time poets got round to narrative again; that Australian poets had never attempted it. . . . It got harder and harder; and I think I finished it out of sheer obstinacy, and in the hope that I may get on with something else." A much longer account of the origins came in reply to correspondence several years after the epic appeared in print:

I think the genesis is, as it were, threefold. The time seemed ripe for direct narrative to be added to Australian literature, as opposed to indirect by means of dramatic monologue, ballads in series, lyrics in series, etc. That thought had been in the back of my mind for some time, and the suspicion that I had a suitable equipment or technique for the task, as suitable as any of my contemporaries, and might well give a lead; though I had this thought long before I had any idea of what such a narrative might be about, and believed I had not sufficient powers of invention (to match that technique) to handle a narrative, which obviously to be of any use towards pointing a way towards narrative in Australia must not have a northern, eastern, or western setting, even less anything like a Biblical or a classical setting—Genesis No. 1.

Then I was tired of being referred to as a "philosophical poet." To some extent that is a contradiction in terms. Certain philosophical ideas had interested and excited me. The poetry was of the excitement and not of the philosophy. Still less did I like being treated as a philosopher and having my so-called "philosophy" ripped to pieces by critics with a real philosophical bias. That, alas! still happens. Yet I had certain ideas which I wanted to express: if I were to express them in somewhat the way I had become accustomed to, the cry would again go up: "intellectual poet!" "philosophical poet!", again with loudly expressed doubts about both the philosophy and the intellect. What better then than to present them under the guise of narrative?—Genesis No. 2.

Everything thus pointed to using my own experience in the tropical Pacific as a basis. I turned over my Fijian diaries; I glanced through [William] Lockerby. I read Williams and the other missionary writers. There did not seem to be anything there. While looking at Lockerby—which unfortunately was not in my hands long enough for a thorough study—I recalled a newspaper article I had read years before in Fiji to the effect that it was while Lockerby was in Bua that the *Favourite* called in and that it was while she had Mariner on board. Hence it was possible, even very likely, though neither Mariner nor Lockerby says so, that these two similar adventurers had met. So, happening to see a *Mariner's Tonga* going for two guineas in a bookshop secondhand, I bought it. Here was clearly what I wanted. As for my lack of powers of invention, why I need not invent anything. My first thought was to alter all names, even turn Mariner into Lockerby, since I knew nothing of Tonga or Tongans but knew the Fijians so well. But my second thought—which was what I did— was to take complete liberty with all events and characters, telescoping some, like the two Finaus, and not giving a damn if my Tongans became Fijians—Genesis No. 3.[2]

II   *An Island Napoleon or Perhaps Chaka*

The structure of "Between Two Tides" is threefold. Part I, "Landfall," gives the story of Will Mariner up to the time when he expects a violent death at the hands of the Tongan attackers but is told: "You are to live; you are to go to the king./Finau has sent for you." The middle section, consisting of three parts—"Shadows Under Trees," "Tongan Tragedy," and "Canoes for Hapai"—is set in the group of islands over which Finau II, a Polynesian Caesar or Alexander, fights and plots to hold sway. The final part, "Downstream," is an aftermath that might answer the question, "What is the upshot of all these events?"

The date of Part V is that of Mariner's accidental death on the Thames. The focus shifts from Dr. Martin, avid scientist in Lisbon who realizes that "science alone would never be quite enough," to Micaela, a matron in Lima who recalls the lad at Tola to whom she gave a shoe-buckle. Next is shown a Tongan wife, Laifotu, who gives not a thought to the Toki she had forsaken. Then the meditations of Mariner, sedate stockbroker sailing his skiff, are reported. He is still trying to reconcile the linkage of past and present, still questing for answers, unaware that there will be no time for answers, since "Death had become the sea and called him back into his youth." Life runs *da capo:* "Once there had been another place and year"—a line repeating the opening of the third stanza of Part I. The final focus of Part V is upon John Martin, who believes that Mariner was the eyes of the tale and Martin's were the hands, but that "that tale was Finau's." "Lives were so linked . . . that dropped in the tide by ones they were still together." The action is ended— if action ever does end.

"I read *The Ring and the Book* again and again before I wrote

'Between Two Tides,'" the poet once stated.[3] However, he did not follow Browning's device of the dramatic monologue. Instead, he used the method of the omniscient narrator who can report thoughts as well as actions and shift the focus from one to another character. "FitzGerald is telling the story of Dr. Martin's book. Dr. Martin is telling the story that Mariner has given him. Mariner tells the story of Finau. And Finau often enough puts his own case. So it is like a series of Chinese boxes, one inside the other."[4]

The tale is indeed Finau's. The various characters play their roles. "Mr. Mariner seen behind was always shadow," thinks Martin. At first a likeness of Captain Duck, the lad is later "Finau in outline," so that through the businessman's coat jutted naked shoulders.[5] The only invented character is Laifotu, young Toki's sweetheart. The love story had to be supplied by FitzGerald; for oddly enough, nowhere in the thousand pages of the book usually called *Mariner's Tonga Islands,* which discourses learnedly of Polynesian marriage customs, is there a hint that Will loved a Tongan girl.

If the tale is Finau's, then the theme must deal with man as a political animal. "That tale was Finau's—except as, mystically, it was man's. . . ." A number of subthemes may be found, but the main one circles around the idea of choice of action. As early as Part I, the governor of Tola remarks of Francisco Pizarro's conquest of Peru: "Life's like a wave breaking, not good or ill,/or right or wrong, but action and pressing forward. . . . Every hour holds its choice. We do the choosing;/but events present the straws. The ends are hidden;/who knows the short from the long?" Again man is faced with the warp and woof of free will and necessity.

All the characters in the poem are significant because of the choices they make.[6] As in 'Fifth Day," attitude matters; bearing. But action now is a search for the unattainable on earth.

> *All aims, all effort*
> *seek to fill somehow emptiness of hands reaching*
> *to what the heart would have which still desires*
> *(beyond man's little capacity) something not known—*
> *except as mirrored in symbols. . . .*

The chief symbol in the book is found in the title. "There's a line drawn in the sand. And a wave breaking—/life, the necessity

for advance in action." Human striving is like writing on the sand
of a beach, lasting only half a day and then wiped out by the incoming tide. ("Tide" is but the older word for "Time.") Action
is necessary, but life is short. The symbol is repeated: the reader
will note that "between two tides" occurs in each of the three stanzas
that open Part II of the poem.

> . . . and here are marks on the sand between two tides—
> the receding tide of morning that scoured under
> crumbling untrodden banks, and Time's other tide
> rising and seeping and smoothing everything away.

The meter of this epic poem is blank verse. It is not, however, the
syllabic unrhymed iambic pentameter of Shakespeare, Milton, or
Wordsworth, but a very loose line. Ordinarily, though, it keeps
five good stresses. Only rarely are there ten syllables; more often the
line runs to a dozen, thirteen, or even fourteen syllables. The choice
of blank verse for this effort in the modern epic needs no technical
justification. The theme is a grand one, and the elevated style is
suitable. Even a critic who feels that the story might better be told
in prose admits that "Between Two Tides" is "a first-rate piece
of writing" and adds: "Although the detail is lively, the strength
lies in the tone and general movement. Few narrative poets have
handled so well the flats between the moments of dramatic crisis."[7]
The poem is organized into verse paragraphs of unequal length,
a device suitable for large, expansive narrative, dramatic, and
meditative topics. The reflective passages, the narrators' philosophiz-
ing, are generally the longest paragraphs; the pure story, the action,
the recorded conversations generally are the shortest. There is a
similarity between this sort of arrangement and that found in prose,
and occasionally—in fact, to be expected in a long poem—the pace
tends toward prosiness (as, indeed, it does in *The Ring and the
Book*). The diction is often lofty, and at times—inevitably in the
political sections—reaches the oratorical.
The author's comments in "Between Two Tides" are actually
few; most of the general ideas are expressed by one or another
character. This verse epic is more enjoyable each time it is read—
especially if the reader has a knowledge of the Martin book and
the Pacific background. Perhaps it will not survive as long as some

of FitzGerald's shorter verses since, as the author points out, it is too long for an anthology and "Extracts might provide entertainment but could show nothing of the real intention or direction of the narrative."[8] But it will survive. H. M. Green's judgment probably comes closest to critical unanimity: "A long narrative poem, it falls but little short of FitzGerald's highest standard. It does fall short, because, in the main, of three defects: there are several breaks in the continuity of the story which it would be hard to justify; it is hard to believe that the protagonist, an island Napoleon, or perhaps Chaka, would have submitted so tamely to eclipse and death from the priests; and, most important, the stage is too small for the theme. Nevertheless, it is among the finest long narrative poems written in this country."[9]

III   *A Memorial Arch after Fire Falls*

The section headed "Southmost Twelve (1953–1962)" in *Forty Years' Poems* covers a decade of poetry, mostly lyrical, which appeared in the 1962 volume of the same name. Three pieces in the volume were omitted in the section, and the opening poem, previously unpublished in book form, was added.

Dedicated to Tom Inglis Moore, "The Tempered Chill" (197), which appeared in the *Bulletin* on June 29, 1949, under the title of "This Understanding," brought one reviewer to say: "The poem puts its gentle finger on the central worry of a poet: simply growing older cannot be responsible for poetic failure, for it is by growing older originally that one came to write poetry; so it must be a failure of will, if only one knew what 'will' meant."[10] The metaphor by which the poet makes his point is that of a cutting tool, "the edge-tool of sense." (Steel is tempered by "chilling" during its experience in the foundry.) Of this poem F. H. Mares wrote: "Image, idea, and expression are indivisible. This is poetry that can stand with the work of Hardy and Frost in its unqualified integrity."[11]

In seven quatrains "What Coin Soever" (198) tries to justify, to dead friends and rivals, the survival of a lesser talent. "This must serve: to saunter forward/still, where wattle's yellow wave/breaks on spring."

"Edge" (199) opens with a startling image, a knife at the throat, and concludes with the same. Other edges are mentioned, places where the known and the unknown ends are defined. Two stanzas of unequal length are unrhymed and give the effect of free verse, although four strong stresses to each line may be found.

"Southmost Twelve" (199–201), title poem of the 1962 book, refers to Australia—or possibly New Zealand—presumably the southernmost region of the globe where one celebrates the ringing out of the old year at midnight. (Patagonia apparently does not count.) The celebrant is cautioned not to assume that the sun will rise tomorrow; it is, moreover, logically possible that it will rise in the west. Thereupon the speaker elaborates his attack on formal logic, "the cold cause-and-effect of mass and force." Still a romantic, an optimist, "creature of instinct," he calls intelligence "knowledge of what I touch—what's bared to sense/as real itself, real in what lies beneath." The eight stanzas are made up of six lines rhyming *abbacc* and have a steady beat of five good stresses in a line. Paradoxically, the poetic argument against logic proceeds in a logical progression from point to point, and the whole structure is a polished sequence.

A first-and-only visit to a place, in company with one's beloved, is the occasion for "The Waterfall" (201–2), which shows an awareness, along with Heraclitus, that all is flux, that the only reality is change. "Doubtless all that we knew/is gone now. Water over the fall/in terms of atoms, molecules, drops, eddies,/is not that water." But the experience is "a thing surely of spirit . . . and so it survives," though it is never repeated. The four stanzas qualify as verse paragraphs. Of its form the poet commented: "It is written in a normal blank verse (with extra syllables and dropped syllables such as are normal in all blank verse)" and "in *every* line of it a light syllable is dropped at least once, bringing two accented syllables into juxtaposition. This was not done deliberately as the poem started. I found that I was writing it that way: that it suited the subject-matter; and I carried it on to the end."[12]

The series of lyrics under the title of "Eleven Compositions: Roadside" (202–10) is held together by common references to man as a traveler through time. The smoky trunks of the bluegum trees are background for the distance that hardly occurs "except/as posts mark off a five-wire stave/in bars of song through freehold." The poet sees a farmstead, but his eye "falls short of my love for just this land." The duty of the soil beneath the paved road (whose path he might have surveyed with chain and theodolite) is "to hold, bear,/pressure and strain." Fortunately, "Not yet the dust in man/comes to that pass;/earth, flesh for a span,/springs with the grass." The crowd passing along, morning and evening, is "but one face made up of all," for "there are no persons in a throng." The same tide never returns—here is an echo of "The Waterfall"— but "life's not what bubbles and goes past/but flow itself, through time, through me." Survive if you can the threat of dispossession by a barbaric stranger. You "are the killer in the dusk/of all that's gone;/but you are the grain in the husk,/the spark in the stone." There is a bar between your conception of your own generation and previous ones—"past one's birth, there's nothing seen;/an hour's no less than fifty years." Scour your heart of the last dregs of hate, for somewhere in the world it is the eleventh hour. The final short poem—the only one forsaking the pattern of quatrains rhyming *abab*—consists of two six-line stanzas rhyming *ababcc.* "Thick dust . . . paints red the roadside; but beyond/how clean are leaf and frond!" Yet "there's a new dust"—atomic radiation—which might "set the last green leaf ablaze/with none to rage thereat." We who travel had best keep to the known road, warily. The "Road-side" sequence accumulated in the middle 1950s and, at one time, nineteen linked verses were collected in typescript. Eight were weeded out before the remainder appeared in *Southmost Twelve.*[13]

"Verities" (210–11) accepts the truism that there is a bond between man and dog, going back to the time of the cave dwellers. It is also true that the roof of the cave, against which man—who is not solely a creature of instinct—knocks his head, is another "verity."

The couplet poem called "Grace Before Meat" (211–12), formed of eleven quatrains rhyming *aabb,* is a jocular tract against vegetarianism. "Meat" here is literally flesh of cattle, good for body and mind; those who are neither slaves, beggars, nor saints should eat their share of the world's food "with fork and bright steel."

"One Day's Journey" (213–14) repeats the idea of the driving quest for the world's end. The journeyer is still untiring. Four stanzas contain six lines, each having four strong beats; oddly, only the second, fourth, and sixth lines of each stanza rhyme with each other.

Of "Song in Autumn" (214) one critic remarks: "The well-worn image that offers the end of the year and the end of the day for old age is given new vitality by the comparison of morning and evening cold. In the morning 'cold then was a lens/focussing sight, and showed that riggers' gear,/the spider's cables,/anchored between the immense/steel trusses of built grass.' Here the reference to engineering work (besides showing FitzGerald's concern with the 'practical man') suggests the excitement of achievement, the purpose and activity of the young man in the morning cold. But it also, and quietly, puts that activity in its place; if spiders' webs are riggers' gear, then riggers' gear are spiders' webs.''[14] The imagery of neat engineering structures in the second stanza contrasts markedly with the irregularity of the rhyme scheme and the varied prosodic elements of this poem about the approach of old age.

Conversely, "Drift" (215) has a meter too markedly regular to reflect the haphazard nature of the theme. Again the message is to avoid wasted hours and challenge life's "square headlands and taut ships."

The two parts of "Bog and Candle" (215–16), one of FitzGerald's best poems, deal with facing the end of life. The first urges the listener to "pray for a clean death," since the test is harder if one must endure cancer or paralysis. The second part relates the story of the blind man who set in his window a lighted candle so that he could "know the world as wider." Thus it is "body's business . . . still to resist . . . the putting-out of the candle in the blind man's room." Both parts are formed of quatrains rhyming *abba,* and the lines regularly have six stresses.

"Insight: Six Versions" (217–21) contains six parts, again in quatrains but here rhyming *abab.* The first evokes the image of the Kaaba in Mecca, the building housing the Black Stone that is the goal of Moslem pilgrims and the point toward which all true believers face when they pray. Those who are not Moslems might be led to worship God in a spire of dust and forget reality—except that they are aroused by "the creak of the crow."

Part II advises the dunce to trust to his ignorance when climbing the ladder of knowledge; "praise laughter and romance/and the low lilt of tongues/which bid the unlettered heart/climb and gaze out." Part III asks why thought, "the eagle," cannot be studied as we study the habits of lesser birds. Part IV remarks that even the unobservant man must pause in the crowd when his eyes meet those of a friend. Part V praises the sudden recall of a scene of youthful days. The final "insightful" poem cryptically points out "this place" under "the spread of sky/men build of words" affords little shelter, but might serve as a "memorial arch/after fire falls as rain." Then "words, past power to confuse/with lie, promise or tract,/might serve for a stark use—/might point at fact."

IV *The "Ring" versus the "Book"*

"Strata" (222–23) recalls young FitzGerald's geology lessons at Sydney University. The earth's layers of rock have supported "life's whole structure." Today, "so much of the living falls/within the pacified/rock of erected walls" that it is too easy to be content "with a synthetic stuff." Therefore he counts as priceless the gift that from his youth forward he was close to "cliff, creek, ravine,/and red gravel of the ridge," and "some ledge/neighborly to the sun." It is a satisfaction to know that beneath "the street's load" there is the "starved rock-mass" of a solid stratum. The five eight-line stanzas, each of two quatrains, regularly have three stresses to a line. Interestingly, the opening stanza, which describes the im-memorial building of the earth through geological time, is the only one containing exactly six syllables to a line.[15]

"Macquarie Place" (223–24) is a favorite with readers who, like FitzGerald, have lingered at the geographical center of Sydney, a small square where, as in Hyde Park in London, an assortment of crackpot orators are free during the lunch hour to express to the crowd their "rat-bag" ideas. The passerby might be tempted here to set up his own soapbox. He prays to be kept sane all his life, but at the same time "let faint/fervor still reach me from the vast/madness of prophet and of saint." Eight quatrains are needed to add their successive points to the poet's unfolding of his theme. The pattern is iambic tetrameter, with just enough variation to avoid monotony.

With his back to the new "concrete-and-glass city" of Sydney the poet walks in "Quayside Meditation" (224–26) and recalls seeing the old ships—even square-rigged China vessels. His life is thus linked with the wooden ships of war of Nelson's time, so that "what's-to-come no longer looms a place/separate from all being but . . . is even our own." He can then turn about, face the high buildings, and accept them as already familiar. The ideas of recurrence and linkage are strengthened by the verse form, the interwoven rhyme scheme comparable to those in "Rebirth" and "Chaos." The series of tercets has a strong iambic pentameter pattern.

"Tocsin" (226–27)—the word originally denoted a warning bell—relates a ringing in the ears to the approach of death by old age, if not by "cleaver and sickle, sword and shears." The listener usually sees "the dark that must be dared/as no way meant for you," but the threat is always present. This intermittent sound warns the man, while life abides, to grasp all in reach and keep his eyes open to everything that is more enjoyable because of the recurrent reminder. The five stanzas of eight lines rhyme *ababcddc,* and the meter is that of the old ballads, often used for narrative English verse. The usual effect of this form is lively and might not be suited to a poem about death; however, the possibility that such a meter could be used for meditation was shown, for example, by Emily Dickinson.

"Protest" (227–28) briefly begs that rebellion should not be stifled and legends should not be stripped to dull fact merely because rebels were usually greedy, lawless, and cruel, like Francis Drake, Ned Kelly "the tin-shirted Australian," Grenville, and Raleigh. This poem gathers its strength from its terse quatrains and visual compactness.

Three poems follow that recall Fijian experiences a generation earlier. "This Between Us" (228–29) is a eulogy of a nameless chief known only by his grass-grown grave. The poet explained: "Lovo is an uninhabited valley in Cakaudrove, Fiji, with a stream through it and traces of a deserted village beside the stream. Also by the stream is a burial mound, and my tent was pitched beside it through a period of impatient delays from various causes. A long time ago; but this is one of those poems carried around in the head for many years before anything materializes. Nasorolevu is the highest mountain in Vanua Levu. The Yasawas are outlying islands to the west."[16] The three stanzas are unrhymed and are made up of lines of irregular length.

A longer poem, tighter metrically, is "Relic at Strength-Fled." FitzGerald wrote that this piece was "a development of a story told me on top of the Main Divide, Vanua Levu, and tucked away in my mind for more than a quarter of a century before it fitted in with anything I wanted to say."[17] The narrative, telling of a defeated, fleeing band of warriors who bury their chief on a boundary ridge, is not difficult to follow. More than a score of quatrains give a rhyming pattern, but the line stresses are irregular—another instance, perhaps, of giving the poem "a bit of a Fijian beat."

The third Fijian poem, "Embarkation," describes the setting out of a canoe expedition forced to explore the ocean because of population pressure. The people leave nothing behind except "those who remain/with a little more room to die in/and one less canoe to be buried in/on this bank of the death by parting." The poet might have seen in the overloading of people on an island a presage of the future overloading of our planet, where embarkation for empty land is more of a threat. The eight quatrains are unrhymed and vary in stresses. This disorder of the metrical system reflects the disorder of the scene of departure from home.

"Caprice" (234–35), which repeats in 1958 the youthful idealization of whim, might well have been written in 1928, except for the mature prosodic skill of the four stanzas of eight lines in couplets.

"As Between Neighbors" (235–36) advises the older man that silence is the best response. He should chain his laughter; "that the old should be merry is offensive to the young." The tone is ironic, since the poet has always enjoyed laughter and conversation. The three stanzas are made of closed couplets, suitable for sage—or ironic—advice since the days of Alexander Pope.

"The poem that best illustrates most of his best qualities at their best is 'The Wind at Your Door'" (236–41) is an opinion most critics would share. "It is flawless in technique and construction. It deals with some great, if grim, adventures. It recalls old days in Ireland. It is concerned with Australian nationhood. Its ultimate theme is human conduct; and, dealing with the flogging of an Irish convict, the whole is embodied in a terse, vivid, and most moving narrative."[18]

The subject of this longer poem is the flogging in 1804 of the "Castle Hill rebels," a band of Irish convicts, political prisoners flogged for refusing to tell where their weapons were hidden. The verses open a doorway to a violent past, and the poet, whose ancestor is mentioned in the first line, feels implicated both with those who inflict punishment and those who are its victims. His earliest forebear in Australia was Dr. Martin Mason, on his father's mother's side, who arrived first in Australia in 1798.[19] FitzGerald came across the account of the flogging in a collection of old records and discussed it with his friend and fellow poet, Dame Mary Gilmore. "As I walked away from her flat," he recalled, "along Darlinghurst Road, after talking to the old lady, it suddenly occurred to me that this was a poem right into my hands; and a couple of months or six months or twelve months later I started to write it."[20]

The hardiest victim of the flogging happened to be a convict named Maurice FitzGerald. While on the one hand picturing him as "an ignorant dolt," the poet applauds the sufferer's fortitude in harsh circumstances and declares: "I'd take his irons as heraldry, and be proud." With this FitzGerald he would like to find "more than a surname's thickness as a proved/bridge with that man's foundations." The theme uses ancestry and kinship to repeat, as in "Essay on Memory," the influence of the past upon the present, and the recalling of the past to influence the future. The wind blowing on the day of the flogging is still blowing: "That wind blows to your door down all these years./Have you not known it when some breath you drew/tasted of blood?"

The setting is a jail, although the historical flogging took place in the open. The poet recalled, "I had the old jail on Cockatoo Island in mind: the thick walls contain rooms."[21] This distortion of history "is not just ignorance but deliberate," he said elsewhere. "It should be very clear to anyone reading it that Joseph Holt is my 'source' but equally clear that Holt says the flogging was in the open with the victims tied to a tree. I put it in a jail—which may not even have been built at the time—for my own purposes. Poetic truth. The 'Ring' versus the 'Book.' The obviousness of the source should make the deliberateness of the distortion of history equally obvious."[22]

The form of "The Wind at Your Door" is rigid—the rhyme royal or Chaucerian stanza, of which, wrote FitzGerald, "George Gascoigne saith that it serveth best for grave discourses."[23] The nineteen stanzas vary in pace from pure narrative to personal statement; the final two conclude with reflection and decision. The interweaving of sections of thought and action results in a unified whole.

"The Wind at Your Door" is, then, a narrative poem, highly personal in tone. Its meaning cuts to the bone. We all share guilt, but must live with it, having our "own faults to face." There is violence in the lines, but as Alec King observes:

The poem is continuously thoughtful; and the original violence of the flogging is never allowed to come out in mere violence of word and image, unmastered by the controlling mode of reflective poetry; the crudity is pointed to rather than presented. This poem is not the original violence of real life re-imagined as myth so that its violence remains, but as a deep tremor in the universality of human life; it is further removed still from its origins—a meditation on the poetic mind finding its way towards myth. Its leisurely stanzas; its structure, turning and returning about its theme; and its personal manner, are all in keeping. Such a way of dealing with life suggests the need for a profound poetic modesty; and I think this modesty is built into the poetry in form, in idiom, and phrases, in avoidance of unmanageable heroics, false bravura. The poem feels certain of itself and its mode.[24]

Any poet would be proud to end his collection of "forty years' poems" with a masterwork like "The Wind at Your Door."

FitzGerald's volume is not quite ended, however; the final poem is justly called "Beginnings." The poet regrets his loss in not having lived in the time when "Caesar/clamped down on savage Britain;/ or, moving closer, not to have watched Cook/drawing thin lines across/the last sea's uncut book." Even in Australia, he was born too late to have seen "Hargrave of Stanwell Park"—a pioneer in the study of aerodynamics—"a crank with a kite—steadied above a cliff." It would be pleasant to walk in the past, but it is more important to "choose this day's concern/with everything in the track." The book ends with the lines: "I regret I shall not be around/ to stand on Mars." Perhaps FitzGerald would settle for a trip to the moon.

V *A Fijian Dies in the Arctic*

The scope of the present study does not include reviewing the unpublished volume *Product,* still in typescript. A number of fine poems by FitzGerald, however, have appeared in periodicals since 1963. These are listed in the Bibliography. Several are significant for a proper view of FitzGerald's development in his sixties, and a few are outstanding testimonies to his unflagging talent.

In "One Such Morning" (*Bulletin,* May 14, 1966, 51–53) the poet returns to narrative in the rhyme royal stanza. It is a long poem that he felt was "evidence that retirement had not meant idleness." It relates a story told him by his father about a fellow commuter on the Hunters Hill ferry who was shortsighted, "almost blind," but was accustomed in his youth each morning to swim naked in Tarban Creek. Losing his spectacles—which he had to wear even while swimming—he went astray, yet had to hide from the eyes of ladies or laughing men until he could feel his way home, up a cliff and through rocks and scrub. The tone is chatty, and the rhymes are often Byronic.

"Sorting Papers" (*Meanjin,* XXV [No. 4, 1966], 417) is a meditation on the time when one must clean out the files of a lifetime. "One cannot own the earth;/therefore I burn these papers in my yard/ wishing I could sort values out so soon,/and choose and bind the handful to be kept," and then, afterward, "be no longer ashamed to let drift by/this bait or that. . . ."

"The Road North" (*Morning Herald,* March 4, 1967, 15) tells of a "conditionally pardoned" convict who served as acting mineralogist on John Oxley's expedition to the west, and later headed his own exploring group of five men, "to crack the undented north." They were forsaken by others, food ran out, they circled, and were lost to human ken. Parr failed, but another man learned of his route and pushed on through. Having surveyed in these mountains, FitzGerald could picture the trials of the pathfinder, and had seen a stiff crest still called "Parr's Brush." The poem acclaims, then, an "unhistoried man and his reward."

In "Of Studies" (*Southerly,* XXVII [No. 4, 1967], 232) the poet acknowledges his debt to other men's thoughts—"not that this fact should taunt me or annul/anything bound or welded in some deft/bundle of re-arrangement." He has produced many such poetic bundles in a life which might have been spent as an active scientist. Rather than repent, he now knows that one should turn, late as it is, "to studies and to what/wisdom is made of words; though still the blood/revolts at quietude/and could find more in living than just to learn."

"Deep Within a Man" (*Morning Herald,* Oct. 1, 1966, 17), "Lawbreakers" (*Ibid.,* Aug. 17, 1968, 19), "Ghost Rally" (*Ibid.,* Aug. 30, 1969, 20), and the sonnet "The Denuded World" (*Australian,* May 10, 1969, 18) are all poems of political protest, showing grief and compassion in time of war. The best of these, in which at times propaganda inhibits poetry, is "Lawbreakers," which was read by its author at the "Arts Vietnam" festival. He evokes the spirits of Robert Emmet, John Hampden, and the men of the Boston Tea Party. Yet a stronger protest is found in a nonviolent man like James Ruse, who after serving seven years at Botany Bay for theft became Australia's first farmer. "But how bring justice on the law/ where it is law that is the crime?" He concludes that never has such wrong been righted until "a few have put the law to test,/broken it, suffered for their deeds."

Best of the later poems is undoubtedly "Invocation of Joseph Asasela."[25] Of it the poet wrote: "I carried the idea around in my head for years, made several attempts to write it; then suddenly it came good."[26] The men of the Fijian island of Kandavu, it is said, have a desire to wander in foreign lands, to ship in trading vessels. Asasela, born to loneliness, went to sea, deserted in Mexico, somehow found his way to the far north, and spent his remaining years "as trapper and craftsman in fur,/skilled at fashioning a glove/or handling dogs in the snow/of the climate he came to love/above the warm long-ago." Alone, he died on "pack-ice driven adrift— reft from his frozen coast." The poet ponders the motives of this son of the tropics who fled to the "utter end of the earth" and concludes that he was "man the seeker," caught in the "primal appeals/of challenge and daring choice." Here is one more fine poem of tribute to the men of dark skin such as FitzGerald had known in his Fiji days.

The form of this "invocation" shows a return to the eight-line stanza rhyming *ababcdcd,* the double quatrain earlier used in "The Road North" and elsewhere. A tricksome touch is added, however, by internal rhymes in the last two lines of each stanza ("adrift/ reft," "thought/distraught," "defeat/retreat"). The simplicity of the diction and the personal tone of reflection are suitable to recall the simple urges of a lone pioneer.

The last four chapters have been devoted to comments upon the selections in FitzGerald's *Forty Years' Poems* and upon a few later pieces. Most of these comments have dealt with the subjects and themes of the poems, since criticism is seldom valid if the critic does not know "what the poem is about." Other comments have indicated some qualities of the versification, since a poet is one

who puts his meanings into their best form, risking all the while
an error in the choice of diction that might ruin his effect. The poet's
main task, however, is to create a unified work of art that arouses
a warm response from the reader; and this response can only
be obtained if the reader goes himself to the poem and, armed with
full preparation, opens his mind to all its possible contributions.

CHAPTER 9

A Kind of Life's Work

TO assess the work of a man's lifetime in a few pages is impossible; but it is possible, in a final chapter, to comment briefly upon his achievements and attitudes. Robert David FitzGerald's career, reflected in a mass of critical comments, produced a body of work that is the most solid and extensive in the history of Australian poetry, and well repays careful scrutiny.

With justice, he once called his collected verse "a kind of life's work."[1] During that lifetime, he practiced two professions with distinction—those of land surveyor and author. With him, writing poetry was a moonlighting task. As he said in a letter to R. G. Howarth on September 15, 1940: "Poetry is a religion with me; and like many another man's religion it has to be kept for Sundays." Yet he went on writing even under difficult conditions—sometimes in a tent in the jungle, often in the small hours of the night. *Nulla dies sine linea* as Pliny the Elder wrote, never a day should pass without writing at least one line. FitzGerald got this idea not from Pliny but from Norman Lindsay, who preached "that poetry is a conscious exercise of effort and of keeping one's hand in in that way. Actually a conscious going out and looking for ideas. Ideas don't just come to you, you've got to go out and look for them."[2] Fitz-Gerald felt that "Inspiration cannot be 'turned on' at will, it is true; but it comes most readily and frequently to the craftsman at work, tuned to it by his own persistence."[3]

I *Patriots Half a World Away*

"By hard work" seems to be the answer to the question: "How do you write a poem?" Yet there is some joy in writing. "It's a positive agony," he remarked in an interview, "but it's a rewarding agony. Yes, on the whole, I think I enjoy that particular kind of agony. But once the poem gets started—is really going, and you're away and you can see how it's going to go on, unfolding in front of you, and you know how it's going to end—then it's very exciting. Yes, I think I enjoy it."[4]

Answering the next question—"Do you write easily?"—Fitz-Gerald exclaimed: "Far from it. Far from it. Everything that I write is absolutely *bashed* out, done over and over again. I write in school exercise-books, and when the poems reach a certain state, then I switch to loose pieces of paper. To write quite a small lyric, I can fill a wastepaper basket with thrown-out bits of paper and fill whole exercise-books."[5]

FitzGerald, like most writers, found that giving rein to the writer's critical powers while trying to create a new work is like attempting to ride two horses at the same time. "For the poet espe-cially it can be quite damaging to try to combine creative impulse with critical doubts of it," he once stated; "he must suspend the critical faculty until he comes to revise or reject."[6]

Revision is apparently almost as important to him as putting down a first draft. As he wrote once to a graduate student: "I re-vise and revise, too, to get the right word. Then that will throw a rhythm out of balance. Then other alterations have to be made; and finally a kind of compromise has to be struck between what is happiest in one way and what in another, making adjustments and sacrifices. All very different from the public idea of a poet dashing things off under the stress of inspiration."[7]

Owing to FitzGerald's practice of emptying his wastebasket fre-quently and destroying every manuscript as soon as a revision is copied, the opportunity to study his methods of revision is rare. To compare original versions of some pieces with their appearance in *Forty Years' Poems,* however, would reveal his continued efforts to improve upon earlier drafts. It would be salutary, for example, to contrast "The Stranger Lad" (*Bulletin,* Jan. 14, 1931, 42) with "Of Some Country" (25). The later version goes far be-yond making the "stranger-lad" into a "fidget-lad" and a "coarse" track into a "blown" track. Entire lines are changed to create a tone much more grim than the original rather sentimental idea that at times men will escape into a world of their own. Equally valu-able would be a study of the poems omitted by the author from his collected volume of 1965. Poems rejected are usually pieces express-ing youthful bathos, those containing bizarre terms, or those—es-pecially ones written for a particular occasion—considered not up to the later standard.

FitzGerald's attitude toward expecting some monetary reward

for the publication of his writings is markedly professional, as well as generous. "Payment is something an author may or may not demand according to his needs," he wrote to C. B. Christesen, editor of *Meanjin,* on July 31, 1951. "But it is a rough measure, useful to himself, of the worthwhileness of his work, whether or not he *can* get paid for it, and how much; the only other measure, the judgment of posterity, he is not in a position to avail himself of. Moreover, he is entitled to expect a return. That does not mean that he should debar himself from giving, which is often a privilege; I have found it so, and all creative writing is to some extent a gift from its creator to his victims."

What does the poet think about his literary style? "I've never set out to have a style distinctly my own," he told the interviewer. "I despise that sort of synthetic originality. The main purpose of style is to fit the subject. The style must be suited to the subject and I've tried to make my style suit my subjects. I have deliberately tried to change my style from time to time, as subject-matters seemed exhausted; as an expression of the ideas which I wanted to express, it was necessary to find new styles to express the change of subject-matters. Two or three times in my life, I think, I have consciously tried to change my style, but never with the idea—as you first put it—of trying to get a style distinctively my own. . . . As a matter of fact, a new style will help find a new subject."[8]

A widely read man (except for fiction), FitzGerald was early impressed by the achievements of other writers. Influences cannot always be documented, and often certain ideas are in the air and available to any writer; but some similarities—or at least concurrences—with other writers can be found upon examination of styles and imagery. FitzGerald has made no attempt to conceal his admiration for certain other poets. His father made him acquainted with "Matthew Arnold's poems, a big influence in my own work which none of the critics seem to have spotted."[9] The young poet's association with Norman Lindsay made him feel early that life is a process of continual self-development through "creative effort" (the title of a 1920 book by Lindsay). He has acknowledged the inspiration given him by reading the poems of Christopher Brennan, who for five years served as a professor of modern languages at Sydney University. Brennan did not affect greatly a choice of subject matter, but "something of the rhythm and tonal qualities."[10] Keats and Browning were lifelong favorites. Modern poets that the Australian admired include William Butler Yeats, Robert Bridges, A. E. Housman, Ezra Pound, and Dylan Thomas.

If there is any close American counterpart to FitzGerald, it is Robert Frost. This is not to say that either influenced the other, or that there are not as many differences as similarities in their lives and works. However, the best poems of both these Roberts will stand close comparison. Subjects for verse often spring from observations of nature in a particular mood, a view of stars or a bend in a stream, a momentary vision that becomes a broad symbol, a notion about life that is worth the trouble of fixing it imperishably in simple but fitting words. Both preferred the uses of rhyme and rhythm and traditional stanzas; FitzGerald would agree with Frost's dictum that writing free verse is like playing tennis with the net dropped down. Their mastery of forms and types ranges from the short, sharp lyric to the lengthy speculative poem ("Essay on Memory" might well be mentioned along with Frost's "Masques"). Use of the dramatic monologue in "Heemskerck Shoals" could be compared with that in "The Witch of Coös" or "Build Soil." Both men like to insert gnarled apothegems into their lyrics. At times the very language of the Australian resembles the hickory-wood diction of the New Englander born in San Francisco.

The lives of these men were lived on opposite sides of the globe, but both held a philosophy basically optimistic even though bruised by experience. Both went abroad early, but preferred most of the time to stay in their own region and see universality from Vermont or Hunters Hill. As they left young manhood, the romanticism of happy courtship and marriage became less obvious in their themes than their views of the human beings around them. Both were men of the countryside, avoiding pale bookishness and feeling at home in timberland; but both were often called to address academic audiences on their art. Both were broadly compassionate but were also intensely patriotic and saw little to be gained by opening their homelands to floods of migrants of other races—for, without being bigots, both felt the most confidence in the traditions of the Caucasian race. Men may closely resemble one another even if one is American and the other is Australian.

II *What a Reviewer Should Watch*

Although a third-generation Australian proud of his country, FitzGerald was never a chauvinist, a "dinkum Aussie" unaware of any other culture. (His down-under accent, by the way, does not reveal itself in his writing; those who wish to mark the poems for rhythm or pronunciation need not worry about nonstandard English.) The landscape of his native continent is seldom obtrusive in his writings; his attitude is somewhat suburban, and he sometimes presents the lonely outback landscape as awesome to the intruder. His residence in Fiji gave him a view of foreign parts. Although he admired Henry Lawson, his tradition was broader than that of the bush balladists. And he stood aside from joining the "Jindies" or the "Angries"—two extreme and contrasting movements in Australian writing that promoted, respectively, leaps into the aboriginal past and the surrealist future.[11]

FitzGerald's attitude toward literary censorship, at a time when the laws of his country provided a dangerous anti-intellectual weapon, was courageously professional. "It is not an author's duty as an author, though it is as a citizen, to keep within laws, but to awaken consciousness. That awakened consciousness is the basis of order—of which laws are simply the expression. . . . The fact is that by the curiously unmoral standards of censorship, literature can quite readily be pornographic, and pornography is frequently literature. To distinguish what elevates and awakens consciousness by beauty and sincerity from what debases the mind by crudity or hatred of human efforts and desires requires a rather higher morality than can be imposed by a police force, whether armed with batons or prayer books."[12]

FitzGerald's finest statement, perhaps, concerning the role of the poet in Australia was made in 1939, at the conclusion of an essay on modernism. He believed that the writer in that country had undergone a healthy encounter with technical experiments. On the use of the Australian environment, he felt that the quality of the verse was more important than the intensity of local color. Admiring Christopher Brennan's poetry, FitzGerald said of him that he took it so for granted that he was Australian that the fact is seldom discernible in his work, although it left its impress on his outlook. "The problem for the modern verse-writer in Australia, as I see it," he wrote, "is to achieve again self-realization, and to establish a relationship with his surroundings at once unforced and inseparable." This achievement, he felt, was highly desirable in the year of the outbreak of World War II. "Prophesy is futile," he concluded; "but it is not impossible that from accidents of geography it may be Australia's duty and privilege to save from the wreck of civilization the little upon which we may build again."[13]

The ideas of Robert D. FitzGerald on the functions and techniques of poetry have been discussed at length in previous chapters. His achievements as poet and critic of poetry have likewise been noted. It remains to comment on his lifelong outlook on the world around him, and on his reputation among his compatriots.

It is absurd to raise the question: "Is he philosopher or poet?"—as if a man could not be both, or neither. Again, FitzGerald has been dismissed as "too intellectual"—as if any poet, or any human being, could have too many brains.[14] The Professor of Australian Literature at Sydney University, FitzGerald's alma mater, once properly condemned critics who make an artificial distinction between form and substance and pointed out that the poet succeeds when his thought is made concrete and convincing. "One's disagreement with a man's ideas, or lack of sympathy with his attitudes, does not make him an unsuccessful poet, nor entitle one to ignore what he says, while admiring his way of saying it. When FitzGerald succeeds, it is by thinking poetically—that is, by achieving precisely the union of form and substance of which he writes."[15]

Clearly, FitzGerald is not a metaphysician or a professional philosopher—to begin with, he lacks any "system" and has found no universal *summum bonum*. Hugh Anderson, in a lengthy essay, has more logically classified the poet as a "humanist." This author concludes: "There is no undue extension of FitzGerald's meaning to say he has realized the times do not call for the poet who writes solely from subjective experiences. It is 'all efforts . . . of mankind,' since man is in every way dependent upon the society of which he is a living part, since he can only express his personality through society; the poet no less than the man-in-the-street—for, in an important sense, he is the man-in-the-street."[16]

FitzGerald has also, with some justice, been labeled an "incurable romantic."[17] He promptly added, in a letter, "and proud of it!" Some of his late poems still show traces of the youthful yearning for a world of color, pagan enjoyment of the senses, and lust for adventure. There is no real contradiction of terms between "Romanticism" and "Realism"—the two are sides of the same coin, and FitzGerald is entitled to dream while repeating that stones are stones and trees are trees. He can depict objects with almost scientific exactness and, like William Wordsworth—the early English Romanticist who decried the vague diction of the neoclassicists he displaced—can render landscapes in startling detail. Admittedly not a practicing Christian, FitzGerald is rather a pantheist, rejoicing in the multiplicity of gods in nature. He would probably agree that the Almighty is too important to be entrusted to clergymen, but he shows a devout admiration for the world revealed to him by senses and mind.

If a one-word label must be attached to the poet, perhaps the most fitting would be "activist." With him, to live is to strive. "I am always interested in any verse-activity," he wrote in 1941; "it is all of value; the absence of activity is death. New schools of thought, new methods, new statements, all stir things up. Youthful violence, for instance, often immediately destructive, is valuable in the long run both because much that is destroyed is valueless and because it is violence. . . . In short, I believe myself to be in complete disagreement with what I believe to be your aims, but loudly applaud your having such aims in a time somewhat aimless mentally and completely chaotic physically."[18] Thirty years later he joined a group of fellow countrymen who were publicly protesting the conscription of young men to fight in Vietnam and proclaimed in a speech that "not only as a duty to civilization but also for the vitality of their craft itself, poets must participate in the world about them." As a professional poet, he is concerned with the fate of all mankind.

FitzGerald shows his professional attitude once again in his sensitiveness to the comments of reviewers through the years. It is a part of his desire to be heard, to expose his ideas to the minds of others. "I feel I have something to say that is worth saying," he told an interviewer. "I am not one of those poets, such as Brennan says he was, who don't care whether anyone reads their work or not. I want to communicate."[19]

Himself a frequent, and generous, reviewer of the books of other poets, he held a theory of the function of criticism that is well expressed in a letter to C. B. Christesen on November 17, 1953:

I believe in dealing with what the poet himself has to say rather than in
examining very closely what he owes to others. How he fits in with "movements" or "tendencies" may be, or is, fit subject for inclusion in extended
critical examination of a poet's whole contribution such as I have never
tackled yet, but not for a review. Partly, no doubt, my reluctance to
examine by process of comparisons is due to academic ignorance; I am,
after all, an untaught sort of writer on critical subjects; but more it is due
to a conviction that what a writer is himself doing is what a reviewer
should keep his eye on rather than points of comparison (odious or otherwise!) with other writers.

III   *Two Poets Mark a Watershed*

It has been difficult for FitzGerald—an individualist who founded
no school and left no disciples—to obtain critical guidance in a
country with a population less than that of the state of California,
a country that has produced not one literary critic of the stature,
say, of Edmund Wilson in America. FitzGerald has been the recipient, on the whole, of frequent and careful treatment of his work,
and his reputation has steadily grown. But reviewing in Australia,
unfortunately, has often been biased by the reviewer's ancestry,
schooling, social class, or religion. Moreover, many of the self-
appointed critics are also creative writers who feel that they are
competing with those being reviewed. As one Australian editor
recently put it: "Criticism (on the whole) is poor—for reasons that
seem to be related to the 'learning' of another culture."[20]

Almost universally, reviewers have been friendly to FitzGerald,
as a sampling of the items in the Bibliography will testify. It would
be tedious in this study to try to refute wrongheaded, caviling, or
spiteful comments. Rather, it has been more valuable to assess the
outstanding contributions of the poet than to seek "faults" that
often turn out to be faults of the reader—lack of perception, narrow
taste, or a dull ear.

Nevertheless, the harshest comments upon FitzGerald's work
are here put on the record. "He seems to have a grudge against the
language," wrote Evan Jones, "a grudge that has been deepened
by its recalcitrance over the years till he is prepared to twist and
torture it ruthlessly."[21] Vincent Buckley has been openly
hostile; for example, he says: "'Essay on Memory' is the more

'dramatic' work, and is an uneasy structure indeed; yet it does show the tortured and rather desperate echoes of FitzGerald the lyricist. If previously the Irishman had assumed an Australian swagger, now he is turned German and plunges along with an arthritic goose-step."[22] James McAuley, in reviewing *Forty Years' Poems,* wrote:

One can find lines or passages that are exceptional, but the general impression the verse makes on me physically is depressing and uncomfortable. It is toneless and unmusical. It lacks color. The phonetic textures are coarse and abrasive, the movement and syntax ungraceful, not only where these things could be justified as an expressive means, but equally where they cannot. In reading FitzGerald I have to anaesthetize myself against the unnecessarily insensitive phrasing. . . . This complaint is perhaps governed by temperamental differences; and, though I feel bound to make it, I don't want to discourage other readers who may react differently to the balance of qualities in FitzGerald's work.[23]

In his review of *Forty Years' Poems,* Grahame Johnston said: "I find little rhythmical sense in FitzGerald's verse; certainly no rhythmical ingenuity. And looking through this book it is easy to discover whole pages which do not definitely declare themselves as poetry, or even as verse. . . . FitzGerald is a man of humanity, courage, and endurance, with a strong sense of moral responsibility. These qualities emerge in his verse, and give it character; but I do not think it is remarkable or memorable in any other way."[24]

On the other hand, many reviewers over the past quarter of a century have acknowledged FitzGerald's power and skill. "The Greater Apollo" was given full reviews in 1927 by writers such as Hugh McCrae and Philip Lindsay. The following year, Nettie Palmer published a lengthy appreciation of a FitzGerald poem, "The Sea-Eagles."[25] A decade later he was acclaimed by A. R. Chisholm: "Here we have a true poet and, if we are justified in judging him by one composition, a great poet. In fact, I doubt whether anything written in English in the past thirty years could be fairly said to surpass this 'Essay on Memory.'"[26] Philip Lindsay wrote in a 1941 book: "Indeed, Fitz is the voice of Australia, the one man who has managed to speak of the growing torments of a nation that struggles, half-desiring to succumb, against the primitive peace of its surroundings. Always his verse is afire with the conflict of mind against

body, man against the self-satisfaction of Nature feeding upon itself, a rage of thought, and sometimes of terror, storming the silent
sensuous trees, flinging the gage of restless man into the unrespon-
sive grave of unthinking life."[27]

Finally, a lengthy comment in the introduction to a fine recent
anthology links FitzGerald with the late Kenneth Slessor as two
young poets who appeared in the early 1920s and would "work a
permanent change in Australian poetry—in the range of themes it
could successfully address, in the level of professionalism at which
it would conduct itself." There is little doubt, proclaims Professor
Harry Heseltine,

that Kenneth Slessor and R. D. FitzGerald thrust Australian verse forward with an imperious force unknown since its foundation in the lines of
Charles Harpur. . . . Their joint triumph was to seize on the central preoccupations of the Australian poetic imagination, and, for the first time, to
realize them in a language of complete adequacy and assurance. Not even
excepting the work of Brennan, their poems more thoroughly than ever
before fused aspiration and execution. . . . For Australian poetry, Slessor
and FitzGerald brought the idea of time within the boundaries of what can
be known and used. Their other great act of liberation concerned the re-
presentation of the self. . . . To prolong this contentious history beyond the
watershed achievement of Slessor and FitzGerald is to risk bringing it onto
that dangerous ground where historical interpretation may pass, unnoticed,
into critical directives as to the proper reading of contemporary poets or
poems. The risk, however, must be accepted, if only for the sake of sketching
in the main channels through which Australian poetry has flowed on the
near side of the watershed. . . . What, as a result of Slessor and FitzGerald,
happened to our poetry may be stated something like this: for the first
hundred years or so of our history, Australian poets struggled fretfully
with the lumpy data that time, place, and cultural circumstance had offered
to their imaginations. Since Slessor and FitzGerald, they have been freed
from their limiting, because unsolved, fixations.[28]

On Robert David FitzGerald's seventieth birthday, few readers
in Australia or elsewhere would deny him the title of the foremost
living Australian poet.

Notes and References

Chapter One

1. Hereinafter, to avoid excessive footnoting, page numbers of references appear in the text in parentheses after a passage or title. Page numbers of poems not otherwise attributed refer to the most recent, easily available, and complete edition of FitzGerald's verse, *Forty Years' Poems* (Sydney, 1965).

2. A recent article about the grandfather is Donald McLean's "The Surveyor Who Loved Orchids," Sydney *Morning Herald,* April 17, 1972, 22. In it, the poet grandson is quoted: "On this block [in Hunters Hill], in the days when it was bushland, my grandfather identified more varieties of terrestrial orchids than have been found on any other similar place on earth. My own father has often told me that when he was a boy his father would take him walking in search of orchids. 'Now then, my boy,' grandfather would say, 'I'll give you a shilling if you find a new genus of orchid and sixpence for a new species.'" A close friend and fellow poet, Douglas Stewart, pays tribute both to the poet and to his grandfather the botanist in "Sarcochilus FitzGeraldi" in *Rutherford* (Sydney, 1962), pp. 10–11, which begins:

> *Here's a word for you, Robert D. FitzGerald:*
> *I met your grandfather living under a stone,*
> *Changed to a small orchid; where the knobbled*
> *Dripping red cliff-face towered and the creek fell down*
> *Through bracken and wattle, rock-fall and wilderness*
> *To the chasm where the lyrebird sang; yes, there he stood,*
> *Safe on the very brink of bushfire and flood,*
> *Sarcochilus fitzgeraldi, no less!*

3. Sydney *Morning Herald, A Century of Journalism,* quoted in Fred Johns, *Australian Biographical Dictionary* (Sydney, 1934), p. 122. Fitz-Gerald the poet disavowed connection with the author of the *Rubáiyát.* "So far as I am aware, I can only claim relationship to Edward Fitz-Gerald insofar as all FitzGeralds of the Geraldyn line are related (of which the capital G is evidence, as the absence of hyphen is, I understand, evidence of legitimacy—so you see, I am not one, whatever you may have thought reading some of my recent letters!)," he wrote to Tom Inglis Moore on March 24, 1946. "It is a tradition (or rumor, which is much the same thing) that we do claim some connection with both Gray and Goldsmith;

but I replace E. F. G. with a more immediate ancestor ('the ruined banker's son, Charles Darwin's friend') [his botanist grandfather], since you seem to require a pedigree and have brought in J. Le Gay on my mother's side."
    4. R. D. FitzGerald, "Uncle Jack Was a Vagabond at Heart," Sydney Sunday Herald, Feb. 21, 1948, 6.
    5. From boyhood FitzGerald was proud of his Irish heritage and pictured himself as a worthy descendant of the battling clans of the Kerry hills. He once made a study of the FitzGeralds and found that the record is filled with fratricide. The prominence of Celts and Gaels in Australian literature has frequently been noted and is easily revealed by a glance at the names in the contents of any fairly complete anthology. As Frank Wilmot ("Furnley Maurice") once noted: "From a love of good law the English have come to respect all law good and bad. From a fear of bad law the Celt (or Irish Celt) has come to hate all law. The Englishman has a dogma he will fight for, but the Celt's is a mystical distrust which he writes beautiful poems about."—"Celtic Writers," in Romance (Melbourne, 1922), p. 79. In an undated letter to T. Inglis Moore, responding to an invitation to inaugurate a Yeats memorial, FitzGerald wrote: "As an Australian poet, by claim, it gratifies me to be picked by you to do honor to an Irish poet. As Irish myself by descent and temperament, very conscious and proud of the Irish in me, I am again gratified. And on a third count, Yeats was the greatest poet of his generation and I am glad, indeed, to be put in this part to assist this particular cause. There is no literary recognition I could get the pure joy from that I get from this."
    6. In those days, Brereton's special distinction on the campus was going hatless. "In later years," his nephew recalled, "when I began writing verses myself I was often told: 'You are getting more like your Uncle Jack every day: next thing, you'll be going round without your hat, I suppose."—"Uncle Jack Was a Vagabond at Heart," 6.
    7. Lindsay in 1950 painted an oil portrait of FitzGerald as an experiment. This portrait hung in the hall of the poet's home for years, but the family felt that it was not a good representation. As FitzGerald wrote to C. B. Christesen on May 17, 1952: "It is not generally thought a good likeness by those who know me well. . . . I rather take the view that if N. L. says I'm like that, like that I am. But I hope I'm not like the reproduction, which is villainous, makes me look like one of his worst wowsers [killjoys]."
    8. R. D. FitzGerald, "Philip Lindsay," Meanjin, XVII (No. 1, 1958), 183.
    9. Jack Lindsay, The Roaring Twenties (London, 1960), p. 94.
    10. Philip Lindsay, I'd Live the Same Life Over (London, 1941), p. 105. FitzGerald commented on this passage: "That was an outrageous statement of Phil's. I never risked damaging a theodolite in my life." Elsewhere, Philip Lindsay wrote: "Our society of two or three was named by

Fitz the 'Pre-Kiplingites,' such being his impatience with the 'modern' patter of juggled words without roots; and truly through Fitz have those 'Pre-Kiplingites' achieved more than even they ever dreamed of achieving."—"Poetry in Australia: Robert D. FitzGerald," *Poetry Review* (London), XL (Oct.–Nov., 1949), 351.

11. Letter of June 14, 1934, from Lovo, Wairiki Province. The novel was written after Phil had joined Jack in London, where the latter founded the Fanfrolico Press and wrote a long list of books. FitzGerald's tribute to Phil given in Note 8 above appeared after Phil's death in 1923.

12. Jennifer Kerry was born in 1932. Rosaleen Moyra was born in 1934. Robert Desmond was born in 1939 and Phyllida Mary in 1942.

14. Stokes memoir, p. 11.

15. On February 4, 1938, back in Australia and working in a Sydney suburb, FitzGerald wrote to Stokes: "That's what I miss more than anything, being one of a team." He kept in touch with other members of the "Fiji mob" and wrote proudly of the history of his profession in the foreword to a 1962 volume, *Knights and Theodolites: A Saga of Surveyors,* by F. M. Johnston.

16. FitzGerald stressed the aid given to his early work by his friend the late Ross Gollan, journalist and unheralded poet. "Ross Gollan gave a lot of attention to 'The Hidden Bole,'" he told the present writer, "none to 'Essay on Memory,' though I sent it to him, and seldom to any later pieces. I think he felt that his minute examination of my stuff word for word was making me too cramped and restrictive, and the time had gone by for it. The last he ever saw was, ironically, 'Tocsin.' He suggested the title."

Chapter Two

1. The first ten copies were printed on special paper. The late Sir William Dixson, founder of the Dixson Library in Sydney, paid a hundred guineas for one of these on publication. According to Geoffrey Farmer (*Private Presses and Australia,* Melbourne, 1972, p. 16), *Heemskerck Shoals* is "probably the most impressive book ever printed in Australia."

2. Mary Gilmore, poet and worker for social justice (FitzGerald was later to edit two volumes of her selected verse), had been created a Dame of the British Empire seven years earlier.

3. Sydney *Morning Herald,* Sept. 24, 1965, 6.

4. *Australian Poetry, 1965* (Sydney, 1965), p. 27.

5. Published in Sydney *Morning Herald,* Aug. 16, 1968, 19.

6. Letter to Professor Brian Medlin, March 18, 1969.

7. Letter to Guy Morrison and Caroline Weate, Jan. 13, 1969.

8. "Those young men whose principles will not permit them to register under the present National Service Act, and who refuse to be coerced into

any war which they believe to be immoral and unjust, have my whole-hearted support, encouragement and aid. If I were required to register under present conditions, I would refuse. Therefore, while young men may serve two years' gaol because they have the courage to defy conscription and oppose the Viet-Nam war, I am compelled to stand with them."

9. "Uncle Bob Sorry He Paid the Fine," *Australian,* Nov. 13, 1969, 4.

10. Sydney *Morning Herald,* Nov. 17, 1969, 2.

Chapter Three

1. "Some Aspects of Vers Libre," *New Outlook,* I (July 26, 1922), 172. Almost forty years later, he wrote: "Theory leading to practice is a halter strangling a mule. I could never see that poetry could be written to fit theory and even less that lives could be fashioned so."—"The Lives of Jack Lindsay," *Meanjin,* XX (No. 3, 1961), 324. Still later he stated in a radio interview: "Theories can be helpful, but anything which restricts poetry is wrong."—"Poetry in Australia: R. D. FitzGerald," *Southerly,* XXVII (No. 4, 1967), 239.

2. Letter to Tom Inglis Moore, 1938 or 1939.

3. *Ibid.*

4. Letter to Douglas Stewart, Feb. 9, 1959.

5. "Form and Matter in Poetry," *Meanjin,* XV (No. 2, 1956), 196.

6. *Ibid.*

7. *Ibid.,* 204.

8. *New Outlook,* II (June 9, 1923), 228.

9. "Another Neglected Australian?," *Bulletin,* May 28, 1930, 5.

10. *Australian Quarterly,* XI (Dec., 1939), 55. FitzGerald was to write further about his friend McCrae in a review of *Forests of Pan* (*Southerly,* VI [No. 2, 1945], 54–56) and in "Tributes to Hugh McCrae," (*Meanjin,* XVII [No. 1, 1958], 73–76), in which he quotes a long letter of appreciation by McCrae of the "Three Australian Poets" article. A selection of McCrae's letters, edited by FitzGerald, was published in 1970.

11. *Ibid.,* 59.

12. *Ibid.,* 62.

13. *Ibid.,* 64.

14. "Comment on 'Five Bells,'" *Meanjin,* V (No. 2, 1946), 159–60.

15. *Southerly,* IX (No. 3, 1948), 151.

16. *Ibid.* This essay expresses FitzGerald's attitude through much of his life, although he confesses to the technical attractiveness of Eliot and in a footnote admits that Eliot's dramas are "constructive work of a high standard." FitzGerald—an admirer of the earlier Ezra Pound, Eliot's editor and master (especially as editor of *The Waste Land*)—felt that

Eliot replaced Pound's gusto with defeatism. "An Attitude to Modern Poetry" as a whole is a firm defense of the moral duty of the poet, traditional or modernist.

17. *Meanjin,* VI (No. 4, 1947), 276.

18. "The Poetry of Peter Hopegood," *Meanjin,* VII (No. 2, 1948), 91. FitzGerald wrote to Tom Inglis Moore on Jan. 27, 1955: "I don't hold with the sort of poetry that requires footnotes."

19. *Ibid.*

20. *Ibid.,* 94.

21. "Conversation Piece: Cinderella and Others," *Morning Herald* (Sydney), Jan. 23, 1949, 12. Bill the surveyor, who says: "Prettiest thing I know is a wave breaking; same with a fire—I can watch a fire till it burns me" is a modern companion of the bargemen and carters in Wordsworth's Preface to the *Lyrical Ballads* (1800), using "the very language of men."

22. *The Elements of Poetry,* p. 21.

23. *Ibid.,* p. 31.

24. *Ibid.,* p. 53.

25. *Ibid.,* p. 54. This lecture deserves to be read in full, not only for its comments on reality and illusion, but on the moral values of art, art-for-art's sake, theories of poetic composition, and the preservative value of verse. This final lecture was reprinted in *Texas Quarterly,* VII (1964), 94–110.

26. "Mary Gilmore: Poet and Great Australian," *Meanjin,* XIX (No. 4, 1960), 343.

27. *Selected Verse by Mary Gilmore* (Sydney, 1948), p.v.

28. *Teaching of English,* No. 3 (Oct., 1963), 6.

29. *Ibid.,* 14.

30. *Ibid.,* 10.

31. *Ibid.,* 15.

32. *Ibid.,* 21.

33. *Southerly,* XXVI (No. 1, 1966), 23.

34. "Bruce Beaver's Poetry," *Meanjin,* XXVIII (No. 3, 1969), 410, 411.

35. Martin Haley, *The Central Splendour: Chung Hua* (Brisbane, 1970), xi.

Chapter Four

1. Paul Fussell, Jr., *Poetic Meter and Poetic Form* (New York, 1965), p. 92.

2. *Australian Poets: Robert D. FitzGerald* (Sydney, 1963), p. ix. Previously, when writing to Douglas Stewart (May 26, 1960) to praise the technique of Stewart's "Rutherford," he commented: "I have quite a good technique myself; in fact, it is one of my strongest points, though for some

158 ROBERT D. FITZGERALD

reason a virtue in me which critics seem least disposed to recognize." In a letter (Dec. 14, 1949) to R. G. Howarth he said: "It is the inference that my failure to conform to certain technical standards—particularly modern ones—indicates lack of interest in technique; that is not true. I may and do lack technique, but not an interest in it!" Even as late as 1966 he wrote to a graduate student, Maureen Cassidy: "It is interesting to have someone analyzing the technique which my critics are in the habit of saying I haven't got. Rather by way of defending myself inwardly against them, I tend in an exaggerated way to express agreement with them, never however conceding that I regard technique as anything but of the highest importance, whether my own is any good or not. I pay tremendous attention to my techniques; but cannot accept the usual analyses of them or of techniques generally."

3. Judith Wright, "R. D. FitzGerald," in *Preoccupations in Australian Poetry* (Melbourne, 1965), p. 164.

4. *Ibid.,* p. 156.

5. H. M. Green, *A History of Australian Literature,* II (Sydney, 1962), pp. 876–77. According to Green, FitzGerald's rhythms "depend on beat, not syllable, but that is no new thing in English poetry; and they run more freely than was usual in the days of our fathers and grandfathers, but they would have been acceptable to [Christopher] Brennan; nor are they, in themselves, particularly individual, though constituents in a style that is strikingly so. FitzGerald uses any meter that comes handy, preferring as a rule the five-beat line, rhymed as a rule, but irregularly. . . ."

6. Ed. Louis Lavater (Melbourne, 1922).

7. "Deep Within a Man," Sydney *Morning Herald,* Oct. 1, 1966, 17, and "The Denuded World," *Australian,* May 10, 1969, 18.

8. "Some Aspects of Vers Libre," *New Outlook,* I (July 26, 1922), 1972.

9. "The Poet-Laureate's Experiments," *Bulletin* (Sydney), April 8, 1926, 3.

10. Concerning FitzGerald's musical background, he wrote (June 7, 1965) in answer to a query by A. Grove Day: "Am not musical. Am not tone-deaf by any means but quite tone-dumb. I like songs and a good tune. A piano almost always, a violin seldom. A full orchestra not at all, not at all. Switch off that blasted wireless!"

11. "Three Australian Poets," *Australian Quarterly,* XI (Dec., 1939), 58.

12. "An Attitude to Modern Poetry," *Southerly,* IX (No. 3, 1948), 154.

13. Letter from FitzGerald to Howarth, Dec. 1, 1949. In a postscript to a letter to A. Grove Day, April 18, 1966, FitzGerald wrote: "I have read Guy Howarth's 'Modern Poetic Technique' but long after it could

have any influence on my style (if any); and anyway it is not an influencing kind of book."

14. Fussell, p. 39.

15. "Modern Poetry and Its Interpretation in the Classroom," *Teaching of English*, No. 3 (Oct., 1963), 10.

16. "Verse Technique of Robert David FitzGerald," unpublished master of arts thesis No. 806, College of Arts and Sciences, University of Hawaii, Jan. 1, 1968. The present author served as chairman of Miss Cassidy's thesis committee and was able to furnish a number of materials for her painstaking analysis of the technical aspects of all the selections in FitzGerald's *Forty Years' Poems*.

17. Karl Shapiro and Robert Beum, *A Prosody Handbook* (New York, 1965), p. 3.

18. *Ibid.*, p. 2.

19. Hereinafter, numbers in parenthesis after a poem will refer to pages in FitzGerald's *Forty Years' Poems* (1965), the indispensable collection for any study of this author's verse.

20. Cassidy, pp. 49–50, 52.

21. *Ibid.*, pp. 50–51.

22. *Ibid.*, p. 45.

23. *Ibid.*, p. 32.

24. *Ibid.*, p. 40.

25. *Ibid.*

26. *Ibid.*, p. 67.

27. *Ibid.*, p. 68. However, the copy of the original edition given to the present writer by Mr. FitzGerald is inscribed: "The earliest versions, since revised half-a-dozen times." A study of the revisions is instructive.

28. *Ibid.*, p. 71.

29. *Ibid.*, p. 73.

Chapter Five

1. *Hermes*, XXVIII (No. 2, 1922), 130.

2. *Australian University Verse, 1920–22* (Melbourne, 1922), pp. 25–26.

3. *Vision*, I (No. 3, 1923), 8; reprinted in *To Meet the Sun* (Sydney, 1929), p. 18.

4. *Australian Little Magazines* (Adelaide, 1964), p. 15.

5. *Vision*, I (No. 4, 1923), 7.

6. "Vision of the Twenties," *Southerly*, XIII (No. 2, 1952), 62–71.

7. *The Roaring Twenties* (London, 1960), p. 96.

8. FitzGerald wrote in 1939 in a review of a collection of McCrae's poems: "I contributed to *Vision*, which I shall claim as an unshadowable

distinction till earth breaks me in little pieces. It need hardly be said, then, that McCrae has been a star in my firmament"—"Three Australian Poets," *Australian Quarterly*, XI (No. 4, 1939), 57. In 1955 FitzGerald wrote for the Sydney *Bulletin* (Feb. 2) a fine poetic tribute to the *Vision* founder, Norman Lindsay.

9. This section is based upon the article, "R. D. FitzGerald in Fiji," by A. Grove Day, *Meanjin*, XXIV (No. 3, 1965), 277–86. The article was based on some fifty letters written by FitzGerald to Henry Stokes, a lengthy memoir by Stokes, interviews with Herbert Norman Murray, and examination of FitzGerald's personal diary during his five Fijian years.

10. "Titles have always given me trouble, but the changes are mostly due to the fact that I had forgotten what I called the pieces in the first place rather than any preference for the second choices"—note by Fitz-Gerald, July, 1965.

11. (Sydney, 1960), p. 15.

12. Chicago, 1938.

13. "Narrative Poetry," *Southerly*, XXVI (No. 1, 1966), 12.

14. Since the present writer has had access to a number of letters, private papers, and personal comments by Mr. FitzGerald and his friends, frequent inclusion of quotations from such unpublished sources seems justified.

The three main questions to ask when approaching a poem might be: What do you think the author was trying to accomplish in this poem? How well do you think he succeeds in accomplishing this intention? Do you believe that this purpose was worth attempting?

Often it is impossible to answer these questions precisely, without first answering some of a number of more specific questions. Analysis might reasonably include the suitability of many of the following elements: theme (main meaning); title; length; form (a broad area, including prosody); structure (the arrangement of the sequences in the order of their presentation and the magnitude of their importance); inner congruity; diction (a vast area of competence); imagery (including figures of speech and symbolism); allusions; patterns (repetitions, usually with variations); revisions; type; mood; tone; intensity; pace; and special contributions (philosophical attitudes, historical fact, general information, reflections on social customs or manners, ideas about human problems, moral messages, good characterization, story interest); and so on. After such analysis, the reader then might decide whether the poet has successfully combined such various elements into a unified whole. The successful handling of any of these aspects may be a source of enjoyment for the appreciative listener. Finally, critical questions such as the following may be raised with profit: What place does the poem occupy in the author's career? Would our appreciation be increased by a knowledge of the author's life? Of the particular circumstances of the poem's composition? Of other works by this author?

Of works by other authors of this period or other periods? For a fairly lengthy "explication" of a poem by FitzGerald, see the discussion of "Heemskerck Shoals" in Chapter 7.

15. *Forty Years' Poems* (Sydney, 1965), p. vii.
16. *Australian Poets: Robert D. FitzGerald* (Sydney, 1963), p. viii.
17. Maureen Cassidy found such a number of parallelisms in this poem as indeed to give evidence of a concern for technical complexity. "(1) The rhyme scheme in both stanzas is identical. (2) The last word of the first line rhymes with the fourth syllable of the succeeding line in both stanzas: 'part/heart,' 'gone/done.' (3) The last word of the fifth line rhymes with the sixth syllable of the following line in both stanzas: 'succeed/undecreed,' 'amiss/than this.' (4) Structurally, each stanza divides itself into two quatrains with a period at the end of the fourth line. (5) The last word of the seventh line alliterates with the second word of the final line in both stanzas: 'world/wild' in Stanza 1, 'keep/captive' in Stanza 2. (6) Rhythmically, each stanza follows this pattern: lines 1, 2, and 3 are iambic tetrameter; line 4 is iambic trimeter; lines 5, 6, and 7 are iambic tetrameter, line 8 is iambic trimeter. Lines 4 and 8 of the second stanza each contain seven syllables (the feminine rhyme is responsible for the additional syllable)."—"Verse Technique of Robert David FitzGerald" (University of Hawaii, 1968), pp. 80–81. In a letter to the present writer of June 14, 1968, FitzGerald added another: "The third line in each stanza is a half-rhyme with the seventh: 'willed/world,' 'scope/keep.'"
18. *A History of Australian Literature,* II (Sydney, 1962), p. 871.
19. Cassidy, *ibid.,* p. 93.
20. "A Pilgrimage in the Sud-ouest," *Meanjin,* XXV (No 2, 1966), 189.
21. *Bulletin,* May 26, 1927, 5.
22. *Ibid.,* May 5, 1927, 2.

Chapter Six

1. T. Inglis Moore, *Social Patterns in Australian Literature* (Sydney, 1971), p. 115.
2. A phrase originated by A. A. Phillips in an article, "The Cultural Cringe," *Meanjin,* IX (No. 4, 1950), 299–302, to depict a sense of inferiority felt by Australians when comparing their artistic output with the inherited "intimidating mass of Anglo-Saxon culture."
3. Moore, *ibid.,* p. 299.
4. "The Poetry of R. D. FitzGerald," *Twentieth Century* (Australia), IX (No. 1, 1954), 20. Hereinafter cited as Todd.
5. Vincent Buckley, *Essays in Poetry, Mainly Australian* (Melbourne, 1957), pp. 126–27. Buckley's opinions are controverted in a lengthy analysis of "Return" by T. L. Sturm, "Robert D. FitzGerald's Poetry and A. N.

Whitehead," *Southerly,* XXIX (No. 4, 1969), 290–93 (hereinafter cited as Sturm).

  6. *Australian Poets: Robert D. FitzGerald* (Sydney, 1963), p. 56.

  7. "Australian Poetry Since 1920," in *The Literature of Australia,* ed. Geoffrey Dutton (Baltimore, Md., 1964), p. 109.

  8. *Ibid.,* p. 107.

  9. "Robert D. FitzGerald," *Overland* (No. 25, 1962–63), 32.

  10. *New Triad,* I (No. 2, 1927), 23.

  11. "Thus FitzGerald depicts 'the untiring Sun' summoning his dancers on Manly surfing sands, where they are 'squanderers of mirth.' He is no less a Sydneysider when he begins his song by the clarion cry: 'I go to meet the sun with singing lips.' He calls his first volume *To Meet the Sun,* just as he rightly capitalizes 'the untiring Sun' like God to signify that he is a true Australian, a sun-worshipper."—Moore, pp. 299–300.

  12. Buckley, pp. 159–60. For the bush balladists, see R. W. Ward, *The Australian Legend* (London, 1958).

  13. Maureen Cassidy, "Verse Technique of Robert David FitzGerald" (Hawaii, 1968), p. 113. The poet wrote to Miss Cassidy on September 15, 1966: "Did you notice that the same scheme is used in 'Rebirth,' 'Chaos,' and 'Quayside Meditation'—a continuing scheme which I think is my own invention . . . requiring modification, of course, at the beginning and the end if all lines are to rhyme. I shall use it again some day." Actually, the schemes in "Chaos" and "Quayside Meditation" differ somewhat, but in all three poems, joining the rhyming lines forms a pattern of interwoven links.

  14. In a personal essay, "Places of Origin" (*Overland* [No. 33, 1965], 19), FitzGerald writes affectionately of his visit to Dublin and mentions that his father's ordinary speech "often gave place to a distinct brogue," although he was born in Australia and had never been to Ireland.

  15. "There is in 'Legend' an example of regularly recurring interior rhyme ['famed him/framed him,' 'fine horses/discourses,' 'jumble/tumble,' 'so exciting/so inviting,' 'muddles/puddles,' 'name him/acclaim him']. This interior rhyme, besides creating an air of levity, has a unifying effect since it occurs only once in each stanza and always occurs in the fourth line of each stanza. The reader tends to look forward to it and use it as a jumping-off place."—Cassidy, p. 118.

  16. "The final two lines contain an interesting double image. Dark Loma may in one sense be in charge of a puppet (the tune). Hidden behind the lattice work of the strings she jerks them quickly and the puppet moves 'light-footed.' Much more obviously, Loma is a hidden musician idly picking at a stringed instrument, and the melody is given the qualities of a dancer."—*Ibid.,* pp. 139–40.

  17. Sturm, 288–90. Note when reading this essay that, after it was

published, FitzGerald informed Mr. Sturm that at the time he wrote "The Hidden Bole" he had not yet read Whitehead's *Adventures in Ideas* (see *Southerly,* XXX [No. 1, 1970], 80).

18. Todd, 25.

19. Perhaps the author's liking for this piece derived from the fortunate ease with which it was written. As he wrote to Tom Inglis Moore on July 19, 1950: "My philosophy of poetry has grown to be and for many years has been that one should write sense if possible in the most adequate forms available and let the poetry look after itself as incidental—the happiest of accidents that can befall, but never deliberate. Never except in 'The Hidden Bole' have I felt that the accidents have befallen me at all lavishly. It is, I feel, perhaps my one claim to being considered as a poet; I'd hate to find it after all no better than later verses."

20. "I doubt if the banyan tree is Fijian; I don't recall seeing one there. I think I had in mind my botanist grandfather's account (which I have) of Lord Howe Island, which he visited about 100 years ago, one of the first scientists to do so. He was very impressed by the banyans there."—Note from FitzGerald to A. Grove Day, July, 1965.

21. "We cannot point to the hidden bole or know whether it is purposeful or not since it is the very ground of our experience of beauty; the moment we try to say something about it we abstract it from the experiential core to which it alone gives meaning, and become involved in the falsifying metaphysical categories previously rejected in the poem, projecting artificial permanences on what can only be experienced in time."—Sturm, 299.

22. "The Achievement of R. D. FitzGerald," *Meanjin,* XIII (No. 1, 1954), 71.

23. "R. D. FitzGerald—Philosopher or Poet?," *Overland* (No. 33, 1965), 16.

24. T. L. Sturm, "The Poetry of Robert D. FitzGerald," *Landfall,* XX (No. 2, 1966), 165-66.

25. "Six Australian Poets," pp. 207-8.

26. *Australian Poets: Robert D. FitzGerald* (Sydney, 1963), p. 57.

27. "Poetry in Australia," *Southerly,* XXVII (No. 4, 1967), 236.

28. "As a matter of fact, Eulogy apart—which is embarrassing rather than anything else when one knows one's own defects and limitations pretty well, I am very pleased with this article; he seems to have followed the argument closely. In the one place where he slips he is hardly to blame since, being anxious to get over a bit of necessary dry argument as briefly as possible, I compressed to the point of obscurity. What is meant by the passage is '*But* this line of argument I've been following leads to the conclusion that there is no such thing as individual existence even briefly. This "heart desires eternally." *However,* Memory provides an answer by

linking up a bird's "many flights upon one thread of keen-eyed bird."' Nowhere else does he go astray, though of course I don't follow a lot of his
references and philosophical terms. I *have* by the way possessed a Sartor
Resartus for years but have not read it."—Letter from FitzGerald to Tom
Inglis Moore (1938?).

29. T. L. Sturm, "Robert D. FitzGerald's Poetry and A. N. Whitehead,"
Southerly, XXIX (No. 4, 1969), 288–304 and T. M. Cantrell, "Some
Elusive Passages in 'Essay on Memory': a Reading Based on a Discussion
with Robert D. FitzGerald," *Southerly*, XXX (No. 1, 1970), 44–52.
Cantrell includes on p. 51 a letter to him from FitzGerald that explains
something of the poet's idea of a universal mind.

30. Cantrell, 44–45.

31. *Ibid.*, 47–48.

32. "Here the imagery, rich and vivid and often vigorous, illuminates
and, as many will think, is a medium for coherent thought. This may seem
unexpected, for the images, though at first sight chiefly visual, are in their
main effect kinesthetic: they have a sort of physical pressure, of material
impact, and this is in keeping with the idea of molding forces that is the
theme of the poem. But the physical and the conceptual are not normally so
tied. So that FitzGerald works with resistant devices and yet triumphs. . . .
There is no other poem in Australian literature of comparable conceptual
subtlety that is so packed with such devices so successfully employed."—
Cecil Hadgraft, *Australian Literature* (London, 1960), p. 221. For an
unfavorable opinion of the imagery, however, see Leonie Kramer, "R. D.
FitzGerald—Philosopher or Poet?," *Overland* (No. 33, 1965), 17.

33. H. J. Oliver, "The Achievement of R. D. FitzGerald," in G.
Johnston, ed., *Australian Literary Criticism* (Melbourne, 1962), p. 72.
Vincent Buckley's remark that in "Essay on Memory" FitzGerald attempts
"to wrench the heroic couplet to a task for which it is by nature unfitted"
(*Essays in Poetry, Mainly Australian* [Melbourne, 1957], p. 38) reflects
some commitment to "the fallacy of form." Alexander Pope used the
heroic couplet for several essays in verse without violating form. In any
event, FitzGerald's couplets are not "heroic," or end-stopped in neoclassical style.

34. FitzGerald's philosophical stance in the essay poems is illuminated
by a letter he wrote on September 12, 1945, to C. B. Christesen, commenting on a critic who mistakenly thought that the poet's theory "admitted
some form of transcendentalism, which it decidedly does not." The letter
continues: "Labels are useless: for God's sake don't fasten either label on
it so as to stick; but I would suggest that the philosophy expressed *ap-
proaches* a pantheistic-atheism or an atheistic-pantheism. Neither term
has much meaning for me; it's closest to pantheism. . . . The attitude, since
there is obviously an element of worship, is religious rather than theo-

logical or philosophical—atheism, let us say, elevated to a religion itself rather than a negation of it, a kind of atheism which, as it were, cannot acknowledge the existence of anything else *except* God, so does not recognize *any separate* god, any 'one that is.'"

Chapter Seven

1. *A History of Australian Literature,* II (Sydney, 1962), 881. Hereinafter cited as Green.
2. *Australian Poets: Robert D. FitzGerald* (Sydney, 1963), p. 57. Hereinafter cited as *Australian Poets.*
3. *Ibid.*
4. *Preoccupations in Australian Poetry* (Melbourne, 1965), p. 161. Hereinafter cited as Wright.
5. *Australian Poets,* pp. 57–58.
6. FitzGerald divulged further "factory secrets" about the sources of "Heemskerck Shoals" in a letter of August 5, 1945, to R. G. Howarth: "All the implications are out of my head; I have no idea if Tasman was that sort of man or thought those sorts of thoughts. You may say then that the principal source of information is the map on the floor of the Public Library, which is also in a little pamphlet I possess (Tomholt has one too). I also read the relevant parts of Tasman's journal—Heere's volume, likewise in the Public Library. But as a matter of fact nearly everything relevant is in G. C. Henderson's *Discoverers of Fiji.*"
7. The Slessor lines are to be found, among other places, on page 18 of *Voyager Poems* (Brisbane, 1960), edited by Douglas Stewart. In his introduction Stewart, who also includes in this fine anthology FitzGerald's long poem "The Wind at Your Door" and who believes that his selections "are the most substantial, the most impressive, yet written in Australia," tries to account for this similarity of material. "I dislike going into niggling little questions of dates to try to prove which of the poets of the present century was first with a voyager theme or which may have influenced the others; and indeed, even with the dates, I would find it impossible to determine whether Slessor influenced FitzGerald, or FitzGerald influenced Slessor; whether both simultaneously influenced each other, or whether both did not come independently to the same kind of themes. . . . It seems to me quite likely, though this would not have been the only influence at work on them, that both these writers took some of their impetus from Norman Lindsay, whose pictures of pirates (more noteworthy figures than nowadays we recognize) may have led to a general interest in adventurers of the ocean, and so to Cook and Tasman" (p. 13). Stewart does not here need to go back to Lindsay's pirates to justify such historical verse. FitzGerald had spent five years in Fiji, and "Heemskerck Shoals" is about the

first ships in Fijian waters. In any event, no Australian poet needs justification if he writes about such discoverers as Tasman and Cook.

8. "The Politics of Mrs. Tompkins' Nose," *Nation* (Sydney), Feb. 14, 1959, p. 13.

9. "Browning at the Dark Tower," *Bulletin* (Sydney), LXVI, June 20, 1945, 2.

10. "FitzGerald is the accepted leader in Australian poetry today, and 'Heemskerck Shoals' is a significant step in his development. By it, with some evident hesitation, he advances from the comparative remoteness and staticism of philosophical poetry to the arena of life and action—Shakespeare's world and Browning's; the creation of character, its revelation and dramatization in event. . . . FitzGerald's quiet style is deceptive; he has done more to make the reader 'see' this near-shipwreck than may be apparent at a first reading."—Douglas Stewart, "Australian Poetry, 1944," *Bulletin* (Sydney), Aug. 15, 1945, 2.

11. "The best contemporary American and British poets, after canvassing the possibilities of an apparently 'freer' metric, have returned to a more or less stable sort of Yeatsian accentual-syllabism . . . and have gravitated toward the system of accentual-syllabism which, for over four centuries, has been found to be the staple system for poetry in Modern English."—Paul Fussell, Jr., *Poetic Meter and Poetic Form* (New York, 1965), pp. 88–89.

12. *Australian Poets,* p. 58.

13. T. J. Kelly, *The Focal Word* (Brisbane, 1966), p. 290.

14. Wright, p. 164.

15. *Ibid.,* p. 166.

16. T. L. Sturm, "Robert D. FitzGerald's Poetry and A. N. Whitehead," *Southerly,* XXIX (No. 4, 1969), 303.

17. *Ibid.,* 304.

18. Wright, p. 167.

19. Kelly, p. 290.

20. "Robert D. FitzGerald," in *The Literature of Australia,* ed. Geoffrey Dutton (Baltimore, Md., 1964), p. 334.

21. G. A. Wilkes and J. C. Reid, *The Literature of Australia and New Zealand* (University Park, Pa., 1970), p. 103.

22. Green, I, 869.

23. Wright, p. 165.

24. *Australian Poets,* pp. 58–59.

25. "It is tight, dry, compact; every phrase is pointed and not a word could be left out. . . . This poem also reads better each time one reads it."—Green, I, 886–87.

26. "Places of Origin," *Overland* (No. 33, 1965), 20.

27. Vincent Buckley, *Essays in Poetry, Mainly Australian* (Melbourne, 1957), p. 135.

Chapter Eight

1. For a briefer account of this episode see "Will Mariner, the Boy Chief of Tonga," Chapter 9 of *Rascals in Paradise* by James A. Michener and A. Grove Day (New York, 1957).

2. Letter to A. Grove Day, August 5, 1956. The letter opens with a response to a query about a Robert FitzGerald who survived the *Port-au-Prince* massacre: "Robert Fitzgerald who escaped to Port Jackson was no relation so far as I am aware. Nor did I get so far in my reading of *Mariner's Tonga* before the scheme of the poem was already in my head: the fact that there was a Robert Fitzgerald on the *Port-au-Prince* was interesting and stimulating, but it had no influence in determining me to write 'Between Two Tides.'"

3. "A Kind of Life's Work," Sydney *Morning Herald*, Aug. 9, 1965, 13.

4. Cecil Hadgraft, *Australian Literature* (London, 1959), pp. 222–23.

5. "Mariner has to be toned down into the eyes of the tale, eventually existing by an act of resolution, but that makes it hard to see his personal appearance even; he gets described too late; in desperation I give him blue eyes. I should have made 'em pink; that might have meant something and got somewhere. Yet to bring him up any clearer might be to involve him in some action which would remove the focus from Finau, who is hard enough himself in all conscience. . . . "—Letter from FitzGerald to Douglas Stewart, April 23, 1950.

6. "The idea that choice is available to us, that we in fact consist of and *are* our choice, is a big advance from the vagueness of 'Essay on Memory.' We determine what we are by choice—limited choice—and the sorting-factor (God if you prefer) chooses *us* but without the same limitations. Our choice is itself action, but is the outcome of attitude and bearing. . . . Incidentally, I am usually amused and annoyed by being classed as a philosophical poet, but even more amused that the only real philosophical poem I've committed—'Between Two Tides'—is not recognized as such."—Letter from FitzGerald to T. Inglis Moore (undated).

7. Arthur Phillips, review in *Meanjin*, XII (No. 1, 1953), 119–20.

8. *Australian Poets: Robert D. FitzGerald* (Sydney, 1963), p. vii.

9. *A History of Australian Literature*, II (Sydney, 1962), 1401.

10. Alec King, *Quadrant*, VII (No. 3, 1963), 84.

11. "Six Volumes of Verse," *Australian Literary Review*, II (No. 6, 1963), 90.

12. Letter to A. Grove Day, June 14, 1968.

13. "Re the *Roadside* series. I had no sooner finished it than other pieces seeming to belong to the same impulse presented themselves and were written. After I revised *Roadside* and cut out that 'cripple' piece, I

altered the order a bit, added the new pieces, one older piece that always seemed to belong, and other older and newer pieces that seemed as though they could be rung in; and so extended the series to 19 compositions. . . . But I'm not sure that I've done the right thing in expanding the series; I may have altered its direction and intention too far."—Letter to R. G. Howarth, Aug. 3, 1958.

14. F. H. Mares, "The Poetry of R. D. FitzGerald," *Southerly,* XXVI (No. 1, 1966), 10.

15. "Other poems [after the end of 1958] are a new form of lyric: to be read as testimony still, but with the strident manner of the earlier verse yielding to an eloquent simplicity. All the central preoccupations are found again here, caught in a finer lens. Within the compass of a poem like 'Strata' FitzGerald can see present civilization as the latest cooling in the process of geological change, and at the same time find an athletic pleasure in its 'tangibles and actualities' still."—G. A. Wilkes, "The Poetry of R. D. FitzGerald," *Southerly,* XXV (No. 4, 1967), 258.

16. *Australian Poets,* p. 60.

17. Written on the flyleaf of a presentation copy to A. Grove Day of *Southmost Twelve.*

18. Douglas Stewart, "Robert D. FitzGerald," in *The Literature of Australia,* ed. Geoffrey Dutton (Baltimore, Md., 1964), p. 340.

19. "Martin Mason arrived in Australia in July, 1798, as surgeon of the *Britannia.* He was Acting Assistant Surgeon to the colony in 1799; and in 1801 became a magistrate of the District of Parramatta and Toongabbie. He practised his profession at Windsor, the first private medical practitioner in Australia. He was a quarrelsome man and had a reputation for cruelty, but professionally was esteemed. . . ."—*Australian Poets,* p. 60.

20. Interview, *Southerly* (No. 4, 1967), 237. The account runs, in part: "Fitzegarrel Receiv'd his 300 lashes. Doctor Mason (I never will forget him) use to go to feel his pulls and he smiled and sayd 'this man will tire you before he will fail,—go on.' It is against the law to flog a man past 50 lashes without a Doctor, and during the time he was getting his punishment he never gave as much as a word; only one and that was saying, 'Dont strike me on the Nick, flog me fair.' When he was let loose two of the Constibles went and tuck hould of him by the arms to help him in the Cart. I was standing by he said to them, 'let my arms go,' struck both of them with his elbows in the pit of the somack and nock them boath down and then step in the Cart. I herd Doctor Mason say 'that man had strength in nuff to bear two hundredd more.'"—*True Patriots All,* ed. Geoffrey C. Ingleton (Sydney, 1952), pp. 22–23.

21. Letter to Douglas Stewart, Oct. 3, 1958.

22. Letter to Douglas Stewart, undated.

23. Letter to Douglas Stewart, Oct. 3, 1958.

24. *Quadrant,* VII (No. 3, 1963), 86.
25. *Meanjin,* XXVII (No. 2, 1968), 146–49. This is one of the nine pieces by FitzGerald chosen for inclusion in *The Penguin Book of Australian Verse,* ed. Harry Heseltine (Ringwood, Victoria, 1972), pp. 182–86. In an unpublished note the poet wishes to make clear the Fijian origin of the real Asasela: "The first name should, more correctly, be 'Jemesa.' I wrote from memory. But since the poem slightly modifies historical records also, it seems consistent to let the name stand now as 'Josefa.' The records themselves are not consistent. It has been pointed out to me that the *Pacific Islands Monthly* of December 20, 1932, noted Jemesa Asasela's death in the Arctic Circle, but referred to him not as a Fijian but as a Samoan. This does not accord with other information. The *Fiji Times* of March 20, 1933, referred to him as Ratu Asesela Robanakadavu Nimiti of the village of Nakoronawa, in the district of Nakasaleka, on the isle of Kadavu (Kandavu); and *Na Mata* of October, 1932, called him *nai taukei e viti*—a Fijian—as, indeed, the Fijian chiefly title of 'Ratu' given him by the *Fiji Times* would imply. In any case *Josefa* Asasela is going to remain a Fijian."
26. Letter to A. Grove Day, July 10, 1969.

Chapter Nine

1. "A Kind of Life's Work," *Morning Herald,* Aug. 7, 1965, 13.
2. "Poetry in Australia: R. D. FitzGerald," *Southerly,* XXVII (No. 4, 1967), 240.
3. Review of James Devaney, *Poetry in Our Time, ibid.,* XIV (No. 4, 1953), 256. Elsewhere he wrote: "Inspiration does not come through hard work, but by favor of the goddess, who may very well withhold it; but hard work is what is most likely to win that favor—the 'conscious and persistent effort' advocated by the mentors of my youth, the process of mental struggle and of abortive attempts on paper which, judging by my wastepaper basket, must gladden any stationer's heart. However it may come to him, it is only by virtue of inspiration that a poet can claim to be a creative artist."—*The Elements of Poetry,* pp. 70–71.
4. "Poetry in Australia," 239–40.
5. *Ibid.,* 240. Elsewhere the poet confessed, concerning his writing of prose: "I find in doing anything like this I rough out a certain amount in type—I'm a one-finger artist—and a certain amount in handwriting that then is transferred to type. That may be done over and over again; but the result is still what I call a 'first draft' and is a mess, both as a composition and as legible matter, being full of handwritten corrections and ballooning interpolations and transpositions. A second typed draft becomes essential. That I then work on and pull the thing round into final shape or

very near it, by which time it is again illegible. A third typing becomes
essential."—Letter to C. B. Christesen, March 5, 1960.

6. "Modern Poetry and Its Interpretation in the Classroom," *Teaching of English,* No. 3 (Oct., 1963), 16.

7. Letter to Maureen Cassidy, Sept. 15, 1966. The importance of
revision is also stressed in a letter to R. G. Howarth, Dec. 15, 1949: "My
own verses are slogged into shape by hours and hours of revision, line
after line, word by word, almost syllable by syllable." Again, he wrote to
C. B. Christesen on June 21, 1960: "Here is the poem; and what a tussle it
has given me. I don't think there is a word in it that hasn't been altered
twenty times."

8. "Poetry in Australia," 235–36.

9. "Modern Poetry and Its Interpretation in the Classroom," 19.

10. "Poetry in Australia," 235.

11. Rex Ingamells first used the term "Jindyworobak" in 1935 as "an
aboriginal word which means to annex, to join. It should appropriately
indicate what I have tried to do in the poems published here: namely, to
express something of the Australian place spirit which baffles expression
in English words."—J. Tregenza, *Australian Little Magazines* (Adelaide,
1964), p. 49. "I could never agree with Ingamells," FitzGerald once
stated, "whom I regret I never met. I considered he wished to make the
Australianity or otherwise of its content the test of the value of Australian
poetry, whereas I had quite other standards."—*The Elements of Poetry*
(Queensland, 1963), p. 19. Further concerning the Jindyworobak aims,
FitzGerald wrote to R. G. Howarth on Aug. 17, 1940: "They are interested
in Australian poetry; and I am not interested in Australian poetry at all,
only in poetry, and regard the national label as purely fortuitous. I fail
to see even yet (though it is 17 years since *Vision* died) that a bad poem
is any better for being Australian or a good poem any worse for omitting
all references to gum-leaves. Granted a real poem will always or usually
spring from, and be directly or indirectly colored by, environment, the
Australianity of Australian verse is nevertheless purely incidental, the
poetry is what counts." The *avant-garde* "Angry Penguins," taking their
image from a little magazine edited by Max Harris and others in the early
1940s, dabbled in subjectivity and Freudian free linkage—convinced, in
Harris's words, "that poetry had to be liberated from all poetic diction
and conventional association."—"Conflicts in Australian Intellectual
Life, 1940–1964," *Literary Australia* (Melbourne, 1966), p. 23. FitzGerald
chuckled, as did most of Australia, when the Penguins discovered that
"Ern Malley"—the untutored genius to whose "Batrachic Ode" and fifteen
other pastiche poems an entire issue of *Angry Penguins* was devoted in
1944—was the creature of a hoax by two more conventional poets. The

exposure of the Penguin gaggle inspired FitzGerald to remark occasionally: "Ernie soit qui Malley pense!" Later, he felt that "Malley" wrote "better poetry—and with much more meaning—than his conjurers were aware of at the time," and thought that Max Harris was punished too severely.— "Form and Matter in Poetry," *Meanjin,* XV (No. 2, 1956), 198.

12. "Authors on Censorship," *Bulletin,* Sept. 29, 1948, 2.

13. "An Attitude to Modern Poetry," *Southerly,* IX (No. 3, 1948), 154–55.

14. "Certainly it will be fair to warn such a student not to be deceived by labels such as that stuck on my work long ago: 'Intellectual'—a term I can only accept as a general classification covering also several other poets with whom I may have certain affinities. But so many have followed suit since that great critic A. G. Stephens, shown some early rhymes of mine by a friend, made but the single comment 'All head; no heart,' that by reaction I have become now first an 'anti-intellectual,' which is bearable because inaccurate, and more recently a 'so-called intellectual,' which seems gratuitously contemptuous—only one degree less so than 'pseudo-intellectual,' which I await with no great qualms. . . . The use of intellect in any poem is normal, however, though secondary, and occurs in the rationalizing and synthesis of these relationships and in their ordering within the framework of craftsmanship."—*Australian Poets: Robert D. FitzGerald* (Sydney, 1963), pp. viii–ix.

15. Leonie Kramer, "R. D. FitzGerald—Philosopher or Poet?," *Overland* (No. 33, 1965), 15–18.

16. "Robert FitzGerald, Humanist," *Southerly,* XIX (No. 1, 1958), 9.

17. H. J. Oliver, "The Achievement of R. D. FitzGerald," *Meanjin,* XIII (No. 1, 1954), 48.

18. "Correspondence," *Meanjin,* I (No. 3, 1941), 12.

19. "A Kind of Life's Work," 13.

20. Donald Horne, *The Next Australia* (Sydney, 1971), p. 95. This author adds: "In Australia the fact that the learned-off culture is of another place [Britain] produces extra difficulties. If applied with real knowledge of other cultures it can produce a mere testiness. Without special recognition of Australian distinctiveness, it can become ignorant bullying. In writing it is often applied with the wrong knowledge. No one would be so crazy as to make English painting or English music the standard by which to judge all other painting or music, but the standards of Eng. Lit. can sometimes be the only thoroughly known standards of literary critics" (p. 96).

21. "Australian Poetry Since 1920," in *The Literature of Australia,* ed. Geoffrey Dutton (Baltimore, Md., 1964), p. 109.

22. *Essays in Poetry, Mainly Australian* (Melbourne, 1957), p. 129.

23. *Morning Herald,* Aug. 7, 1965, 13.
24. *Australian,* Sept. 25, 1965, 11.
25. *Illustrated Tasmanian Mail* (Hobart), Feb. 29, 1928, 5.
26. "Mr. FitzGerald's 'Essay on Memory,'" *Australian Quarterly,* X (No. 3, 1938), 71.
27. *I'd Live the Same Life Over* (London, 1941), p. 105.
28. *The Penguin Book of Australian Verse* (Sydney, 1972), pp. 45–48.

Selected Bibliography

An extensive listing appears in *R. D. FitzGerald: A Bibliography* (Adelaide: Libraries Board of South Australia, 1970), in the Bibliographies of Australian Writers Series, compiled by Jennifer Marjorie Van Wageningen and Patricia Anne O'Brien. Items published after 1969 are included as a supplement in the annual cumulation of *Index to Australian Book Reviews*. The Adelaide bibliography was indebted to the Fryer Memorial Library of Australian Literature, University of Queensland, for help in compiling the more than 450 entries. The present author, with the aid of Mr. Hugh Anderson of Melbourne, has found a few items not listed by the Adelaide researchers. In their bibliography may be found dates of appearance of individual poems in periodicals and inclusions of poems in several dozen anthologies, as well as listing of biographical notes, portraits, and reviews of Mr. Fitz-Gerald's books.

A valuable chronological list, giving dates of first publication, is Hugh Anderson's "A Checklist of the Poems of Robert D. FitzGerald, 1917–1965," *Australian Literary Studies,* IV (May, 1970), 280–86.

The items below are given chronologically, except for "Other Sources," which are given alphabetically. Some Australian periodicals do not use volume numbers. It should also be remembered that in the Southern Hemisphere a "winter" number might appear in July.

PRIMARY SOURCES

1. Books: Poetry

The Greater Apollo: Seven Metaphysical Songs. Sydney: privately printed, 1927, 14 pp. "This pamphlet is for private distribution by gift among the author's friends only. No copies are for sale." 250 copies.
To Meet the Sun. Sydney: Angus & Robertson, Ltd., 1929, 53 pp. Thirty-three poems, including *The Greater Apollo* series. 500 copies.
Moonlight Acre. Melbourne: Melbourne University Press, 1938, 71 pp. Nineteen poems, 500 copies. 2nd ed., 1944; No. XII ("All the moon's couriers descend") is removed and the numbering adjusted accordingly.
Heemskerck Shoals. Lower Fern Tree Gully, Victoria: The Mountainside Press, 1949, 36 pp. Decorated by a map and fifteen designs after drawings by Geoffrey C. Ingleton. Eighty-five copies: Nos. 1–10

printed on Arnold's Handmade paper; 11–85 on Georgian semi-rag paper. Signed by the author.

Between Two Tides. Sydney: Angus & Robertson, Ltd., 1952, 79 pp. Frontispiece by Norman Lindsay.

This Night's Orbit. Melbourne: Melbourne University Press, 1953, 41 pp. Nineteen poems, 230 copies.

Roadside: Nineteen Compositions in Series. Sydney: typescript, 1957. Three copies. "For Tom Inglis Moore." (Most of these were later printed in *Southmost Twelve.*)

The Wind at Your Door: A Poem. Cremorne, N.S.W.: Talkarra Press, 1959, 17 pp; 275 copies.

Southmost Twelve. Sydney: Angus & Robertson, Ltd., 1962, 60 pp. Twenty-eight poems, including an introductory verse to Tom Inglis Moore.

R. D. FitzGerald: Selection and Introduction by the Author. Sydney: Angus & Robertson, Ltd., 1963, 60 pp. Australian Poets Series. Thirty-one poems.

Of Some Country. Austin, Texas: Humanities Research Center, University of Texas, 1963, 46 pp. Tower Series No. 4. Twenty-seven poems, with drawings by Sister Mary Corita.

Forty Years' Poems. Sydney: Angus & Robertson, 1965, 242 pp. Contains most of his later work and a section called "Salvage" which retains, with revisions, all poems the author wished to preserve from the period 1922–30.

2. Books: Prose

The Elements of Poetry. St. Lucia: University of Queensland Press, 1963, 72 pp. Three lectures delivered at the University of Melbourne in July, 1959, afterward rewritten and delivered at the University of Queensland in June, 1961. On both occasions the lectures were given under the auspices of the Commonwealth Literary Fund.

3. Books Edited or Published with Introductions

Australian Poetry, 1942. Selected by Robert D. FitzGerald. Sydney: Angus & Robertson, Ltd., 1942.

Selected Poems by Andrew White, with preface by Robert D. FitzGerald. Sydney: Australasian Publishing Co., 1944.

Selected Verse by Mary Gilmore, with foreword by Robert D. FitzGerald. Sydney: Angus & Robertson, Ltd., 1948.

Knights and Theodolites: A Saga of Surveyors by F. M. Johnston, with foreword by Robert D. FitzGerald. Sydney: Edwards & Shaw, 1962.

Mary Gilmore. Selection and introduction by Robert D. FitzGerald. Sydney: Angus & Robertson, Ltd., 1963. Rev. ed., 1969.

The Central Splendour, Chung Hua: An Anthology from the Chinese, translated by Martin Haley. Preface by Robert D. FitzGerald. Brisbane: Smith & Patterson, 1970.
The Letters of Hugh McCrae. Selected, with foreword, by Robert D. FitzGerald. Sydney: Angus & Robertson, 1970.

4. Articles, Letters, and Interviews

"Some Aspects of Vers Libre." *New Outlook,* I (July 26, 1922), 172–73.
"A Defense of Slang." *Ibid.,* II (June 9, 1923), 228–30.
"Old Magic." Sydney *Bulletin,* May 21, 1925, 2. Based on *A Sailor's Garland* by John Masefield.
"The Poet-Laureate's Experiments." *Ibid.,* April 8, 1926, 3. Reply to "Two Poets and a Gossip" by Hilary Lofting in *ibid.,* March 18, 1926, 2–3.
"From Robert D. FitzGerald." *Ibid.,* May 19, 1927, 5.
"Another Neglected Australian?" *Ibid.,* May 28, 1930, 5. On Henry Lawson.
"Vertical Curves." *Australian Surveyor,* VII (No. 4, 1938), 238–40.
Letter. *Meanjin,* I (No. 3, 1941), 12.
"Comment on 'Five Bells.'" *Ibid.,* V (No. 2, 1946), 159–60.
"Interview with FitzGerald." *Australasian Book News,* II (July, 1947), 5–6. Interviewer, Douglas Stewart.
"Uncle Jack Was a Vagabond at Heart." Sydney *Morning Herald,* Feb. 21, 1948, 6.
"The Poetry of Peter Hopegood." *Meanjin,* VII (No. 2, 1948), 91–94.
"An Attitude to Modern Poetry." *Southerly,* IX (No. 3, 1948), 148–55.
"Authors on Censorship." *Bulletin,* Sept. 29, 1948, 2 (symposium).
"Conversation Piece: Cinderella and Others." Sydney *Sunday Herald,* Jan. 23, 1949, 12.
"Something Personal: Mostly About Bones." *Morning Herald,* May 7, 1949, 8.
"On Payment." *Everyman,* I (1954), 2.
"A Garibaldi Veteran." *Bulletin,* April 25, 1956, 21–22.
Letter on play "Ned Kelly." *Morning Herald,* May 15, 1956, 2. Answering letter from Frederick Aarons of May 10.
"Form and Matter in Poetry." *Meanjin,* XV (No. 2, 1956), 196–204.
"Reduction to Meridian of Circum-Meridian Observations." *Australian Surveyor,* XVI (No. 6, 1957), 343–47.
"Tributes to Hugh McCrae." *Meanjin,* XVII (No. 1, 1958), 73–76.
"Philip Lindsay." *Ibid.,* XVII (No. 1, 1958), 183–85.
"The Politics of Mrs. Tompkins' Nose." *Nation,* Feb. 14, 1959, 13.
"Mary Gilmore: Poet and Great Australian." *Meanjin,* XIX (No. 4, 1960), 341–56.

"The Lives of Jack Lindsay." *Meanjin,* XX (No. 3, 1961), 322–25.
"Modern Poetry and Its Interpretation in the Classroom." *Teaching of English,* No. 3 (Oct., 1963), 4–22.
"Poetry's Approach to Reality." *Texas Quarterly,* VII (1964), 94–110. Reprint of Part III of *The Elements of Poetry.*
"A Kind of Life's Work." *Morning Herald,* Aug. 7, 1965, 13. Interviewer, C. McGregor.
"Places of Origin." *Overland* (No. 33, Dec., 1965), 19–23.
"Narrative Poetry." *Southerly,* XXVI (No. 1, 1966), 11–24.
"A Pilgrimage in the Sud-ouest." *Meanjin,* XXV (No. 2, 1966), 179–89.
"History of the New South Wales Division." *Australian Surveyor,* XXI (No. 5, 1967), 15–19.
"The Rights and Wrongs of a Cruel War." *Australian,* Oct. 21, 1967, 10. Response by Owen Harris, *ibid.,* Oct. 28, 11.
"Poetry in Australia." *Southerly,* XXVII (No. 4, 1967), 233–42. Interviewer, J. Thompson.
"Nationalism and Internationalism." *Ibid.,* XXVII (No. 4, 1967), 260–65.
"Propaganda and Arts Vietnam." Letter, *Australian,* Oct., 29, 1968, 6.
"Vale John Thompson." *Poetry Magazine* (Australia) (No. 5, 1968), 6.
"Kenneth Slessor." *Australian Literary Studies,* V (No. 2, 1971), 115–20.
"Australian Women Poets." *Texas Quarterly,* XV (No. 2, Summer, 1972), 75–97.
"Verse and Worse." *Southerly,* XXXIII (No. 2, 1973), 156–66.

5. Short Story

"His Blameless Youth," *Bulletin,* Feb. 8, 1933, 34.

6. Book Reviews by R. D. FitzGerald

The Aspen Tree and Other Verses, by Winifred Shaw [a fourteen-year-old girl]. *Hermes,* XXVII (Aug., 1921), 88–89.
Alma Venus! and Other Verses, by Bernard O'Dowd. *Ibid.,* XXVIII (May, 1922), 15–17.
Our Earth, by Kenneth MacKenzie. *Australian National Review,* II (Oct., 1937), 92–94.
Green Lions, by Douglas Stewart. *Ibid.,* II (Dec., 1937), 80–82.
I Look Forth, by Henry Boote. *Ibid.,* III (May, 1938), 77–79.
The Young Desire It, by Kenneth MacKenzie. *Ibid.,* III (June, 1938), 79.
Vintage, by Harley Matthews. *Ibid.,* IV (Oct., 1938), 82–84.
A Beggar's Opera, by Mary Finnin. *Ibid.,* IV (Nov., 1938), 83–84.
Poems in Praise of Practically Nothing, by Samuel Hoffenstein. *Ibid.,* IV (Dec., 1938), 84–86.
Vaudeville, by Ronald McCuaig. *Ibid.,* V (Feb., 1939), 84–85.
Hermes (magazine of the undergraduates of the University of Sydney).

Ibid., V (Feb., 1939), 88.

Beauty Imposes, by Shaw Neilson. *Ibid.,* V (April, 1939), 79–80.
"Three Australian Poets" (on Hugh McCrae, Mary Gilmore, and Kenneth Slessor). *Australian Quarterly,* XI (Dec., 1939), 53–64.

Forests of Pan, by Hugh McCrae. *Southerly,* VI (No. 2, 1945), 54–56.

Shipwreck, by Douglas Stewart. *Meanjin,* VI (No. 4, 1947), 274–77.

Selected Verse, by Mary Gilmore. *Ibid.,* VIII (No. 3, 1949), 182–84.

Language of the Sand, by R. Robinson. *Ibid.,* IX (No. 1, 1950), 73–74.

The Ship of Heaven, by Hugh McCrae. *Ibid.,* X (No. 3, 1951), 307–11.

With a Hawk's Quill, by James Picot. *Ibid.,* XII (No. 4, 1953), 452–57.

Poetry in Our Time, by James Devaney. *Southerly,* XIV (No. 4, 1953), 252–56.

The Old Ladies of Newington, by Peter Bladen. *Meanjin,* XIII (No. 1, 1954), 143–46.

Poems, by W. S. Fairbridge and *Lifted Spear,* by E. G. Moll. *Southerly,* XV (No. 2, 1954), 108–11.

Fourteen Men and Other Poems, by Mary Gilmore. *Meanjin,* XIII (No. 4, 1954), 622–24.

The Burden of Tyre, by C. J. Brennan. *Southerly,* XVI (No. 1, 1955), 18.

Selected Poems, by Henry Kendall. *Overland,* No. 11 (Jan., 1958), 36–37.

Life Rarely Tells, by Jack Lindsay. *Nation* (Australia), No. 2 (Oct. 11, 1958), 22–23.

The Roaring Twenties, by Jack Lindsay. *Meanjin,* XX (No. 3, 1961), 322–25.

Modern Russian Poetry, selected and translated by Jack Lindsay. *Ibid.,* XX (No. 3, 1961), 346.

Spiegel the Cat, by D. Martin. *Overland,* No. 22 (Dec., 1961), 49.

Poems, by V. Vallis. *Southerly,* XXII (No. 1, 1962), 49–51.

Cock Crow, by Rosemary Dobson. *Southerly,* XXVI (No. 2, 1966), 132–37.

Studies in Australian Bibliography, by Harry Chaplin. *Southerly,* XXX (No. 1, 1970), 74–76.

7. Poems Published Since 1963

"Proceedings of an Historical Society." *Meanjin,* XXIII (No. 4, 1964), 366.

"This Righteous Twist." *Australian Poetry,* 1965. Sydney: Angus & Robertson, Ltd., pp. 27–28.

"Currencies." *Overland* (No. 33, Dec., 1965), 18.

"One Such Morning." *Bulletin,* May 14, 1966, 51–53.

"Sorting Papers." *Meanjin,* XXV (No. 4, 1966), 417.

"The Road North." *Morning Herald,* March 4, 1967, 15.

"Deep Within a Man." *Ibid.,* Oct. 1, 1966, 17.

"Of Studies." *Southerly,* XXVII (No. 4, 1967), 232.

"Invocation of Joseph Asasela." *Meanjin,* XXVII (No. 2, 1968), 146–49.

"Lawbreakers." *Morning Herald,* Aug. 17, 1968, 19.

"The Denuded World." *Australian,* May 10, 1969, 18.
"Society." *Overland* (No. 41, Winter, 1969), 7.
"Ghost Rally." *Morning Herald,* Aug. 30, 1969, 20.

8. Unpublished Sources

Fiji diaries of R. D. FitzGerald, 1931-36.
Correspondence between FitzGerald and Henry X. Stokes of Lautoka, Fiji; R. G. Howarth, editor of *Southerly;* C. B. Christesen, editor of *Meanjin;* Professor Tom Inglis Moore, Department of English, School of General Studies, Australian National University; and A. Grove Day, Department of English, University of Hawaii.
Twenty-five-page memoir on FitzGerald by Henry X. Stokes, 1964.
Interviews by A. Grove Day with Herbert Norman Murray, Douglas Stewart, C. B. Christesen, Tom Inglis Moore, R. G. Howarth, and many others.
Collection of papers and clippings given by R. D. FitzGerald, Mitchell Library Manuscript No. 2318, containing folders on preparation of *The Letters of Hugh McCrae,* on FitzGerald's participation in "Arts Vietnam," and on his experience as a member of the Committee in Defiance of the National Service Act.
"Product," typescript of "later verses," published or unpublished, since 1963, lent by Mr. FitzGerald. On title page: "For C. B. Christesen" and a quotation from *Sartor Resartus.*
Conversations between R. D. FitzGerald and A. Grove Day since 1955.

9. Recording

"Robert D. FitzGerald Reads from His Own Work," with accompanying text. St. Lucia: Queensland University Press, 1971.

SECONDARY SOURCES

1. Criticism: General

MILLER, E. MORRIS. *Australian Literature.* Melbourne: Melbourne University Press, 1940, pp. 60, 101-2, 337, 818, 825, 827, 960.
SECCOMBE, H. G. "A Contemporary Australian Poet," *Australian Quarterly,* XIII (No. 1, 1941), 65-72.
LINDSAY, PHILIP. *I'd Live the Same Life Over.* London: Hutchinson, 1941, 104-6.
MOORE, T. INGLIS. *Six Australian Poets.* Melbourne: Robertson & Mullins, 1942, pp. 187-213.
GREEN, H. M. *Fourteen Minutes.* Sydney: Angus & Robertson, Ltd., 1944, pp. 130-36.

Selected Bibliography   179

LINDSAY, NORMAN. "Browning at the Dark Tower," *Bulletin* (Sydney), June 20, 1945, 2.

PALMER, NETTIE. *Fourteen Years.* Melbourne: Meanjin Press, 1948, pp. 29–30, 48–50.

LINDSAY, PHILIP. "Poetry in Australasia, No. 4: Robert D. FitzGerald," *Poetry Review* (London), XL (Oct.–Nov., 1949), 348–51.

MOORE, T. INGLIS. "Australian Poetry," *Fortnightly* (April, 1950), 260–65.

MURPHY, ARTHUR. *Contemporary Australian Poets.* Melbourne: Marunyah Press, 1950, pp. 36–40.

LINDSAY, JACK. "Vision of the Twenties," *Southerly*, XIII (No. 2, 1952), 62–71.

MCLEOD, ZELIE. "Poet Who 'Cracks Great Barrels of Song,'" *Sydney Daily Telegraph,* Feb. 28, 1953, 13.

OLIVER, H. J. "The Achievement of R. D. FitzGerald," *Meanjin,* XIII (No. 1, 1954), 39–48; also in *Australian Literary Criticism,* ed. Grahame Johnston, Melbourne: Oxford University Press, 1962, pp. 69–78.

TODD, F. M. "The Poetry of R. D. FitzGerald," *Twentieth Century* (Australian), IX (No. 1, 1954), 20–29.

"Australian Literary Series, No. 19: R. D. FitzGerald," *Morning Herald,* Sept. 3, 1955, 12.

WRIGHT, JUDITH. *A Book of Australian Verse.* Melbourne: Oxford University Press, 1956, 1962, p. 105.

MILLER, E. MORRIS and MACARTNEY, F. T. *Australian Literature.* Sydney: Angus & Robertson, Ltd., 1956, pp. 177–79.

BUCKLEY, VINCENT. *Essays in Poetry, Mainly Australian.* Melbourne: Melbourne University Press, 1957, pp. 70–78, 122–41, and *passim.*

ANDERSON, HUGH. "Robert FitzGerald, Humanist," *Southerly,* XIX (No. 1, 1958), 2–10.

HADGRAFT, CECIL. *Australian Literature: A Critical Account.* London: Heinemann, 1960, pp. 219–24.

STEWART, DOUGLAS, ed. *Voyager Poems.* Brisbane: Jacaranda Press, 1960, pp. 7–16.

LINDSAY, JACK. *The Roaring Twenties.* London: Bodley Head, 1960, pp. 94–96, "FitzGerald and Marlowe."

EWERS, J. K. *Creative Writing in Australia,* rev. ed. Melbourne: Georgian House, 1962, pp. 112–15.

GREEN, H. M. *A History of Australian Literature,* Vol. II. Sydney: Angus & Robertson, Ltd., 1962, pp. 868–88 and *passim.*

STEWART, DOUGLAS. "Robert D. FitzGerald," *Australian Surveyor,* XIX (No. 4, 1962), 243–44.

KEESING, NANCY. "Robert D. FitzGerald," *Overland* (No. 25, 1962–63), 31–32.

HOPE, A. D. *Australian Literature, 1950–1962.* Melbourne: Melbourne University Press, 1963, pp. 4–5.

180   ROBERT D. FITZGERALD

WALLACE-CRABBE, CHRISTOPHER, ed. *Six Voices: Contemporary Australian Poets.* Sydney: Angus & Robertson, Ltd., 1963, pp. 19–33.
STEWART, DOUGLAS. "Robert D. FitzGerald, a Background to His Poetry," in Dutton, Geoffrey, ed., *The Literature of Australia.* Baltimore, Md.: Penguin Books, 1964, pp. 332–41.
TREGENZA, J. *Australian Little Magazines, 1923–1954.* Adelaide: Libraries Board of South Australia, 1964, pp. 12, 17–18, 23–26, 79, 88, 91.
DAY, A. GROVE. "R. D. FitzGerald and Fiji," *Meanjin,* XXIV (No. 3, 1965), 277–86.
KRAMER, LEONIE J. "R. D. FitzGerald—Philosopher or Poet?," *Overland* (No. 33, 1965), 15–18.
WRIGHT, JUDITH. *Preoccupations in Australian Poetry.* Melbourne: Oxford University Press, 1965, pp. 154–69.
"Surveyor-Poet Wins Half £ 5,000 Award," *Morning Herald,* Sept. 24, 1965, 6.
MARES, F. H. "The Poetry of R. D. FitzGerald," *Southerly,* XXVI (No. 1, 1966), 3–10.
KELLY, T. J. *The Focal Word.* Brisbane: Jacaranda Press, 1966, pp. 285–90.
WILKES, G. A. "The Poetry of R. D. FitzGerald," *Southerly,* XXV (No. 4, 1967), 243–58.
CASSIDY, MAUREEN. "Verse Technique of Robert David FitzGerald." Unpublished master of arts thesis No. 806, College of Arts and Sciences, University of Hawaii, Jan. 1, 1968.
STURM, T. L. "Robert D. FitzGerald's Poetry and A. N. Whitehead," *Southerly,* XXIX (No. 4, 1969), 288–304.
CANTRELL, T. M. "Some Elusive Passages in 'Essay on Memory': A Reading Based on a Discussion with Robert D. FitzGerald," *Southerly,* XXX (No. 1, 1970), 44–52.
WILKES, G. A. and REID, J. C. *The Literatures of Australia and New Zealand.* Ed. by A. L. McLeod. Pennsylvania State University Press: University Park and London, 1970, pp. 101–5.
MCLEAN, DONALD. "The Surveyor Who Loved Orchids," *Morning Herald,* April 17, 1971, 22.
MOORE, T. INGLIS. *Social Patterns in Australian Literature.* Sydney: Angus & Robertson, Ltd., 1971; University of California, 1971.
HESELTINE, HARRY. *The Penguin Book of Australian Verse.* Sydney: Penguin Books, 1972, pp. 45–48.

2. Criticism: Specific Full Reviews

The Greater Apollo

"The Greater Apollo," *Morning Herald,* April 9, 1927, 10.
MCCRAE, HUGH. "Robert D. FitzGerald," *Bulletin,* May 5, 1927, 2.

"L. PHILLIPS" [PHILIP LINDSAY]. "The Greater Apollo," *Bulletin,* May 26, 1927, 5.

"Mr. FitzGerald's Poems," *Morning Herald,* May 25, 1929, 12.

To Meet the Sun

HEWINS, I. "A Book of Poems by R. D. FitzGerald," *Australian Quarterly* (No. 2, 1929), 101–4.

PALMER, NETTIE. "Robert FitzGerald's Poems," *All About Books,* I (No. 7, 1929), 207.

MANN, CECIL. "R. D. FitzGerald," *Bulletin,* June 19, 1929, 2.

"Essay on Memory"

[MOORE, T. I.] "Notable Poem," *Morning Herald,* April 9, 1938, 7.

"Prize Poem: Salute to FitzGerald: Professor Chisholm's Study," *ibid.,* Sept. 10, 1938, 20.

CHISHOLM, A. R. "Mr. FitzGerald's 'Essay on Memory,'" *Australian Quarterly,* X (No. 3, 1938), 65–71.

LANCASTER, K. J. "On the Slopes of Parnassus," *Southerly,* XIII (No. 2, 101–4).

Moonlight Acre

"Poetry of Power: Mr. FitzGerald's New Book," *Morning Herald,* Dec. 31, 1938, 8.

"Moonlight Acre," *Bulletin,* Jan. 18, 1939, 2.

"A New Australian Poet," *Poetry Review,* XXX (July–Aug., 1939), 329.

SLESSOR, K. "The Flowering of a Poet," *Desiderata* (No. 39, 1939), 26–28.

SECCOMBE, H. G. Review, *Australian National Review,* V (No. 27, 1939), 26–28.

"Modern Poetry," Adelaide *Advertiser,* April 6, 1940, 10.

Australian Poetry, 1942

"The New 'Australian Poetry,'" *Bulletin,* Feb. 10, 1943, 2.

"Review," Melbourne *Age* "Literary Supplement," March 6, 1943, 5.

"Good Selection of Australian Verse," *Advertiser,* March 13, 1943, 3.

MITCHELL. A. G. Review, *Southerly* (No. 4, 1943), 26–27.

Heemskerck Shoals.

STEWART, DOUGLAS. *The Flesh and the Spirit.* Sydney: Angus & Robertson, Ltd., 1948, pp. 208–12.

182   ROBERT D. FITZGERALD

Between Two Tides

[STEWART, DOUGLAS]. "Story from Tonga," *Bulletin,* Nov. 5, 1952, 2.
BARTLETT, N. "Philosopher Poet," Sydney *Daily Telegraph,* Nov. 8,
    1952, 14.
BUCKLEY, VINCENT. Review, *Austrovert* (No. 9, 1952), 6–7.
E.C. Review, *Morning Herald,* Dec. 20, 1952, 8.
THWAITES, M. "Recent Australian Verse: Life, Variety and Energy,"
    Age, Jan. 10, 1953, 12.
PHILLIPS, A. Review, *Meanjin,* XII (No. 1, 1953), 118–20.
OLIVER, H. J. "Story and Theme," *Southerly,* XV (No. 1, 1954), 28–31.

This Night's Orbit

M.I.G. "Contrast in Poetry and Attitude to Life," *Age* "Literary Supple-
    ment," Oct. 31, 1953, 14.
STEWART, DOUGLAS. "FitzGerald's New Poems," *Bulletin,* Dec. 2, 1953,
    2, 35.
HOPE, A. D. "The Poetry of FitzGerald," *Morning Herald,* Dec. 12, 1953, 10.
"An Australian Poet," *Times Literary Supplement* (London), Oct. 22,
    1954, 674.
THOMPSON, J. "Poet in Progress," *Southerly,* XVI (No. 2, 1955), 90.

The Wind at Your Door

STEWART, DOUGLAS. "Tribal Ancestors," *Bulletin,* Sept. 30, 1959, 2.
JOHNSTON, G. K. W. Review, *Observer* (Australia), Oct. 31, 1959, 699.
HODGES, H. "The Doctor, the Convict, and the Poet," *Biblionews,*
    XII (Oct., 1959), 40.
BUCKLEY, VINCENT. "R. D. FitzGerald in 1959," *Nation* (Australia),
    XXX (Nov. 7, 1959), 21.
PHILLIPS, A. "Poetry Chronicle," *Meanjin,* XVIII (No. 4, 1959), 459.
CLARK, R. Review, *Australian Letters,* II (Dec., 1959), 59–60.
THOMPSON, J. "Compressed Poetry," *Southerly,* XX (No. 4, 1959), 233.
KING, F. "The Savagery of Manunkind," *Westerly,* (No. 3, 1959), 33–34.
"S[IDNEY] D[ORNE]." Review, *Bonfire,* I, (No. 1, 1960), 62–63.
Review, *Bonfire,* I, (No. 1, 1960), 62–63.
MCAULEY, J. Review, *Quadrant,* IV (No. 2, 1960), 91.

Voyager Poems

JONES, E. "Six Voyagers," *Observer* (Australia), Nov. 12, 1960, 33.
MOORE, T. I. "Exploring the Explorers," *Bulletin,* Nov. 23, 1960.

Southmost Twelve

McCUAIG, R. "Poets Taken by Surprise," *Bulletin,* Jan. 19, 1963, 36.
CROSS, G. "Australian Poetry," *Morning Herald,* Feb. 2, 1963, 16.
HARRIS, MAX. "Regrading the Seniors," *Nation* (Australia), Feb. 23, 1963, 21.
LEE, S. E. "Poetry of Distinction," *Southerly,* XXIII (No. 2, 1963), 140–41.
MACAINSH, N. "New Poetry," *Overland* (No. 26, April, 1963), 40.
MARES, F. H. "Six Volumes of Verse," *Australian Literary Review,* II (No. 6, 1963), 90.
KING, A. Review, *Quadrant,* VII (No. 3, 1963), 84–87.
"The Australian Idiom," *Times Literary Supplement,* July 30, 1964, 670.
JONES, EVAN. Review, *Prospect,* VII (No. 1, 1964), 29–30.

The Elements of Poetry

MAIR, I. "An Australian Poet on His Controversial Art," *Age,* June 29, 1963, 18.
PORTEOUS, A. "Anti-Christian," *Bulletin,* Aug. 31, 1963, 40.
BRISSENDEN, R. F. "R. D. F. as Critic," *Australian Book Review,* II (Sept., 1963), 176–77.
JONES, E. "Better Late," *Prospect,* VII (No. 1, 1964), 29–30.
"Australian Poetry," *Press* (Christchurch, N. Z.), Feb. 1, 1964, 3.
MACAINSH, N. "Three Lectures, Seven Books," *Overland* (No. 29, April, 1964), 61–62.

Robert D. FitzGerald: Selection and Introduction by Author

"Australian Poetry," *Press,* Feb. 1, 1964, 3.
JONES, T. H. "Able to Be Romantic," *Quadrant,* VIII (No. 2, 1964), 73.

Forty Years' Poems

McCUAIG, R. "FitGerald's Colonial Echoes," Canberra *Times,* July 24, 1965, 10.
McAULEY, J. Review, *Morning Herald,* Aug. 7, 1965, 13.
"FitzGerald's Poetry: Critic's Singular Malady," letters to the editor by T. I. Moore and A. Grove Day in answer to review above. *Ibid.,* Aug. 14, 1965, 2.
"Task of the Reviewer," rejoinder by J. McAuley on above letters. *Ibid.,* Aug. 19, 1965, 2.
ELLIOTT, BRIAN. "Poetry, Verse, Etc.," *Australian Book Review,* IV, Aug., 1965, 178.
HALEY, M. "FitzGerald's Poems," Melbourne *Advocate,* Aug. 26, 1965, 9.
SMITH, V. "FitzGerald's Iron Strength," *Bulletin,* Aug. 28, 1965, 52–53.

PHILLIPS, A. "The Poems of R. D. FitzGerald," *Meanjin,* XXIV (No. 3, 1965), 368–69.
DOUGLAS, D. Review, *Age* Literary Review, Sept. 4, 1965, 23.
C. D. "Life in its Wholeness," *Star* (Auckland, N. Z.), Sept. 18, 1965, 19.
JOHNSTON, G. Review, *Australian,* Sept. 25, 1965, 11.
BURNS, R. "The Isolated Self," *Nation* (Australian), Oct. 16, 1965, 21–22.
THOMPSON, J. Review, *Poetry Magazine* (No. 5, 1965), 28–30.
DUNLOP, RONALD. Review, *Poetry Australia,* VII (No. 7, 1965), 39–43.
WHITEHEAD, A. H. Review, *Methodist,* Jan. 22, 1966, 22.
STURM, T.L. "The Poetry of Robert D. FitzGerald," *Landfall,* XX (No. 2, 1966), 162–76.

3. Other Sources (alphabetically by author)

Australian Encyclopaedia 5th ed. Sydney: Grolier Society, 1965.
BROWN, CYRIL. *Writings for Australia.* Melbourne: Hawthorn, 1956.
CHRISTESEN, C. B. *On Native Grounds.* Sydney: Angus & Robertson, 1968.
CLARK, MANNING. *A Short History of Australia.* New York: New American Library, 1963.
CROSS, G. "Australian Poetry in the Sixties," *Poetry Australia* (No. 5, 1965), 33–38.
DUTTON, GEOFFREY. "Australian Poetic Diction," *Australian Letters,* I (No. 1, June, 1957), 12–16.
———, ed. *The Literature of Australia.* Baltimore, Md.: Penguin Books, 1964.
FUSSELL, PAUL, Jr. *Poetic Meter and Poetic Form.* New York: Random House, 1964.
HORNE, DONALD. *The Lucky Country (Australia Today).* Baltimore, Md.: Penguin Books, 1965, 1971.
HOWARTH, R. G. *Notes on Modern Poetic Technique: English and Australian.* Sydney: Angus & Robertson, Ltd., 1949.
HOWARTH, R. G., SLESSOR, KENNETH, and THOMPSON, JOHN (eds). *The Penguin Book of Modern Australian Verse,* rev. ed. Baltimore, Md.: Penguin Books, 1961.
INGAMELLS, REX. *Handbook of Australian Literature.* Melbourne: Jindyworobak Publications, 1949, p. 9.
JAFFA, HERBERT C. *Kenneth Slessor.* New York: Twayne's World Authors Series, No. 145, 1971.
JOHNSTON, GRAHAME, ed. *Australian Literary Criticism.* Melbourne: Oxford University Press, 1962.
JONES, EVAN. "Australian Poetry Since 1920," in G. Dutton, ed., *The Literature of Australia.* Baltimore, Md.: Penguin Books, 1964, pp. 100–133.
JONES, JOSEPH and JOHANNA. *Authors and Areas of Australia.* Austin, Texas:

Steck-Vaughn Co., 1970, p. 22.

LAVATER, LOUIS. *The Sonnet in Australasia.* Melbourne: Vidler, 1926; Sydney, Angus & Robertson, Ltd., n.d.

LINDSAY, NORMAN. *Bohemians of the "Bulletin."* Sydney: Angus & Robertson, Ltd., 1965.

MACARTNEY, FREDERICK T. *A Historical Outline of Australian Literature.* Sydney: Angus & Robertson, Ltd., 1957.

MACKANESS, GEORGE. *Bibliomania (An Australian Book Collector's Essays).* Sydney: Angus & Robertson, Ltd., 1965.

MORRISON, G. "Arts Vietnam," *Overland* (No. 40, Dec., 1968), 20.

PHILLIPS, A. A. "The Cultural Cringe," *Meanjin,* IX (No. 4, 1950), 299–302.

Poetry in Australia. Vol. I: *From the Ballads to Brennan,* ed. T. Inglis Moore. Vol. II: *Modern Australian Verse,* ed. Douglas Stewart. Sydney: Angus & Robertson, Ltd., 1964; Berkeley and Los Angeles: University of California Press, 1964.

PREMINGER, ALEXANDER S., ed. *Encyclopedia of Poetry and Poetics.* Princeton, N.J.: Princeton University Press, 1965.

SHAPIRO, KARL and BEUM, ROBERT. *A Prosody Handbook.* New York: Harper & Row, 1965.

SIMPSON, R. A. "The 'Bulletin' Poets," Sydney *Bulletin,* Feb. 27, 1965, 44.

WELLEK, RENE and WARREN, AUSTIN. "Euphony, Rhythm and Meter," in *The Theory of Literature,* New York: Harcourt, Brace, 1949, 1956.

Who's Who in Australia. Melbourne: *Herald,* 1971, pp. 304 and *passim.*

Index